Community Policing, Chicago Style

Studies in Crime and Public Policy

Michael Tonry and Norval Morris, *General Editors*

Police for the Future
David H. Bayley

Incapacitation: Penal Confinement and the Restraint of Crime
Franklin E. Zimring and Gordon Hawkins

The American Street Gang: Its Nature, Prevalence, and Control
Malcolm W. Klein

Sentencing Matters
Michael Tonry

The Habits of Legality: Criminal Justice and the Rule of Law
Francis A. Allen

Chinatown Gangs: Extortion, Enterprise, and Ethnicity
Ko-lin Chin

Responding to Troubled Youth
Cheryl L. Maxson and Malcolm W. Klein

Community Policing, Chicago Style
Wesley G. Skogan and Susan M. Hartnett

Community Policing

Chicago Style

WESLEY G. SKOGAN
SUSAN M. HARTNETT

New York   Oxford
Oxford University Press
1997

Oxford University Press

Oxford   New York
Athens   Auckland   Bangkok   Bogota   Bombay   Buenos Aires
Calcutta   Cape Town   Dar es Salaam   Delhi   Florence   Hong Kong
Istanbul   Karachi   Kuala Lumpur   Madras   Madrid   Melbourne
Mexico City   Nairobi   Paris   Singapore   Taipei   Tokyo   Toronto   Warsaw

and associated companies in
Berlin   Ibadan

Copyright © 1997 by Oxford University Press

Published by Oxford University Press, Inc.
198 Madison Avenue, New York, NY 10016

Oxford is a registered traademark of Oxford University Press

Library of Congress Cataloging-in-Publication Data
Skogan, Wesley G.
Community policing, Chicago style / Wesley G. Skogan and Susan M. Hartnett.
p. cm. — (Studies in crime and public policy)
Includes index.
ISBN 0-19-510560-5
1. Community policing—Illinois—Chicago. 2. Crime prevention—Illinois—Chicago—Citizen
participation. 3. Police administration—Illinois—Chicago. 4. Chicago (Ill.).—Police Dept.
I. Hartnett, Susan M. II. Title. III. Series.
HV7936.C83S56   1997
363.2'3—dc20   96—27841

9 8 7 6 5 4 3
Printed in the United States of America
on acid-free paper

To Barbara

To Dennis, Sarah, and Erica

Preface

A vigorous debate is taking place over the role of the police in American society—a debate that is closely linked to a new burst of innovation in police departments all over the country. Although it takes many different forms, this wave of innovation has become known as "community policing."

The concept is so popular with the public and city councils that scarcely a chief wants his department to be known for failing to climb on this bandwagon. This is, of course, a reason for caution. Enthusiasm for the idea of community policing has not yet been tempered by evidence about two big issues: Can it be done, and will it work? The police chiefs that must shoulder the burden of "reinventing" their agencies know that these are unanswered questions. Many fear that they are more likely to fail than to succeed as they are swept down this popular path.

Not only are police departments notoriously resistant to change; but sophisticated observers are even uncertain about how much effect police really have on the trends that are driving down the quality of life in American cities. It is not clear to either group whether community policing can indeed be done, or whether it will work.

This book presents the results of a large-scale evaluation of community policing in Chicago—It answers the "Can it be done?" and "Will it work?" questions for a major American city. During the mid-1990s, Chicago embarked on an ambitious effort to reinvent policing in order to forge a new partnership between police and the city's remarkably diverse neighborhoods. Chicago accomplished a great deal in a short time, which calls for a close look at the city's experience. Indeed, this book presents one of the first detailed portraits of community policing in action. It traces Chicago's program from its inception to its application in the field and examines how well it worked. We first examine the roots of community policing there, detailing its origins in the face of the political, racial, and fiscal realities that confront big-city America; community policing came to Chicago because it promised to speak to those realities. Then we detail how the city developed its unique, homegrown approach to community policing and experimented with it in five parts of town. We describe the impact of the program on community involvement, the quality of life in the city's neighborhoods, and the police officers who were involved in the program.

The first chapter provides a definition of community policing, and describes some of the obstacles to making it work in practice. This is important, for many efforts to implement community policing programs have failed to materialize. Chapter 2 describes the conditions leading to the adoption of community policing in Chicago, while chapter 3 examines the process of planning and the eventual deployment of officers to carry out the program. Drawing on their experience, and learning from the obstacles that thwarted reform in other cities, Chicago crafted a policing plan that became known as CAPS (Chicago Alternative Policing Strategy). The challenge of convincing police officers and their supervisors in the field that the plan could be carried out, and that community policing was there to stay, is described in chapter 4. It details the strategies employed by the department's managers to "bring officers on board," and presents evidence of how effective they were. Chapter 5 examines the public's vital role in community policing and the many forms it took in Chicago's program. It turned out that getting the public involved was as challenging as winning the hearts and minds of the police. Chapter 6 describes how the program actually worked when it finally hit the streets. It examines the all-important linkages that developed between the police and other city agencies, which had a critical role to play if the program was going to work. Chapter 7 analyzes the impact of community policing on the quality of life for Chicago's residents. It examines trends in crime, casual social disorder, and physical decay in the city's experimental police districts, and how they were affected by the program. Chapter 8 reviews some of the lessons that Chicago's experience provides.

Acknowledgments

We would like to thank Chicago Police Superintendent Matt Rodriguez and Deputy Superintendent Charles Ramsey for their support; also, the police research and development director, Barbara McDonald; and the deputy director, Nola Joyce. The remaining list of officers and staff members of the Chicago Police Department who have shared their wisdom with us is a very long one. It includes the commanders of the five districts where the CAPS program was piloted: Abel Presas, Thomas Byrne, Dennis Lesniak, Leroy O'Shield, and Ronnie Watson. Access to reports and data was facilitated by Kevin Morison and Ann Cibulskis. Members of the department's Data Systems Division (especially Pat Moore) have always been helpful. And, of course, we would like to express our gratitude to the hundreds of members of the Chicago Police Department who generously shared their valuable time, insights, and opinions with us.

We are also grateful for the continued interest in, and support of, this evaluation among Chicago's public officials. They include Mayor Richard M. Daley, Gery Chico, Mary Lou Budnick, James Reilly, David Anderson, and Ted O'Keefe.

Valuable advice, support, and financial assistance were forthcoming, at crucial moments, from the staff and board members of the Illinois Criminal Justice Information Authority: Peter Bensinger, Thomas Baker, Dennis Nowicki, Candice Kane, Roger Przybylski,

David Olson, Sharon Bond, Lynn Higgins, and Len Wojciechowicz. Federal assistance and support came from people at the National Institute of Justice: Jeremy Travis, Sally Hillsman, Christy Visher, Winifred Reed, Lois Mock, Craig Uchida, and David Hayslip. We are also deeply grateful to staff members of the John D. and Catherine T. MacArthur Foundation and of the Chicago Community Trust for their commitment to Chicago and to systematic evaluation.

Other supporters in Chicago and elsewhere included Warren Friedman, James K. (Chips) Stewart, Steve Gaffigan, William Geller, Karen Hoover, William Nolan, Susan Popkin, Steward Turner, Cathy Vates, Elizabeth Hollander, and Ani Russell.

Key members of our research team included Justine Lovig, Jill DuBois, Marianne Kaiser, and Tabatha Johnson Robinson. Significant contributions were also made by Scott Althaus, Dana Cole, Gail Dantzker, Sean Davis, Sirgulina Davidsdottir, Noelle Gonzalez, Sheila Houmes, Judee Schejbal, Robert Van Stedum, Jinney Smith, Melissa Miller, Dominique Whelan, and Kristin Donovan. Audrey Chambers provided valuable manuscript production assistance, Jill DuBois furnished ongoing editorial support and played a major role in both the research and writing of this book. Theresa Parker and Laurie Pielak helped us navigate rough bureaucratic waters.

Our fellow faculty researchers in this evaluation effort include Susan Bennett, Richard Block, Paul Lavrakas, Arthur Lurigio, and Dennis Rosenbaum. Alex Weiss contributed a much-valued review of the manuscript. Burton Weisbrod, director of Northwestern's Center for Urban Affairs and Policy Research, provided advice and support at many key junctures, as did the acting director, Fay Lomax Cook.

Contents

Community Policing, Chicago Style

1

Policing at Century's End

One cold March evening, several Chicago beat-team police officers visited a four-story apartment building in a decaying section of their district. For months, neighbors had been complaining about the building at the area's community beat meetings (formal gatherings of police and citizens), so the officers decided to make a careful inspection of it as they followed up on a specific incident. They were appalled at what they found. Inside, the building was in a state of collapse. The doors had been torn off most of the apartments, and the appliances and electrical fittings had been scavenged. Ceilings in the top-floor units were coming down. The halls were littered with hypodermic syringes. None of the exterior doors locked, but that would have made little difference because garbage was piled so high in the alley that anyone could clamber through a rear window. One resident later reported that cockroaches in the building "look like little Volkswagen cars." The officers soon found that the paying tenants had all fled and that they had been replaced by a rotating cast of squatters, gang members, drug dealers and users, and runaway youths.

One of the beat-team officers got the district's commander involved. He had already heard complaints about the building and its landlord at beat meetings he attended, and when he got the whole picture, he became furious. He later noted, "Guys like these are just as bad as the criminals that were arrested in this building. They

. . . don't care for their building and just milk these people dry. I'm not going to stand for that!" He brought a police photographer with him during a walk-through inspection of the building and later took the area's alderman on a guided tour. A search of police records found an enormous number of 911 calls about the building, and a long list of arrests associated with it. There was quick follow-up action by the city's building inspection department, and within two months, the prosecutor's office had delivered an ultimatum to the landlord—a list of what needed to be done to the building. Meanwhile, residents picketed the landlord's office, and the district commander sent a team to back them up. When the landlord did not comply, he was charged and hauled into court. A group of approximately 15 residents, representing the district's court advocacy committee, attended each hearing and made its presence known to the judge and the prosecutor. The landlord was convicted of reckless conduct that violated the state's criminal housing management statute, and he was eventually fined and sentenced to perform 200 hours of community service.

Beat teams? Beat meetings? Building inspectors? Court advocates? Housing management? The escorting of demonstrators? These all represent the changing face of policing, in Chicago and around the country. Everywhere, departments are moving toward a "community policing" model, which replaces traditional crime fighting with a problem-solving and prevention-oriented approach that emphasizes the role of the public in helping to set police priorities. In some cities, this is in the hands of special teams made up of volunteer officers who work mostly in poor and minority areas; in others, it involves a departmentwide transformation in the way police conceive of their role in society. In some places, community policing is equated with foot patrols; in others, community officers travel on bikes or work out of trailers. However, it actually has nothing at all to do with how police get around, but, rather, with how they work with the public to identify and resolve neighborhood problems. Almost everywhere, police find they need close support from other city agencies in order to respond effectively to the issues that people identify as priorities when they are consulted. When asked by police about what really concerns them, neighborhood residents typically identify a broad range of problems, many of which have little to do with crime. Community policing means different things in different communities, and to make it work can involve reinventing government, not just the police department.

This book examines how Chicago reinvented policing, and how it took a few steps toward reinventing local government. Almost everywhere, community policing involves politics, public relations, and hard work by dedicated police officers; and the hype may well outweigh any actual accomplishment. Many cities fail in their efforts to implement community policing, for fostering innovation in police departments is a tough job. By digging deeply into one such effort to plan and implement a serious, large-scale community-policing program, we hoped to learn what it would take to move policing into the twenty-first century. Chicago accomplished a great deal during the first years of its experiment with community policing; and this book documents both what the city did and the impact of the program on the lives of its residents. Whether Chicago provides a paradigm for the rest of the country remains an open question, but it does illustrate how difficult—and potentially rewarding—reinventing policing can be.

What is Community Policing?

In a definitional sense, community policing is not something one can easily characterize. It involves reforming decision-making processes and creating new cultures within police departments; it is not a packet of specific tactical plans. It is an organizational strategy that redefines the goals of policing, but leaves the means of achieving them to practitioners in the field. It is a process rather than a product. Efforts to do it share some general features, however. Community policing relies upon organizational decentralization and a reorientation of patrol in order to facilitate two-way communication between police and the public. It assumes a commitment to broadly focused, problem-oriented policing and requires that police be responsive to citizens' demands when they decide what local problems are and set their priorities. It also implies a commitment to helping neighborhoods solve crime problems on their own, through community organizations and crime-prevention programs.

These principles underlie a host of specific programs and policing tactics. Under the rubric of community policing, departments are opening small neighborhood substations, conducting surveys to measure community satisfaction, organizing meetings and crime-prevention seminars, publishing newsletters, forming neighborhood watch groups, establishing advisory panels, organizing youth activities, conducting drug-education projects and media campaigns, patrolling on horses and bicycles, and working with municipal agencies to enforce health and safety regulations. These activities are often backed up by organizational goals that are spelled out in "mission statements"; and departments all over the country are rewriting their missions to conform to new ideas about the values that should guide policing and the relationship between the police and the community.

There are four general principles. First, community policing relies on organizational decentralization and a reorientation of patrol in order to facilitate communication between police and the public.

Traditionally, police departments were organized on the assumption that policies and practices were determined at the top and flowed down in the form of rules and orders. The job of supervisors was to see to it that these rules and orders were carried out. Of course, this organizational chart did not reflect the reality of policing, which is that operational decision making is radically decentralized and highly discretionary, and that most police work takes place outside the direct control of supervisors. But departments maintained an elaborate paramilitary structure anyway, for it helped sustain the illusion that police were under control. Police were also amazingly successful at maintaining proprietary information about themselves and crime; they released what was useful and were secretive about the rest.

The community-policing model is more in accord with the way in which departments actually work. It involves formally granting neighborhood officers the decision-making authority they need to function effectively. Line officers are expected to work more autonomously at investigating situations, resolving problems, and educating the public. They are being asked to discover and set their own goals, and, sometimes, to manage their work schedules. Decentralization facilitates the development of local solutions to local problems and discourages the automatic application of central-office policies. The police are not independent of the rest of society, where large organizations have learned that decentralization often allows flexibility in decision making at the customer-contact level. To increase responsiveness, police are also emulating the general trend in large organizations toward shedding layers of bureaucracy; most departments that adopt a serious community policing stance strip a layer or two from their rank structures to shorten lines of communication within the agency. Police are also reorganizing to provide opportunities for citizens to come into contact with them under circumstances that encourage an information exchange, the development of mutual trust, and an opportunity for joint or coordinated action. An improvement in relationships between police and the community is a central goal of these programs.

The second principle of community policing is that it assumes a commitment to broadly focused, problem-oriented policing. On its own, problem-oriented policing represents a minor revolution in police work. It signifies a reversal of the long-standing disdain that police held for tasks that were not, in their view, "real police work." It represents a shift away from the crime-fighting orientation that police departments have professed since the 1920s. Adopting that stance was useful at that time. It provided a rationale for disconnecting police from politicians and insulating police management from narrow political concerns. Rigid discipline was imposed to combat internal corruption, and officers were shifted rapidly from one assignment to another, so that they would not get too close to the communities they served. Controlling their work from downtown, via centralized radio dispatching, was a way to ensure that they stuck to the organization's agenda. Later, when big-city riots threatened, focusing on "serious" crime at the expense of maintaining order, and adopting a detached professional manner were ways to keep out of trouble. "Just the facts, ma'am," was all they wanted.

But police departments now are experiencing the liabilities of having disconnected themselves from any close attachment to the communities they serve. Problem-oriented policing encourages officers to respond creatively to problems they encounter, or to refer them to public and private agencies that can help. More important, it stresses discovering the situations that produce calls for police assistance; identifying the causes which lie behind them; and designing tactics to deal with these causes. This involves training officers in methods of identifying and analyzing problems. Police work traditionally consisted of responding sequentially to individual events, while problem solving calls for recognizing patterns of incidents that help identify their causes and suggest how to deal with them. Police facilitate this with computer analyses of "hot spots" that have concentrated volumes of complaints and calls for service (Sherman, 1992). Problem-oriented policing also recognizes that dealing with such incident patterns may involve other agencies and may not, in fact, be police work; in traditional departments, this would be cause for ignoring these problems.

Third, community policing requires that police respond to the public when they set priorities and develop their tactics. Indeed, effective community policing requires responsiveness to citizen input concerning both the needs of the community and the best ways in which the police can help meet these needs. It takes seriously the public's definition of its own problems. This is one reason why community policing is an organizational strategy but not a set of specific programs—how it looks in practice *should* vary considerably from place to place, in response to unique local situations and circumstances.

Listening closely to the community can produce different policing priorities. In our experience, officers involved in neighborhood policing learn quickly that many residents are deeply concerned about problems that previously did not come to the department's attention. The public often focuses on threatening and fear-provoking *conditions,* rather than on discrete and legally defined *incidents.* Residents are often concerned about casual social disorder and the physical decay of their community, rather than traditionally defined "serious" crimes, but the police are organized to respond to the latter. Residents are unsure that they could (or even should) rely on the police to help them deal with these problems. These concerns thus do not generate complaints or calls for service, and as a result, the police know surprisingly little about them. The routines of traditional police work ensure that officers will largely interact with citizens who are distressed because they have just been victimized, or with suspects and troublemakers. Accordingly, community policing requires that departments develop new channels for learning about neighborhood problems.

An important corollary of this commitment to responsiveness is that police need to find ways to evaluate their ability to satisfy the concerns expressed by the public. This is a "customer satisfaction" criterion for assessing the quality of policing. Some police departments use questionnaires to evaluate their programs on a continuing basis. Most mail them to people who have called for assistance, which is a very inexpensive process. Others conduct telephone interviews with residents to assess the visibility and quality of police service.

The fourth principle is that community policing implies a commitment to helping neighborhoods solve crime problems on their own, through community organizations and crime-prevention programs. The idea that the police and the public are "coproducers" of safety predates the current rhetoric of community policing. In fact, the community crime-prevention movement of the 1970s was an important precursor to community policing. It promulgated widely the idea that crime was not solely the responsibility of the police. The police were quick to endorse the claim that they could not solve crime problems without the community's support and assistance (it helped share the blame for rising crime rates); and now they find that they are expected to be the catalyst for this effort. They are being called on to take the lead in mobilizing individuals and organizations around crime prevention. These efforts include neighborhood-watch programs, citizen patrols, and education programs that stress household target hardening and the rapid reporting of crime to the police.

Why Community Policing, and Why Now?

Why is this happening? What lies behind this sudden burst of innovation? Some of the factors that explain it are unique to policing, but community policing did not emerge in a vacuum. Parallel and supportive changes are taking place in society.

In many cities, the most important factor underlying the acceptance of community policing is politics. Groups that too frequently have hostile relations with the police, including African-Americans and Hispanics, are a potent political force in big cities and many smaller ones. While they are certainly concerned about crime, they also have an interest in curbing police abuse, and their leaders profit from promoting a style of policing that serves their constituents, rather than targeting them for enforcement. Political leaders of all backgrounds also share an interest in preventing the kind of collective violence that arose following the televised beating of Rodney King in Los Angeles in 1991. Since the mid-1960s, riots in American cities have frequently been sparked by conflicts between African-Americans and the police. In fact, studies of riots in the 1960s found that half were sparked by abusive incidents, and that tensions between the police and African-Americans were high in the months preceding the violence in every riot city (Kerner, 1967). The threat persists, as evidenced by riots during the 1990s in Los Angeles, Miami, and other cities. When developing departmental policies and choosing police administrators, politicians pay careful attention to how their actions will be received by racial and ethnic minorities. The rhetoric of community policing is favorably received in this political environment.

As a result, being involved in community policing is a way for police officers who aspire to high position to develop their careers. Cities that search for progressive and innovative police chiefs—who will be sensitive to racial tensions—find that a commitment to community policing is an attractive credential. A long list of police chiefs gained their reputations as senior commanders of community-policing projects in Houston, Philadelphia, Los Angeles, and other cities. Upwardly mobile police commanders who are looking to attain visibility in other cities are therefore well advised to become involved in community-policing projects.

Interest in community policing has also been encouraged by the emergence of a cadre of well-educated and sophisticated administrators at the top of prominent police departments. Armed with university degrees in management, law, operations research, and the social sciences, they can be receptive to outside pressures for change. They have been impressed by two decades of research on policing, which has highlighted some of the limitations of the way in which it traditionally has been organized. This research has challenged the effectiveness of routine patrol and of rapid responses to most telephone complaints; detectives' investigation practices; the sufficiency of occasional crackdowns on outdoor drug markets; and the manner in which police handle domestic-violence cases. The efficacy of many of the alternatives to these traditional practices remains unproven, but their weaknesses have been exposed, and the confidence that practitioners and informed outsiders have in many traditional policing practices has been undermined. This all comes at a time of concern about the cost and the effectiveness of the police. The fiscal crisis in American cities challenges police to work within existing financial constraints—there will not be much "more of the same," in the form of more hiring of officers to conduct policing in the traditional style. Both police and their political masters are looking for ways to get more out of less.

The work of policing intellectuals like Herman Goldstein, John Alderson, James Q. Wilson, and George Kelling also laid the groundwork for the appearance of community policing on the policy agenda. Early innovative projects, like the one in San Diego (Boydstun and Sherry, 1975) that encouraged problem identification and problem solving by beat officers, introduced both a community orientation to policing and the idea that experiments should be systematically evaluated. Later, the concept spread because of aggressive marketing by federal agencies and Washington, D.C., think tanks. Their target is not just police chiefs, but also the professional managers that run a majority of American cities. Cities are also encouraged to share ideas, due to the need to write grant proposals in order to secure federal funds; these proposals typically demand reviews of similar programs in other cities and summaries of what research suggests about the effectiveness of proposed programs. Proposals to experiment with new programs are more likely to be funded, because the results will be more visible. The spread of community policing throughout the country has been supported by the development of nationwide networks of police managers, who communicate with each other and with government policy-makers, consultants, professional police planners, and policing intellectuals. They communicate their ideas through conferences, magazine articles, research reports, and professional newsletters. Police officials are now more frequent visitors to other cities, sometimes touring progressive departments to see, firsthand, new forms of policing in action. They know what is going on around the country, and where the policing field seems to be moving.

Lying behind all of these factors are long-run shifts in societal organization that have facilitated the adopting of community policing. These include a general trend toward the decentralization of large-scale organizations into smaller, more flexible and responsive units; a flattening of them, to cut the number of management layers between top management and those who meet the customers; and a widespread impetus to privatize the delivery of public services, coupled with an increasing reliance on markets or marketlike mechanisms, to secure a customer orientation in government agencies. Technology is another powerful force that is driving change in organizations of all kinds. Even policing—traditionally among the least-capital-intensive functions—is being affected. We are now feeling the impact of a mobile-communications revolution that may rival the effect of the first linking of the public to the police via radio dispatch in the 1930s. In some cities, technology is being used to directly connect patrol officers to community residents through cell phones, beepers, and voice mail. In many areas, foot-patrol officers carry electronic paging devices that enable residents of the area to contact them directly while they are in the field. As more citizens and police carry portable communications devices, the immediacy of their messages will increase. As the ability of citizens to directly communicate with individual officers increases, the role of centralized dispatching will diminish, along with the illusion of control over officers' performance that this gave to the top brass downtown.

Finally, community policing is popular because it seems as

American as apple pie. Community policing is characterized by "Officer O'Leary" strolling down the avenue, holding an apple in one hand and twirling a nightstick in the other, shooing away pesky street urchins as he warmly greets passersby. It's the quintessential village constable or the night watchman, who lives in the same community that he serves. At a mythic level, community policing reminds us of a world we think we once had, but have now lost. Of course, it only *seems* that way. Police during that bygone era were often more brutal, lazy, and corrupt than they are today, probably by a wide margin. But these myths have a power that derives not from their accuracy, but from the cultural understandings that they represent (Crank, 1994).

Can it Work?

While there is a great deal of enthusiasm for community policing in many quarters, and many reasons for giving it a try, making it work is another matter. There is indeed a cross-country record of failed attempts to implement community policing. The list of reasons for these failures is at least as long as the list of reasons for trying it in the first place, and they illustrate the enormous difficulty of making change in police departments.

Efforts to implement community policing have floundered on the rocks of police culture. It gets labeled as "social work," the job of "empty holster guys," and not of "real police officers." The frequent enthusiasm that public officials and community activists express for neighborhood-oriented policing encourages its detractors to dismiss it as "just politics," or another passing civilian fad. Police are skeptical about programs invented by civilians, who, they are convinced, cannot possibly understand their job. They are particularly hostile toward programs that threaten to involve civilians in setting standards or evaluating their performance. And resistance does not come just from the bottom of the organization. Mid-level management revolts have sunk community policing in several cities. People at these levels feel bypassed and alienated. They see authority taken from them and pushed to lower levels in the organization (thus losing the power they had to micromanage units under their control), while, at the same time, opportunities for their promotion are being sabotaged by shrinking management layers and the flattening of the formal rank structure.

Police departments are not particularly open to innovation at the top level, either. Supervisors typically are command-and-control oriented and feel most comfortable when everything is done by the book. Their organizational charts feature elaborate bureaucratic hierarchies and rigid chains of command. Discussions of community policing often feature management buzzwords like "empowerment" and "trust," and these make them nervous. Top management worries about corruption and wonders whether officers can be called on to "represent local interests" and steer the allocation of valuable services, and even infrastructure development, without being tempted to share in the advantages this can create. They also have to deal with the reality of the contract that frequently binds their department to work rules, performance standards, and personnel allocations that have been negotiated with powerful employee unions. They may have much less freedom than outsiders imagine in regard to "reinventing" the department.

Police managers and city executives also have to find the people required to staff the program. Policing is labor intensive, and while community-policing advocates promise that it eventually will drive down the demand for police service, it may, in truth, require even more officers during what may turn out to be a lengthy interim period. Finding the money to hire more officers to staff community-policing assignments is a hard job, so departments will inevitably be asked to dig up a contribution from existing resources. This brings them face to face with "the 911 problem." Because the volume of telephone calls to big-city departments skyrocketed in the mid-1970s, the police commitment to respond to these calls as quickly as possible has absorbed the resources of many departments. Programs around the country encountered heavy political sledding when the perception arose that they were diverting resources previously devoted to responding to emergency calls into this untried, new social experiment (Skogan, 1995).

Ironically, it also turns out to be difficult to sustain community involvement in community policing. The two groups involved may not have a history of getting along in poor neighborhoods. Organizations that represent the interests of community members there also may not have a track record of cooperating with police, and poor and high-crime areas often are not well endowed with an infrastructure of organizations ready to get involved. Crime and fear can stimulate withdrawal from community life, rather than involvement in it, and fear of retaliation by gangs and drug dealers can undermine public involvement. Finally, residents of crime-ridden neighborhoods have no reason to think that community policing will turn out to be anything but another broken promise. They are accustomed to seeing programs come and go, due to political and budgetary cycles that are out of their control.

Also, many community-policing efforts have failed to deliver the goods. Adopting community policing inevitably means accepting a widely expanded definition of what police are responsible for. As we noted above, when police meet with the public to discuss neighborhood problems and set priorities, a large number of issues that previously fell outside the police mandate will be high on the list. But while police can note that trash-filled vacant lots are a high-priority problem, they have to turn to other city agencies to get the trash picked up. For a long list of familiar bureaucratic and political reasons, these agencies usually think that community policing is the police department's program—not theirs—and resist bending their own professional and budget-constrained priorities. Interorganizational cooperation turns out to be one of the most difficult problems for innovative departments.

Community policing also threatens to become politicized and polarizing, and there is evidence that it can be inequitable in its application. An evaluation of community policing in Houston (Skogan, 1990) found that the program favored the interests of racially dominant groups and established interests in the community. Whites and homeowners enjoyed most of its benefits, while renters, African-Americans, and Hispanics were excluded. Community policing is difficult in areas where the community is fragmented by race, class, and lifestyle. Groups will be quick to point to each other as the source of local problems. If, instead of trying to find common interests amid this diversity, police deal mainly with the people who step forward to support them, they will appear to be taking sides. It will be very easy for them to focus on supporting those with whom they get along, and who share their outlook. As a result, the local priorities that they represent will be those of some in the community, but not all. Critics of community policing are concerned that it can extend the relationship of police and citizens past the point where detached professionalism and a commitment to the rules of law can control their behavior. To act fairly and constitutionally, and to protect minority rights, the police must sometimes act in a way that is contrary to the opinion of the majority. As Mastrofsky (1988) points out, community policing must develop a process by which officers can be given sufficient autonomy to do good, without increasing their likelihood of doing evil.

In light of this formidable list of obstacles to making it work, critics of community policing have been quick to claim that, in reality, it is just rhetoric. It is certainly true that it *involves* rhetoric, for community policing redefines the goals of policing. Providing a new vision of where a department is heading calls for rhetoric, one of the tools of leadership. Community policing also calls for rhetoric because police departments depend on the communities they serve for financial and moral support, so they must have public and political approval before undertaking a significant change in direction. Rhetoric about community policing informs the community about a set of plans it is being asked to pay for.

The question is, is it *more* than rhetoric? There are many examples of failed experiments, and of cities where the concept has gone awry. On the other hand, there is evidence (summarized in Skogan, 1995) in many evaluations that a public hungry for attention has a great deal to tell police when asked, and it is grateful for the opportunity to do so. When residents see more police patrolling on foot, or working out of a local substation, they feel less fearful. In areas where officers have developed sustained cooperation with community groups and fostered self-help programs, they have witnessed declining levels of social disorder and physical decay.

Organization of the Book

This book presents the results of more than three years of research on community policing in Chicago. We began our evaluation in December 1992, well in advance of the implementation of the program and before many of its main features had been settled on. The program was announced in the spring, and officially began at the end of April 1993. The book tracks its progress through the fall of 1994, when it was expanded from test districts to encompass the entire city. The research on which it is based continued through 1995. During this period, we documented what we learned about all of the issues discussed above, including the origins of the program, its design principles and programmatic features, the problems involved in getting it off the ground, and evidence about its impact. Along the way, the managers of Chicago's program confronted virtually every obstacle to implementation that has cropped up around the country—from police culture to resource constraints to occasional community indifference. What they did about the obstacles is discussed in detail.

Evaluation researchers make a distinction between process and outcome evaluations, and we did both. For two years, we closely monitored the planning and implementation of the program in the city's five experimental police districts. We wanted to assess the program's planning process, the strategic and tactical programmatic decisions made by top managers, and obstacles to making change within the department. In a bold move, the police gave us complete access to anyone, in any district, and welcomed us to watch them in action. We interviewed officers and civilian employees at all levels of the organization, city officials, and community leaders. We attended planning meetings to observe how objectives were set, what problems arose, how they were dealt with, and who participated. We went to the superintendent's office, the mayor's inner sanctum, meetings and retreats of the department's senior managers, planning meetings with district commanders and the heads of city service agencies, and ad hoc trouble-shooting sessions of all types.

The conclusions we drew from all of these are presented in the next two chapters. Chapter 2 examines the origins of community policing in Chicago; it answers the question, "Why community policing, and why now?" In a nutshell, the answer in Chicago was politics. In different ways, community policing seemed to speak to the city's crime, fiscal, and racial problems, and it promised to do so in time for the next election. It was imposed on the department by the mayor, in a move to solve his political problems, and in the end, this turned out to be one of the program's great strengths. Chapter 3 looks at the planning of the program and how it got out on the street. The chapter examines what the department attempted to do and how it hoped to get there. This involved finding leadership, crafting a strategic plan, and mobilizing the resources needed to carry it out.

Most of our work was not done in downtown office buildings, but in the field. During our three-year study, we surveyed more than 7,000 police officers to examine the impact of training and experience in the field on their attitudes and role perceptions. We rode with patrol officers and observed what went on at the district stations. We interviewed the sergeants and lieutenants who were charged with managing community policing on a daily basis. We devoted all of this effort to studying the views of rank-and-file officers, because, around the country, involving them has turned out to be one of the most difficult parts of implementing community policing. Chapter 4 calls this the problem of "winning hearts and minds," and it examines the strategies employed by the department's senior managers to solve it. They changed the nature of many officers' jobs, because work structures people's experiences and views. They tried to change the organization's management and supervision styles, and they worked hard at communicating a vision of the direction in which the department was headed. During the first two years of the program, one of management's most solid accomplishments was the mounting of a serious training effort; and whenever officers were trained, we observed the planning of the curriculum and assessed how well it was executed. By tracking officers' attitudes over time, we found evidence of some success in the process we describe in chapter 4 as "bringing officers on board."

Chapter 5 examines the role of citizen participation in community policing. An important feature of Chicago's program was that it provided multiple channels through which neighborhood residents could make their views known and lobby to influence police priorities. The most important of these were beat meetings—small gatherings (as noted previously) of police and residents held each month in church basements and park buildings located in each of the 54 experimental beats. These meetings were to be the locus for the development of police-citizen problem-solving partnerships at the grassroots level. Each month, we observed a sample of them to monitor what was going on, and we frequently found that they were not working the way the people downtown thought they should. Too many meetings were dominated by police neighborhood-relations specialists, and most of the problem-solving plans they came up with featured traditional enforcement efforts. We also attended all of the meetings of the advisory committees that were set up to inform and counsel the district commanders. While their efforts varied, none were very effective. Chapter 5 also documents the role of community organizations in community policing. We examined how local groups mobilized to influence policing in their districts, and found that organizations that represented white and middle-class constituencies were much more successful in using the opportunities for involvement created by Chicago's program, for it fit more naturally their goals and the ways in which they were organized. Just this element of the evaluation involved interviews with almost 500 community activists.

Chapter 6 presents some details on how the program actually operated in the field. One of the biggest victories during the first year was the successful integration of policing with a broad range of city services. In many cities, the effort to bring the two together has failed. In Chicago, relentless pressure from the top (the mayor) and from the bottom (the district commanders) helped keep service delivery on track, and in the end, many of the most visible successes of the first year could be traced to this component of the program. Chapter 6 then examines case studies of collaborative problem solving by police and citizens, and extracts from them some general lessons about how to sustain such efforts. Collaboration was not easy, and many of them were not particularly successful.

We also assessed the impact of community policing on the quality of life in Chicago's neighborhoods, and the results of this assessment are presented in chapter 7. Using a quasi-experimental approach, we collected a great deal of data from the five test police districts and from a set of matched comparison areas spread around the city. The data included surveys of city residents. These focused on victimization, fear of crime, reports of neighborhood conditions, and popular assessments of the quality of police service. We also assembled a large amount of crime, demographic, and city administrative data using a consistent geographical format. Chapter 7 uses these data to examine the impact of Chicago's program in the neighborhoods. We found changes in the visibility of policing; new optimism about the quality of police service; and evidence that crime, social disorder, and physical decay went down in the community-policing districts. We also found that the benefits of the program were fairly widespread. Every district registered some successes, and there was evidence that homeowners, renters, whites, and African-Americans all benefited as well. Hispanics did not benefit, though, and it appears that they did not even get the message. Thus, they did not get involved, and they did not see a significant improvement in the quality of their lives.

This was not a hands-off study. At one of our first meetings, the commander of an experimental district made *his* expectations clear: We would write a book telling everyone what he did wrong, and it would come out in five years—when it was too late to do anything about it. He did not think this was a good idea, and neither did we. Instead, we were willing, at every step, to feed back to the city the results of our research. We did not do so until we were satisfied that we knew what we were talking about, so sometimes this feedback came slowly; for us, being sure meant collecting and analyzing data. We learned that it is hard for researchers to offer timely data when the subject is a moving, evolving target. We tried to give strategic, rather than tactical, advice. For example, we would not identify *who* was doing a good or bad job; rather, we tried to describe the frequency of good and bad work, and the factors that seemed to contribute to each. This helped us maintain the confidence of the people we were studying. We were also committed to the timely dissemination of our findings to a wider community of stakeholders that coalesced around the program, and, eventually, to the public (we were not interested in getting headlines). We accomplished this through memos and private briefing sessions, detailed reports, and presentations of our findings at a variety of forums. At various times, we briefed the mayor, the superintendent and his senior advisers, district commanders, federal and state money givers, visiting dignitaries, community organizers, and rank-and-file police officers who called us on the phone when they heard about our findings.

We controlled the definition of our role because the evaluation was funded by state and federal research grants and by awards from private foundations, not by the city or the department. (The preface to this book acknowledges their contributions.) However, the enormous cooperation that we enjoyed stemmed in part from our willingness to share what we were learning. Did we have any effect on the program? Perhaps, although the people running it were very well informed, and our reports more often confirmed what they suspected or justified what they wanted to do, rather than surprising them. There would be a community-policing program in Chicago without us, for it was rooted in solid political calculations. And without us, it would have looked pretty much as it did, for the department was committed to inventing a unique new version of itself, one rooted in local experience, not in books. This book is thus not for the department, but for an audience still peering into the future, trying to make out just what community policing is and if it can possibly live up to its billing.

2

Police and Politics
in Chicago

Community policing came to Chicago on April 29, 1993: That was inauguration day for CAPS (Chicago Alternative Policing Strategy), an ambitious plan to reorganize the police department, redefine its mission, and forge a new relationship between police and residents of the city.

Why did the department adopt this new model of policing? Although it would have to be implemented by the Chicago Police Department, the impetus for change was a political one—the idea came from City Hall. In a process that began in 1991, community policing was imposed on the department by a mayor who was facing a short but difficult list of political problems: crime, racial conflict, money, and the next election. There was almost no distinction between these issues since they were so intertwined. Crime was on everyone's mind, but it was not clear if the city could do anything about it, or could afford to. The mayor and his advisers thought he had to do *something* about crime that would appease the media and trump his potential opponents before his next campaign. His biggest political fear was that the opposition would form a coalition of the city's African-American and Hispanic constituencies, for together they would be hard to beat. Community policing turned out to speak to all of his concerns.

Crime

For local officials, crime is like the weather: Everyone talks about it, but they often feel they cannot really do much about it. But by the beginning of the 1990s, it provided an ominous backdrop to discussions about virtually every aspect of life in Chicago. The city's crime count peaked in the summer of 1991, which turned out to be a critical year for decisions about community policing. During 1991, almost 44,000 robberies were reported to the police, up from 37,000 the previous year. Assaults were up by 1,000 over 1990, and up by almost 5,000 since 1989. Burglary and theft numbers were also high (the latter hit an all-time record in 1991), and the number of murders in the city reached its highest point in more than a decade. Chicago's 1991 homicide rate placed it fourth in the nation. In 1991 the city counted 2,400 serious crimes on its buses and trains—also an all-time record.

Equally ominous was the nature of crime in the city, which seemed to be changing. It was becoming both more pervasive and more threatening. Pay telephones were no longer a neighborhood amenity; instead, they were perceived to attract the curse of street drug trafficking. Men who lounged in the vicinity of pay phones were commonly believed to be making deals and waiting for drug customers. The term "drive-by shooting" had just entered the city's lexicon, along with "carjacking." Homicides attributed to gangs grew 160 percent in the five years before 1991. Assaults became increasingly lethal. The firepower employed by gangs and even seemingly random street killers escalated to levels found in the military. Gun use in crime went up—guns accounted for two-thirds of all homicides in the city, and between 1988 and 1994, the number of murders by gun went up by 62 percent. The number of murder weapons that were high-caliber automatic or semiautomatic guns jumped 650 percent over the same period (Illinois Criminal Justice Information Authority, 1995; Block and Block, 1993). The courts were trying a growing number of gun toters who were so young that special measures had to be taken to prosecute them as adults. The number of juveniles arrested for murder grew 230 percent (to 103 cases) between 1985 and 1991. Children were also dying violently in record numbers.

The city was awash with drugs, including, in growing volume, the crack-cocaine combination that previously had missed Chicago. At the beginning of the 1990s, gang wars erupted over the control of lucrative drug-selling sites. Some of the gangs were large and powerful. During the 1980s, the four largest accounted for almost 70 percent of all the gang-related crimes in the city; between them, they had an estimated 19,000 of the city's 36,000 gang members. There was a brief lull in gang-related violence at the end of the 1980's, due to the formation of alliances between several of the major gangs, but the alliances came apart in 1990 and the number of gang-related homicides reached a new record in 1991. In 1990 and 1991, one of the community areas later targeted for community policing was the site of an all-out narcotics war between the Black Gangster Disciples Nation and the Black Disciples (Block and Block, 1993). The homicide count there helped make August 1991 the deadliest single month in Chicago's crime history.

Adding to the problem was the fact that some of the city's most prominent public-housing projects echoed with gunfire almost nightly. In 1991, the violent-crime rate in public housing was almost twice the rate for the city as a whole, and it was 17 times as high as the rate for Chicago's suburbs. Three percent of all Chicagoans live in public housing, but public housing accounted for 10 percent of the city's murders. In a series of meetings beginning in May 1991, the Department of Housing and Urban Development had begun to prod City Hall to respond.

City Hall took note. The mayor's political operatives reported that crime was at the top of people's agendas. The voting public wanted something done about it. The flight of the middle class from the city during the 1970s and 1980s had slowed, according to the 1990 census, but the city's demographic stability remained fragile. A subsequent study by the *Chicago Tribune* (Reardon, 1993) documented the fact that the most frequent reason listed by those who had moved from the city during 1992 was crime. Crime was also most frequently cited by movers with families. The question was, What could the mayor do about the crime rate? City Hall believed the answer was, "Not much." The city did not yet know that the economy was beginning to come out of a deep recession—one which would help drive an incumbent president from office the following year. The city's employment base remained shaky. After decades of Republican administrations in Washington, less remained of the safety net that the city could tighten, and it did not appear that the city could afford to pay for local initiatives that would address the fundamental economic and social ills of the city.

In truth, crime in Chicago was as rigidly segregated as its population, so the highest risks actually were faced by the poor and racial minorities. To document this, we geocoded more than 600,000 police incident reports for 1993, classifying each into one of the city's census tracts. Figure 2-1 examines the ratio of crime rates for Hispanic and African-American neighborhoods in Chicago to those for largely white areas. If risks in their neighborhoods were the same as those for residents of white areas, the ratios would be 1:1, but this was never the case. Burglary rates in both Hispanic and black Chicago stood at just less than twice the rate for largely white areas, but most were more disproportionate. Crimes that took place at the victim's homes (a fear-provoking category) were also more common in minority areas. In general, property crimes were the crimes most evenly distributed throughout the city; but otherwise, depending on the crime category, Hispanics were victimized at about 1.5 times the rate for whites, while the rate for blacks was closer to twice the white rate. Differences between the areas were more dramatic for personal and drug crimes. In fact, residents of black Chicago were robbed and raped at a rate more than four times the white rate; and Hispanics at about twice the white rate. Crimes that involved guns were seven times more common in African-American neighborhoods and three times as frequent in Hispanic areas. The biggest disparity was for rates of drug offenses—the rate for black Chicago was 11.5 times the rate in heavily white areas, and in Hispanic neighborhoods, it was four times the white rate.

The disparate distribution of crime among the city's neighbor-

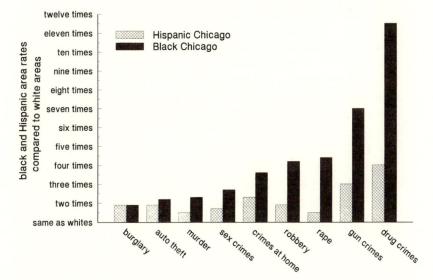

Figure 2-1 Crime rates in black and Hispanic areas compared to rates for white areas.

hoods was also illustrated in analytic crime maps we drew for each of the areas in which Chicago was about to launch its community-policing experiment. Only one of those is presented here, a map depicting the distribution of burglaries, violent crimes, and drug crimes in the 22d District. The map features data for April 1993, the month before community policing was implemented there. It presents "hot spot" clusters that identify extreme *concentrations* of crime rather than the location of hundreds of individual incidents.

Although they share this police district, the black and white communities of the 22d District are as segregated as any other area in Chicago. Overall, the district was about 60 percent African-American and 40 percent white; other groups had virtually no presence there. The location of the white-dominated areas within the police district can easily be deduced from   Figure 2-2. Mount Greenwood, comprising the western side of the district, was 1.2 percent African-American in 1990; Washington Heights, which encompasses the northeastern side of the district, was 99 percent African-American. At the bottom of the map lies the Morgan Park area (65 percent black), and in the middle sits Beverly (25 percent black). Four of the city's fifteen most affluent census tracts are in Beverly, and two more lie in Mount Greenwood. Figure 2-2 illustrates that even within small subareas, the relationship between crime and race was a clear one, accurately reflecting the overall situation of Chicago's white, African-American, and Hispanic communities.

While the mayor and his advisers did not think he could do much about crime problems of this magnitude, and especially about their deep social and economic roots, doing something about the police department was another matter. That lay squarely within his authority. State statutes give the mayor control over the superintendent of police—he picks the superintendent, who serves entirely "at the pleasure of the mayor." He also exercises a great deal of influence over the selection of other top commanders within the department, who are known as the "exempt staff" because their positions are exempted from many civil service rules. Although the authority to select those who filled these positions formally lay in the hands of the superintendent, many who held top jobs in the department had long-standing ties with powerful politicians and political groups. Political leaders jockeyed with the superintendent and the mayor for control of policy-making positions within the agency. Finally, the mayor crafts the city's budget and sets the

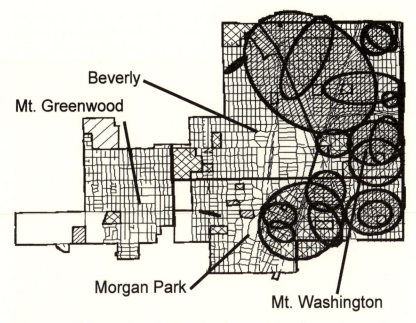

Figure 2-2   Morgan Park violence, burglary and drug hot spots.

agenda for the Chicago City Council's fiscal deliberations. Although he did not wield the machinelike control that his father had exercised over the council, the mayor generally had his way. Some of the mayor's key advisers thought that, by demonstrating an apparent move in the direction of improving policing, he could make a credible claim that he was doing something about crime.

What to do about the police thus became the question of the day. Traditionally, law-and-order politics focuses on the order end of the equation. Getting tough on crime is seemingly every politician's response to a restless electorate. However, the mayor faced several impediments to pursuing that strategy.

First, important advisers did not think it would work. While the mayor's background as a prosecutor predisposed him toward enforcement approaches to crime control, people around him had begun to believe that the levels of policing that Chicago could afford (see the next section) would not be sufficient to reduce crime significantly. Indeed, it appeared unlikely that adding a few officers to the force would make much of a dent in the city's crime rate. The mayor continued to call for tough action by the courts, and for legislation requiring more stringent prison sentences for offenders, but of course none of these efforts would be carried on his budget.

The mayor's advisers also thought that getting tough might not work, because they were fed up with the police department. They did not believe they would get very much for their investment if they just tried to go the law-and-order route. In their view, the department was lazy, poorly-managed, and unresponsive to policy direction. A tradition of mismanagement and a series of costly agreements with the police union had driven up the department's budget, while its efficiency was being eroded. In the early 1990s, the department was still clinging to the reputation for professionalism that it had gained in the 1960s. Interestingly, the reforms of the 1960s were also imposed from outside the department, by the mayor's father. When City Hall's management consultants began looking around, they found overstaffed offices, highly paid officers doing simple clerical tasks, and a bloated group of downtown bureaucrats in blue uniforms. Officers who were listed on districts' books could not be found doing patrol-related tasks. The mayor's advisers suspected that, while the Patrol Division's numbers were quite high, too few officers were actually on patrol duty, relative to how much he was spending on policing. However, they could not get a trustworthy response when they asked simple questions. And when City Hall advisers requested management information from the police department they almost never got a useful response. They had difficulty controlling the department's spending—direct instructions to control overtime spending were ignored; and since it took months to get financial reports from police headquarters, the mayor's budget analysts were always hopelessly in arrears. Consequently City Hall was deeply frustrated by its relationship with the department.

In private, the mayor also proclaimed the department "a boys' club" and "a closed shop." He believed that for too many, a police job was a cozy sinecure: Officers covered up for each other when they made mistakes, jockeyed for inside jobs to get off the street, put in their years, and retired young. At the same time, everywhere he went in the community, he heard complaints that police officers cruised past trouble spots without stopping; drove past citizens who tried to wave down the cars; responded slowly (or not at all) to 911 calls; and provided indifferent service. In the 1980s, investigative reporters revealed that the police department "killed crime" by fraudulently rejecting crime reports, and that it was done by detectives to keep their workloads light (Skogan and Gordon, 1982). In this environment, just hiring more officers did not seem very productive. In the internal debate over what to do about the police,

the mayor insisted on dealing with their insularity, nonrespon-
siveness, and organizational drift.

Money

Chicago's police budget was set by the city council, after hearings
and negotiations that were based on the mayor's initial budget recommendations. In 1991 the department's budget was $629 million,
and it was set at $686 million for 1992. Previously, the police had
consumed about 20 percent of the city's revenue. Subtracting oblig-
atory debt, bond interest, and pension payments, the police accounted for about 25 percent of the city's actual operating budget.
Since policing is a labor-intensive activity, the total department
budget was principally driven by wage levels and the number of
employees on the payroll. In 1992, the average starting pay for a
police officer in Chicago was $30,400, a good salary by national
standards. The fastest growing items on the police budget were salaries and medical benefits. More, and perhaps better, policing
could cost a great deal.

Financing a department of 12,500 officers was not easy in a period of fiscal stress. Federal revenue sharing with the cities had
been abolished in 1986, and block grants to cities were cut drasti-
cally by 1987. During the 1980s, direct federal aid to Chicago fell
to about one-fourth its 1980 total (Ladd and Yinger, 1989). As a
result, most of whatever money the mayor wanted to spend in com-
bating crime had to be raised locally. However, the mayor, also well
known for being fiscally prudent, was praised in the *Wall Street
Journal* and by other conservative sources for responsible municipal management (Glastris, 1993). Unlike many other cities, Chicago
had held the line on municipal spending during the postwar era. It
had avoided going into debt, had resisted short-term borrowing as
a way of paying its operating expenses, and enjoyed a good credit
rating (Fuchs, 1992). The incumbent mayor privatized some city
services, civilianized parking enforcement, and contracted out the
task of collecting parking fines.

All of this found favor among those in the mayor's electoral
base, which was dominated by homeowners and business operators. They shared an interest in keeping property taxes low. Many
of the city's white residents were older, living on fixed incomes
that did not keep up with inflating property values—and thus their
tax bill—during the 1970s and early 1980s. White Chicagoans also
needed to keep city taxes low because they were paying private-

school fees as well as public-school taxes. In 1990, the Census indicated that 49 percent of the elementary- and secondary-school students who were living in largely white areas of the city were attending private—predominately Catholic—schools. Businesses were potentially mobile, and many suburbs would offer them attractive relocation packages in order to secure the jobs and tax revenues that would move with them. The mayor and his allies believed that businesses and homeowners, if threatened with large tax increases to pay for unpopular city programs, would vote with their feet, by moving to the suburbs in even larger numbers. So, for decades, the city served this coalition by keeping taxes low while providing an adequate level of city services in neighborhoods which supported the Democratic machine (Judd and Swanstrom, 1994; Holli and Green 1984). When the mayor faltered in this compact, he learned his lesson: In 1992 he offered an assortment of proposed tax increases, including a large jump in the property-tax rate, which, he argued, was necessary to pay for several hundred new police officers. He was quickly slapped down by the city council and their grumbling constituents. The mayor adroitly replaced his budget director, and the new one engineered a budget for the following year that found the money for new officers by raising various fees and shrinking other city agencies through attrition.

The cost of hiring new officers thus clearly set a limit on the mayor's options for dealing with crime. During his 1990 reelection campaign, he had promised to increase the size of the force by 600 officers, only to learn that he could not afford to follow through on the commitment. By 1991, he was unwilling to spend much more on police if he did not get a promise that greater efficiency or effectiveness would result. When he later became convinced that community policing might accomplish this, he was willing to push harder to find the resources to support it. As we shall note in the next chapter, finding ways of hiring more officers to staff the city's community-policing program was one of the mayor's most important contributions to the effort.

Politics

Both crime and city finances interacted with the most important issue on City Hall's mind—getting the mayor reelected. The city's next general election, pitting him against a typically hapless Republican, would not be held until November 1995. But the real contest would be the March 1995 mayoral primary, in which he certainly would face more credible opposition. In Chicago, campaigns begin about a year in advance of polling day; so the mayor's supporters hoped to begin pointing to his concrete accomplishments by the spring of 1994. However, in 1991, those accomplishments seemed few in number. Much of the mayor's time in office had been devoted to struggles with the governor and the state legislature over a third airport that he wanted constructed within the city's boundaries, and to his efforts to secure casino gambling revenues for Chicago. Neither issue had yet been resolved in any definitive way. Other ad hoc proposals by the mayor, including a plan to let neighborhoods use culs-de-sac to wall themselves off from nearby trouble spots, had generated a great deal of controversy but had not led to any concrete action. The mayor needed more good works to point to during the upcoming campaign.

The mayor's lustrous father once remarked that "good government is good politics"; and community policing promised to provide the governmental half of this equation. The groundwork for discussing the issue had been laid during the late 1980s by community groups that supported neighborhood-oriented policing, a concept which was gaining popularity around the country. The most prominent of them was the Chicago Alliance for Neighborhood Safety (CANS), a coalition of crime-prevention organizations founded in 1981. With the support of a long list of foundations, they examined police services; visited other cities to observe fledgling community-policing efforts; and issued a series of reports that recommended the development of a community-policing strategy for Chicago. Their proposals were endorsed by the city's major newspapers in early 1992. By then, CANS had spun off a separate Community Policing Task Force that represented a broad coalition of neighborhood groups. They, in turn, stimulated a public discussion of policing in the city. The multiracial participation in the debate made it clear that there was broad interest in a new kind of policing and that community policing promised to be a unifying, rather than a potentially divisive, response to the city's crime problems.

Race

At the beginning of the 1990s the mayor of Chicago faced another important political reality: the city's changing voter base. African-Americans, and Spanish-speaking people, whose origins lay in Mexico and Puerto Rico, constituted a majority of the city's population, and they were a potent political force. The mayor teetered on top of the coalition he had assembled to capture the job in this diverse environment, and the parameters of coalition politics were set by the city's demography. In 1990, about 38 percent of the city's residents were white, 38 percent were black, and 20 percent were Hispanic. Whites turned out to vote in much larger proportions, but their numbers were shrinking faster than those of other groups. In 1950 the city had been 84 percent white, but the number of whites declined almost 20 percent between 1980 and 1990 alone. Beginning about 1980, the black middle class and affluent black workers also began to pour out of the city's South and West Sides into the southern suburbs, in search of nicer housing and better schools. Between 1980 and 1990, the city's African-American population dropped by almost 10 percent. As a result, the declining number of African-Americans that remained in the city were poorer and more desperate than before. Only Hispanics (up 29 percent), and a small but burgeoning Asian population (up 39 percent), were growing in number, because of immigration and the fact that many of them were of child-bearing age. A prominent local demographer predicted that Hispanics would become the city's largest group by 2005, comprising 33 percent of the population, while whites were expected to sink to 28 percent (Rodriguez, 1996). A major swing group in city politics was a thin band of relatively affluent and well-educated whites that lived along the lakeshore. They were often Republican in their national politics; despite their being dubbed "lakeshore liberals," George Bush carried the city's Yuppie heartland in 1988. These voters could be convinced to turn out in large numbers (and, significantly, to give money) for "good government" candidates who promised to heal, rather than exacerbate, racial divisions that threatened the city's peace and the value of their pricey real estate.

Thus the mayor's political calculus: He was unlikely to face a notable challenger in his own faction, due to the disastrous consequences experienced by white politicians after a split had occurred among them several years before; a black candidate had then won the Democratic primary and the subsequent general election. An alternative winning coalition could be built only around an African-American candidate, but the black or white winner had to have Hispanic support. The strongest card in the mayor's hand was the fact that blacks and Hispanics were far from being united politically; in fact, they were in fierce competition over housing, schools, and jobs. But as a group, they had at least two important concerns in common: crime and the police. The possibility that African-

Americans and Hispanics might form what was known locally as a Rainbow Coalition—perhaps in response to crime and police issues—had important political ramifications, for it threatened to destabilize the city's dominant electoral coalition and loosen the mayor's grip on power.

The depth of racial division over the police was documented by a survey we conducted in early 1993, in order to establish a baseline for assessing the impact of the community-policing program that was then being readied behind the scenes. We surveyed 2,573 adults living in most of Chicago's police districts. That survey (which will be examined in great detail in later chapters) included a number of questions that assessed popular views of the quality of police service. Four questions inquired about police demeanor—that is, about how respondents felt that the police generally treated people in their neighborhood. We asked them how polite, concerned, helpful, and fair they thought police were. Figure 2-3 examines the results, by race. It illustrates the very large gap between the views of whites, who, by and large, were very satisfied with the police, and African-American and Hispanic respondents. The latter groups were generally twice as dissatisfied, or more so, with the way in which they perceived the police treated people in their communities. Almost 30 percent thought police were typi-

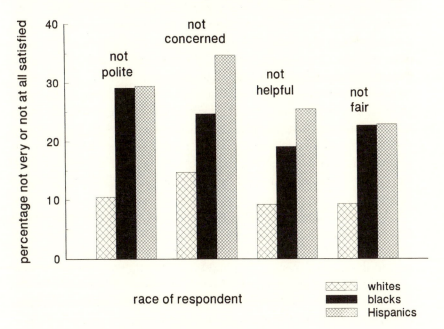

Figure 2-3 Dissatisfaction with police by race.

cally somewhat or very impolite, which was three times the rate among whites. And more than 20 percent of each group thought police were unfair, more than twice the white rate. Minority respondents were more divided on the other two measures. Significantly for the mayor, Hispanics were substantially more dissatisfied than black respondents on several issues.

Other questions about police revealed the same deep racial cleavages. When asked how big a neighborhood problem was that of "police stopping too many people on the streets without good reason," 8 percent of whites thought it was a big problem or somewhat of a problem, but 26 percent of Hispanics and 31 percent of African-Americans thought it merited concern. Fully 40 percent of Hispanics and 33 percent of blacks thought that "police being too tough on people they stop" was a problem, but only 10 percent of whites thought so; and police use of excessive force was at least somewhat of a concern for 34 percent of Hispanics and 32 percent of blacks, but only 8 percent of whites.

The deep racial cleavages in views of policing (revealed in figure 2-3) was potentially one of the most significant obstacles to the formation of police-community partnerships in Chicago. Another deep dividing factor was age—controlling for other factors, younger adults were much more unfavorably inclined toward the police; also, men were somewhat less favorable than were women. At the outset, all these cleavages would make it difficult for police to successfully form alliances with many community members. The split was not new. Surveys conducted by the Census Bureau during the mid-1970s found that differences between whites' views and African-Americans' views on the police were greater in Chicago than in any other major city they studied (Skogan, 1979). Our survey, conducted just in advance of the city's 1993 community-policing initiative, indicated that the cleavages were still profound. Many Chicagoans supported police efforts, but for a large number, the police were another of life's problems rather than a solution to them.

Moreover, both African-Americans and Hispanics felt under-represented on the police force. Blacks constituted only 25 percent of the force, but 38 percent of the city's population. In the highly prized detective division, 91 percent of the officers were white and only 2 percent were Hispanic (Illinois Advisory Committee, 1993). In the past, it also had been charged that police districts in African-American communities were understaffed, relative to the high levels of crime there. A 1983 study of crime, 911 calls, and police personnel allocation revealed that largely African-American districts had more 911 calls and crimes per officer assigned there, and longer periods during which police cars were not available to respond to calls for service (Washington, 1983).

While minority neighborhoods were the most crime-ravaged ones in the city, their political leaders were not interested in supporting tough enforcement efforts that would target their constituents. They also had a stake in curtailing police power, not in expanding it. In 1991, a prominent political issue in Chicago was the revival of allegations of abuse and torture of prisoners by police officers. By then, the city's demography dictated that all politicians had to pay careful attention to how their actions, and those of the police, were received by Hispanics and African-Americans; and the rhetoric of community policing played better than hard-nosed enforcement in this political environment. It seemed that the kind of get-tough-on-crime campaign that could elect a Republican mayor in Los Angeles could simply not net a victory in the 1990s in Chicago, due to its smaller white middle class.

Crafting City Hall's Strategy

At the outset, City Hall's predominant interest was money—more precisely, how to get more police on the streets without spending any more of it. City Hall approached this issue in the standard fashion for the 1990s: It commissioned a management study. The mayor wanted a team with strong analytic skills, one that could give him impartial advice about performance improvement measures like those that were becoming wildly popular in the private sector. The study was conducted by an international consulting firm. Its first report focused on traditional management issues, including such big-ticket items as medical leave; the financing of medical care for police employees; and the replacing of sworn officers with civilian employees so that police could be returned to street duty. The report also examined the savings involved in merging or disbanding various units and bureaus; privatizing some activities; cracking down on overtime; and scheduling officers' court appearances more efficiently. It analyzed 911 operations and department dispatching policies, and it recommended finding alternative ways of dealing with many calls for service. The consultants' second report turned from administrative and support services to operational matters and focused on the department's large Patrol Division. This report included a number of specific suggestions for further reducing operating costs, and it laid the foundation for what was to become community policing in Chicago.

The cost-cutting measures turned out to have significant implications for community policing. One of City Hall's biggest sources of dissatisfaction with the police department was its top-heavy bureaucracy. The mayor and his advisers felt that too many officers had found comfortable hideaways in district station houses and the downtown headquarters building, and that not enough were on the street. The elaborate paramilitary structure of the department seemed to have too many layers for a department in which the bulk of the work was done by patrol officers who were simply responding to radio calls. The second consulting report proposed to stretch existing dollars by reorganizing the city's 25 police districts into 18 larger ones, freeing an anticipated 344 officers at the time in administrative positions, for other duties. It proposed an expansion of the department's modest effort to civilianize station-house clerical and technical jobs, which would eventually free up 1,100 sworn officers. It recommended that the department downsize and redeploy some special units, and use more one-officer cars. The report also envisioned reducing the bureaucracy by closing one area-level administrative office, abolishing one rank level (that of captain), and reducing the number of lieutenants. The consultants advised that many of the functions performed by captains and lieutenants could be handled by lower-ranking and less-well-paid officers. Overall, the plan proposed to free 1,650 sworn officers from their current duties. Finally, the report called for the hiring of a new layer of civilian professionals (eventually, it was decided they would have MBAs) to serve as business managers for the districts.

The cost-cutting proposals advanced by the consulting team got a favorable reception at City Hall. They spoke to the mayor's concerns about bureaucracy and mismanagement. He particularly favored the idea of compressing the rank structure, for he had long suspected that the work performed by most captains did not justify their lofty civil service status. (He once exclaimed to us, "Captains! Nobody can tell me what they do!") Several of the mayor's prominent policy advisers were interested only in recommendations that promised to increase the efficiency with which the department pursued its traditional tasks. Two of the most important mayoral advisers later supported the development of a community-policing plan because they perceived that it would put more officers on the streets and in visible contact with the public. However, other City Hall staff members had a larger vision of what a thoroughgoing

management study might accomplish. Their plan had been to engage a police-oriented organization, such as the Police Executive
Research Forum, to conduct the management review. As a compro-
mise, when a mainstream management consulting firm was hired
for the job, the city specified that the consulting firm's in-house
policing expert should take a prominent role and provide "the police perspective." This decision turned out to be crucial.

The consulting firm's first report included a sketchy six-page
appendix that described a plan for community policing in Chicago.
It was inserted, at the last minute, by the team's policing expert. He
did so over the opposition of some team members, who felt that
posing such a radical and unproven alternative lay outside their
mandate. It was also opposed by the chairman of a civilian advisory
committee that had quietly been formed to guide the management
study. He felt it "sold out" Chicago police in favor of a pop socio-
logical idea. However, the chief consultant got the mayor's ear: At
a meeting with the mayor to discuss the first report, he pointed out
that the officers who would be freed for new duties were costing
the city about $48 million per year. He outlined two courses the
mayor could take with this money. One was to save it by shrinking
the size of the force appropriately through attrition, and, in effect,
returning it to the taxpayer. He then argued for the adoption, instead, of a strategy of keeping the department at its established size
and making alternative use of the hundreds of officers whose time
would be freed up by the recommended management efficiencies.
If their new tasks were not clearly specified, he argued, they would
quickly be reabsorbed by the department. It had a strong business-
as-usual orientation, and the freed-up officers would vanish without a trace. The mayor liked this idea, which responded to his frustration with the organization, and he called for a more detailed
officer-utilization plan as part of the consulting firm's second report.

Although it was soon superseded by events, the second report
set the agenda for later planning efforts by the police department
itself. The report called for dividing district officers into two teams.
Some would be given long-term beat assignments and would answer the calls that came from their area. The others—rapid-
response officers—would pick up overload calls and be quickly assigned to emergency situations. The second report also favored
freeing officers for permanent beat assignments, by cutting back on
the city's traditional commitment to sending a patrol car in response to a large percentage of 911 calls. This was dubbed a policy

of "differential response." The plan also referred to the need for contributions to the effort by neighborhood groups, the private sector, and other city agencies. Using the consulting firm's exhaustive analysis of where idle resources might be found in the organization, the plan documented the argument that the department already had the resources that it needed to begin to reinvent itself.

It was apparent, on the surface, that community policing was going to be a difficult sell. Powerful senior commanders thought it was a bad idea and did their best at every turn to stymie the consultants' investigations. Consulting-team members visited other cities to learn what was wrong with community policing there and tried to respond accordingly in their plan. Their number-crunching did not indicate that community policing was going to be particularly inexpensive, either. Even with the labor that the consultants anticipated saving via the cost-cutting measures, the plan still called for the eventual hiring of an additional 40 to 50 officers for each district, to adequately staff it. The plan called for community policing to be phased in, by beginning it in selected prototype districts.

The mayor had initially been cool to the idea of community policing. It seemed vague to him, "wishy-washy," and appeared to be just a call for better police-community relations. By 1991, discussions of community policing were widespread, and some kind of program called community policing had been adopted in hundreds of American cities. However, this concept had not found root in Chicago, and no one of importance at City Hall even knew about this nationwide movement. At the police department, out-of-town visitors who expressed an interest in community policing were sent to a district where the commander was experimenting with his own program, without downtown support or interest. The consulting team's policing expert had been pushing the concept of community policing in meetings at City Hall, but only a few members of the mayor's staff seemed at all interested. However, in early 1992, the mayor attended an out-of-town conference which included an extensive discussion of community policing, and he came back charged with new interest. What he had heard there reminded him of what the chief consultant had been telling him, and his stock began to rise at City Hall meetings. As one informant described it, the consulting firm's policing expert provided "the big-picture vision" and was "preacherlike in his presentations," in a process that otherwise dwelled on nuts-and-bolts issues. This was important, for battles over a third airport and gambling revenue for Chicago distracted the mayor, and it was difficult to keep his attention focused on the police department. The outside policing expert, lobbying the mayor's friends and advisers, used the argument that he should push ahead because community policing was a program that the mayor could institute without the support of the state legislature or the state's Republican governor. Further, the management study had concluded that the mayor could at least launch it without imposing a tax increase to pay for more officers. When the mayor's airport and gambling initiatives began to falter at the state capital, this argument was taken seriously.

When it finally was launched by City Hall, it was clear that there was going to be considerable difficulty in getting community policing off the ground in Chicago. The department's politically savvy senior command staff was far from convinced that it was a good idea. Many senior managers within the department disagreed with any program that seemed to divert resources from traditional enforcement efforts. Many thought it was another civilian fad. They thought they could wait this one out, as they had done with others in the past. Apart from the command staff, 12,500 police officers would also have to be convinced that community policing was a good idea, or at least that it was a program that their on-the-spot supervisors really expected them to carry out. They in turn confronted a deeply divided community that too often saw the police as another of their problems. Translating the consultants' plan into a real program that would make a noticeable difference in their lives would be a formidable challenge.

3

Crafting a Program

Finding New Leadership

It was a propitious moment for addressing change in the Chicago department, for the incumbent superintendent of police had reached an age at which he could gracefully be retired. The superintendent had been selected several years earlier by a reform-minded mayor, in a decision that was considered surprising at the time. He was a tough and bluff "old school" cop. It was rumored that this had caught the then-mayor's eye, in contrast to other final candidates for the position, who had espoused a more sophisticated management line. Once in office, it was apparent that the superintendent liked the department just the way it was, with himself in charge. So he proved actively hostile to the idea of community policing, and to City Hall concerns about efficiency and responsiveness. He hoped to be retained as superintendent by the new mayor, but City Hall was counting the days until he could be replaced by invoking the department's retirement rule.

The process of finding his replacement began in the autumn of 1991, just as a sketchy plan for community policing was being drafted. In Chicago, the search for a new superintendent is conducted by a civilian oversight committee, which advertises the job opening and interviews semifinalists for it. Among the hurdles applicants faced this time were three essay questions. The second called for them to "discuss the pros and cons of community-oriented policing, particularly as a viable law enforcement philosophy for the Chicago Police Department." The application packet also warned that the department was civilizing administrative jobs, and that a management study had identified "opportunities for improving administrative effectiveness and efficiency."

Most of the consultants' work on their second report, including its community-policing plan, was completed before the new superintendent was selected, in April 1992. The three final candidates recommended to the mayor by the civilian oversight board were briefed individually on the plan by members of the consulting team; the candidates were informed that this was the direction in which the department was heading, and during the briefings they all agreed to support it. Key players at City Hall tried to find out how they had reacted to the presentation, but the consultants tried to stay out of the selection process. The mayor himself interviewed each of the candidates and deliberated about his selection for several months. During the interregnum, his press secretary noted that the mayor wanted to select a superintendent who would use the consulting firm's report "as a blueprint to revamp the entrenched police bureaucracy." A local newspaper opined that "the police management report . . . has become the mayor's bible of police administration, and it gives him a public license for changing the department" (Kass and Stein, 1992). During the news conference at which he introduced his new superintendent, the mayor indicated that he expected him to carry out the report's recommendations.

The candidate that ultimately was selected by the mayor had risen quietly through the ranks, often serving in administrative positions. He had a reputation for being cautious, but for knowing his way around—his father had been a precinct captain. As the president of the civilian oversight board put it, "His career . . . is an example of someone who pays his dues, touches the right bases, and eventually emerges in the number one position" (Stein, 1992). Like the other final candidates for the position of superintendent, he had indicated his support for the emergent plan. But in addition, he had a reputation for being open to community concerns and was one of the department's more effective external spokesmen. City Hall perceived that he would be committed and cooperative, and that he would push the implementation of a more detailed community-policing plan within the department.

The next step was to find a hands-on manager who would direct the day-to-day details of planning and implementing a new model of policing for the city. In the summer of 1992, the soon-to-be-appointed CAPS manager received a call from the superintendent's personal assistant asking him to attend a meeting at the consultants' Chicago office. At that meeting, which was attended by the superintendent and other high-ranking department personnel, he was told that he would be the manager of a community-policing program that would be launched in the coming year.

The new project manager was an assistant to the chief of the patrol division—a job that put him about four layers below the top of the department's organizational hierarchy. He was responsible for seeing that positions in the districts were staffed, cars were in place, and supervisors were on the job. Until this point, his career path had been mostly on the operational, rather than the administrative, side of the agency—most notably, he had directed narcotics investigations. He was the second youngest member (at age 42) of the department's exempt staff. Although lacking downtown administrative experience, he was one of those who had applied when the position of superintendent of police was vacant. He had impressed the oversight board and had been one of the ten candidates on the board's shortlist. The process of applying for the position of superintendent and preparing an answer for the pivotal essay question about community policing had required him to read and think about the topic and talk to experts in the field. Taking on his new role as CAPS manager would force him to develop a more sophisticated view of the entire organization and its political context—a new vantage point for him.

But the CAPS manager needed help. At first, he wore two hats, serving as a deputy chief charged with a host of routine administrative responsibilities as well as his new duties. His eventual source of staff support and leadership assistance was to be the Research and Development (R&D) unit of the department. This was a new job for R&D—as in many departments, Chicago's R&D unit did no research and very little development work. Its role was to read slips from the suggestion box and write directives and policy statements on subjects like uniform requirements and weapon use. The process of writing directives was a long one. As one R&D employee put it:

> There's a certain complexity to all this. You've got unions to work with, and then everything has to be reviewed by 110 exempt people. Depending upon the complexity, it takes various amounts of

time for them to get to final-draft stage. Like disciplinary policy—
that can take 12 years.

Another officer noted:

> R&D is really big on R and real small on D. They like to study
> things to death—it's really frustrating.

As CAPS began to become a reality, R&D had to take on a very
different mission, and become heavily involved in planning and
managing organizational change. This called for a new director, and
one was at hand. She worked for a state criminal justice agency and
knew the superintendent and many key players at City Hall. In the
fall of 1992 she submitted a proposal to the superintendent, titled
"Reinventing R&D in Chicago." It described the steps required to
reinvigorate the unit. The proposal was offered as "a package deal,"
according to insiders, one that included the addition of the new
director as well as several other staff members. The proposal was
well received, and the new director and her staff began working in
February 1993.

The fact that the new R&D personnel were civilians, and that
more were soon hired, was a striking change from the business-as-
usual attitude in the department. From the outset, the civilian staffers knew that they had to prove themselves within the department.
Two of them noted:

> There's a general belief that civilian employees cannot see certain
> things clearly, like some administrative issues.

> The schism [involving civilians and sworn officers] really does ex-
> ist. What has been most difficult for me is dealing with the rank
> structure—designated authority. I sometimes can't get answers in
> a reasonable amount of time because of the chain of command. It's
> a real impediment.

While many officers agreed that civilians brought important
perspectives and skills to the department, they also expressed concern that civilians would never see things as police do—from "the
police perspective." However, even sworn officers in the unit were
pleased that its bureaucratic structure had been flattened, and they
believed that the new civilians would help drive the change process. In fact, later, the new director of R&D was appointed CAPS
comanager, which formalized her role. Eventually, the two comanagers worked as a team to create a vision of what CAPS should look
like, and of the steps that needed to be taken to reach its goals.

A Prototyping Strategy for Organizational Change

The consulting firm's report of July 1992 recommended that community policing be tested in several districts before being implemented citywide. In January 1993, the mayor, his City Hall advisers, top department personnel, and members of the consulting team met to decide how many experimental areas there would be. The police lobbied for one or two test districts, which could easily be staffed with existing resources, but the consultants insisted they could handle more, and some in City Hall wanted more areas in order to signal the city's commitment to the program. The consultants anticipated that an average of 40 additional officers would be needed to fully staff the beat teams and rapid-response units in each of Chicago's police districts. This meant that about 200 officers would need to be found in order to begin community policing in five districts, and a lot more would have to be found quickly to staff an expanded program designed to cover the entire city. Debate raged as to whether such a large number of officers could be found within the department, with the leader of the consulting team insisting that it could be done.

One difficulty was that there were multiple and conflicting sets of numbers given to describe how many district officers were serving in what positions, as well as different scenarios about how many could be freed from their current duties. The department's personnel director, a civilian put there by City Hall to make the agency more responsive to policy directives, had a set of numbers that was based on the payroll, which was an unreliable guide to who was actually doing what. The consulting team had developed its own numbers by auditing the districts' books and checking them against the data on who was reporting for duty, by attending roll-call sessions at the stations. The two sets of figures did not always agree. Ambitious commanders developed bookkeeping tricks to hide the true number of officers they controlled, so that they had backup personnel to police events and to throw into the field when emergencies occurred; this let them demonstrate that they were "can-do" problem solvers. They also needed extra people to make up for the irritating habit of savvy patrol officers who would "drop off the radio" and disappear for large portions of their shift. The consultants themselves were also internally divided about the scenarios by which officers could be freed from their existing duties. The pessimists were crushed by the failure of a reorganization plan that they had crafted to free up the officers that were needed, while the optimists thought there was a great deal of elasticity in the number of officers that the department required for many of its operations. Yet a third set of personnel figures was held by a senior police executive who was opposed to the project. During the planning process, his response to virtually every proposed plan was that officers could not be found to staff it, but he would ultimately produce the numbers he thought his boss wanted. All of the players furiously crunched their numbers as the decision about the test districts approached. City Hall was upset about the whole situation and took it as further evidence that the department was not very well managed.

The number of experimental districts was finalized at a second summit meeting with the mayor. The consultants again lobbied for five districts, and the police for fewer. Although there was continued disagreement about the numbers of officers that could be freed for the program, the mayor decided to begin with the larger number.

The department was asked to submit the names of ten prospective test districts, from which five would be chosen by City Hall. This process set off an intense period of politicking. If the mayor had any doubt that the program was a politically popular one, his fears would have been alleviated by the ensuing citywide scramble for inclusion on the list of community-policing districts; no one wanted to be left out. Aldermen and community organizations tested their clout in the struggle. In the Rogers Park District, a community organization orchestrated hundreds of calls to the mayor's office within a two-hour period to press for selection of their area. The alderman for this community gathered 4,000 signatures on petitions calling for a ward referendum on the area's participation. Eventually, four of the department's choices were selected: Englewood, Marquette, Austin, and Rogers Park. The fifth district that was selected, Morgan Park, was not among the 10 proposed by the department, but was named by City Hall. This mixed-race, largely middle-class area was the home of many city workers and was represented downtown by powerful community organizations that managed, in this instance, to "deliver" for their constituents. One newspaper reported that aldermen for wards that were left out of the program "groused openly" about being "jilted" (Spielman, 1993).

The community-policing areas, which are illustrated in Figure 3-1, broadly represented the city's neighborhoods. They ranged from being fairly affluent to desperately poor, and from being racially heterogeneous to solidly segregated by race. Rogers Park was

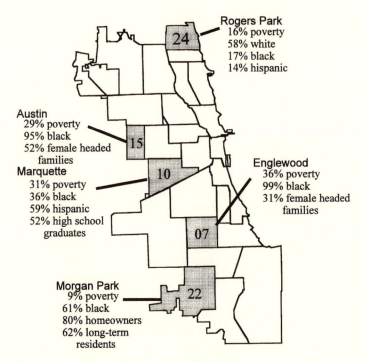

Figure 3-1 Chicago's prototype districts.

the most ethnically diverse area—17 percent of its residents were black, 14 percent were Hispanic, and 58 percent white, with many other ethnic groups comprising the remaining 11 percent. Almost all residents of Austin and Englewood, on the other hand, were African-Americans. Marquette was made up of blacks (to the north) and Hispanics (to the south), with the latter making up almost 60 percent of the total. Only slightly more than half the adults in Marquette had graduated from high school. On the other hand, in Morgan Park, middle-class whites constituted a 40-percent minority, while about 60 percent of the district's residents were African-Americans. Morgan Park residents were easily the most affluent—80 percent were homeowners. Rogers Park residents were significantly better off than those of the remaining districts, but they were the most transient—only 24 percent had lived there for a decade, while the comparable figure for Morgan Park was 62 percent. In Austin and Englewood, about 30 percent of households were headed by females, and almost an equal number of residents were living below the poverty line.

The CAPS manager was pleased with the selections, which became known as the prototypes. He noted the obvious omission of a district that included high-rise family public housing. About 3 percent of the city's residents lived in family public housing, many in blocks of high-rise apartments famous for the extent to which they concentrated human misery in a small space. Though fraught with high rates of violence, guns, and drugs, it would remain unclear how Chicago's public housing projects would fit into the department's new community-policing model.

Learning by Doing

Besides being recommended by the city's consultants, a prototyping process, rather than an elaborately scripted change process, was also required because early CAPS planning efforts failed. The process started too slowly. Although the first CAPS manager was assigned to lead the project in the summer of 1992, he originally had no staff support and precious little time off from his regular assignment. Only after the consultants, and a City Hall staffer assigned to watch over the project, discovered that no progress was being made was the pressure turned up by City Hall: The manager was relieved of his other duties, and the mayor made it clear to an assemblage of top brass in his office that the project manager was in charge of community policing in Chicago. But even then, things moved slowly—in part, because everything that had to be cleared through City Hall got delayed. Early on, it was hard to keep the mayor's attention focused on community policing.

The department's first move had been to form committees. The CAPS manager identified several department areas for change, including training; performance evaluation; neighborhood relations; computerized crime analysis; 911 response; and the organization of field operations. During the summer and early fall of 1992, he formed implementation committees for each topic. Each committee was instructed to develop a mission statement and establish its goals and objectives. In the fall, the superintendent invited all members of the department to participate in the work of the committees. While this stirred new involvement, many committees found themselves stepping backward to incorporate their new members. In January 1993, a retreat was held for a progress review, but while some committees had completed their work, others had made little headway. Ultimately, the CAPS manager asked each committee to turn in a final report on its work and go out of business, but several never put words on paper.

In the end, most of the committees' work did not turn out to be very useful. The participants were, in the words of a seasoned observer, "good tactical planners but poor strategic planners." Their recommendations were prematurely specific, and not prioritized. More important, they were not based on a clear vision of what community policing involved or where the department was headed. This could only come later, when the model became clearer and a department mission statement and supporting documentation could be crafted by the superintendent. Since the committees' recommendations were essentially without a rationale, it was hard to know when to adopt, or how to adapt, them. As a result, the committees provided little useful guidance in the fluid circumstances in which CAPS management found itself.

Furthermore, CAPS was never elaborately planned. That would have taken extensive research; further investigation of projects in other cities; the calculation of elaborate staffing and budget projections; and the drafting of elaborately written plans that would have to be reviewed and approved (and perhaps stalled or killed) at many levels by the department's bureaucracy and City Hall reviewers. The predictability and control that a textbook planning-and-implementation approach would have offered was attractive in the police culture. In addition, the department historically distrusted its employees, expecting many of them to shirk their work and stick only to job requirements "on the books." Many top managers assumed it was their natural inclination to loaf, and that too many officers were potentially corrupt. There were vocal complaints because neat organizational charts and cut-and-dried CAPS job descriptions were not devised before the program was put into the field. As one original committee member put it, "I'd sleep a lot better at night if we just told them what to do." But this kind of planned change was impossible.

Instead, faced with inadequate information about many important matters, too little time to engage in strategic thinking, and surprisingly little staff support for such a high-priority project, CAPS's managers made a virtue out of their situation by adopting a different model of organizational change. They adopted an iterative planning strategy, one for which the original designation of the experimental districts as prototypes proved to be prophetic. They adopted a "try it and see if it works" strategy. Planning became interactive and evolutionary, almost a survival-of-the-fittest process. The prototypes provided a place to try out ideas, identify mistakes, and try fresh approaches when things did not work. Because of the late start, the program development effort had an extremely compressed time frame. As a result, multiple program components were under scrutiny at the same moment. In industrial circles, this approach to product planning is called "prototyping." It involves developing products by testing a succession of rough working models and laboring collaboratively to fix what proves to be wrong with them in the real world. Relentlessly innovative corporations are often prototypers; this process demands flexibility and rapid internal communication among developers about the successes and failures of each iteration. Flexibility and communication were not, however, the department's strong suit, so just the process for planning CAPS called for the organization to change.

Learning by Communicating

The organizational change strategy the department decided on required good communication up and down the organizational hierarchy if it were going to succeed. We have already noted how poor the department's information systems were; it was even difficult to tell how many people were at work. But downtown needed to know what was going on in the field and to learn if it was working. Bad news, along with the good, had to filter upward on a timely basis. As a CAPS manager noted at one district commander's meeting, "I'm not looking for platitudes; I want to know the problems, also. I know you're having problems—we want to hear them, so we can make adjustments." One of the important achievements of R&D was the establishment of new lines of communication within the department, a place which (in the words of one sworn staff member) "has had tremendous difficulty communicating with itself. It's a top-down organization." Within R&D, staffers could now wander in and out of the director's office or call her directly; the chain-of-command principle that controlled communication even within this small unit was broken down. The director, in turn, had a similar relationship with the superintendent. She had direct access to him, and he felt comfortable walking into the R&D office to speak directly with her. The superintendent also developed a pattern of casually dropping in at CAPS-related meetings, just to keep up with what was going on. At key meetings, he often gave opening remarks that clearly communicated his commitment to, and involvement in, the success of the program.

One of the first communication devices to be adopted was weekly district commander meetings. These gatherings were interactive ones, and many problems were ironed out as they emerged. At the meetings, the commanders, their neighborhood-relations staff members, and other district personnel met with the CAPS manager, the R&D director and her staff, and City Hall representatives. The sworn CAPS comanager described his goal for the meetings: "I don't want to hear the wonderful things that are going on. I know that's bullshit. I want to hear about the problems." The meetings provided some of the first opportunities for feedback regarding the implementation and actual operation of CAPS and its reality on the streets; they were a link between program theory and program implementation. For example, it was during the district commander meetings that downtown managers realized that a system of permanent turf assignments for beat officers that they had developed was unrealistic due to foul-ups in the operation of the 911 dispatching system. Later, these sessions were held on a monthly basis, after many major issues were resolved in the field.

Shortly after the inauguration of the prototype commander meetings, City Hall appointed two staff members to serve as liaisons to CAPS, and they regularly attended all important meetings. One liaison staffer virtually joined the management team, and participated in the development of most key program designs. She served as the department's informational conduit to City Hall.

Staff members of the Mayor's Office of Inquiry and Information (MOII), who were charged with coordinating the delivery of city services in support of CAPS, met regularly with the district commanders and the CAPS comanagers to work out service delivery problems. Representatives of various city departments also appeared, depending on the topics at hand. These meetings served several purposes. They gave district personnel an opportunity to identify problems that particular city agencies needed to address. They gave the districts an opportunity to complain to department heads when the problems were not being resolved satisfactorily. They also gave department heads an opportunity to explain to police the legal and bureaucratic issues involved in resolving some of the problems brought to their attention. Finally, the meetings provided MOII coordinators with an opportunity to explain, and get feedback on, various reporting forms and the format of computerized problem status reports that they had devised to document progress on service requests.

Also, an internal newsletter was developed for communicating with rank-and-file officers. It highlighted upcoming events, showcased CAPS successes, and articulated what the program was about. A writer and public-relations specialist was added to the R&D staff to coordinate this and other media products, and staff members went into the field to collect success stories for the newsletter. Each issue highlighted an aspect of CAPS that was related to one of the prototype districts. (Later, all of these products were also featured on the department's community-policing web page, accessible via the Internet.)

R&D staff members and CAPS trainers who were not on assignment were also sent into the field to serve as troubleshooters for problems as they emerged. They rode with officers in beat and rapid-response cars, visited stations, and conducted personal interviews with police officers and their supervisors. Their role was to get the "real" story on how CAPS was operating in the field, and to report back to the R&D office. The sworn CAPS manager knew that executives downtown often did not get enough detail about real-world problems to make appropriate changes when difficulties occurred in the field.

As problems arose, focus groups were assembled to identify exactly what was wrong and how it could be fixed. For example, as CAPS unfolded, it became clear that the role of sergeants was not defined clearly, and that they often felt unsure about what was expected of them. There was confusion about their role in maintaining beat integrity; in the coordination of city services; in the continuing demand they felt in meeting traditional performance standards; and in dispatching problems. These and other issues were hashed out by focus groups, and new procedures and guidelines were then developed. About one month after the program began, another 10 focus-group sessions were held with officers who were working in the prototypes. They revealed that officers did not understand what was expected of them, and that they were not getting clear guidance from their supervisors. They disliked the new paperwork associated with the program and reported that they were not being dispatched in line with CAPS guidelines.

R&D staffers also conducted surveys of officers. In June 1993, they distributed questionnaires to 572 officers (about one-third of the total) serving in the prototype districts. The survey gauged the frequency with which they were attending community meetings; exchanging information across watches; and being called off their beats, rather than maintaining beat integrity. In structured settings, such as training, quality-control surveys were routinely distributed to assess officer's experiences. For example, the department's training-evaluation form consisted of 12 questions that rated instructor effectiveness; participant involvement; and the appropriateness of the materials, methods, and skills taught. The results of these questionnaires were tabulated and returned to the trainers.

Finally, our evaluation provided feedback about selected activities. In particular, our review of the department's early training efforts helped the police evaluate their own internal processes (Dantzker et al., 1994). As a result of our feedback, future training efforts changed a great deal. Our observations also revealed that beat meetings were not being conducted appropriately, and that lower-level supervisors did not share downtown's enthusiasm for the program.

Learning from Other Cities

To a certain extent, the department also learned from the experiences of other cities that had tried community policing. While to outsiders this would seem a natural strategy, Chicago's police department, like many others, had a very insular view of the world. Indeed, a superintendent had not been appointed from the outside since 1960. There was no budget to support staff visits to other cities' departments or trips to conferences. The department did not maintain a news and clipping service that could alert executives to programs and events elsewhere. For a long time, the Chicago police resisted calling what they were doing "community policing," because this would make it seem like the idea came from someplace else. The label they formally adopted—Chicago Alternative Policing Strategy—signaled that theirs was a home-grown product.

Some news leaked in from the outside world, however. While preparing their detailed second report on community policing, the mayor's consultants traveled to other cities to observe programs in action and to abstract lessons they could apply for their client. They had a keen eye for the risks involved in moving in this direction. In New York and Houston, they were alerted to the political risks faced by departments that publicly deviated from a tough-on-crime stance. This opened them to attacks by opponents of the program, who could charge that community policing put the public at risk by diverting resources into untried social experiments. In Los Angeles and Atlanta, they found that officers could not sustain community-oriented projects unless they were somehow freed from responding to 911 calls at frequent and unpredictable intervals; indeed, meeting with the public, researching problems, and orchestrating community and interagency involvement in solving them took time. In Los Angeles, community officers were dissatisfied over the conflict between what they were told to do (which was new) and how their performance was evaluated (by the old standards, including how many arrests they made). Again, both demands competed for their time. In New York, there was conflict over whether community involvement was "real" police work, and officers assigned to it were treated as second-class citizens by their fellow officers. The consultants learned that it was important to avoid letting the inevitable label "social work" stick to Chicago's program. In Houston, mid-level managers felt left out of the planning process and felt their authority was undercut when new responsibilities were passed on to the beat officers. Many became implacable foes of community policing (Booz, Allen & Hamilton, 1992).

News from outside Chicago was also delivered in a series of one-day seminars sponsored by the state's criminal-justice agency. These seminars brought in academics and practitioners in the area of community policing, who shared their experiences with members of the exempt staff. Among them were researchers who had conducted evaluations of community policing, as well as police executives and professional community organizers from around the country. These were interactive sessions that allowed participants to ask questions, challenge the ideas that were presented, and try to relate them to policing in Chicago. In addition, the agency brought in experts who conducted more intimate workshops with commanders of the prototype districts, allowing them to openly air issues in their districts and their personal concerns about CAPS.

Developing the Underpinnings

Running in parallel with practical planning processes was the development of the program theory that it was to reflect. One of the most significant written products of CAPS's first year was the department's mission statement and a supporting report, "Together We Can." Issued in October 1993, this 30-page document described the superintendent's philosophy of community policing and identified, step by step, many of the key components of change needed for the program to succeed in Chicago. The department's mission statement read as follows:

> The Chicago Police Department, as part of, and empowered by, the community, is committed to protect the lives, property and rights of all people, to maintain order, and to enforce the law im-

partially. We will provide quality police service in partnership with other members of the community. To fulfill our mission, we will strive to attain the highest degree of ethical behavior and professional conduct at all times.

"Together We Can" (the title was contributed by one of the consultants) was drafted by R&D staff members and consultants and then extensively rewritten by the superintendent himself. It opened with a "rationale for change" that reviewed the limits of the traditional model of policing that had characterized the department. Drawing on research on policing and the depiction of a crime rate that was soaring (despite the department's best efforts), it argued for a "smarter" approach to policing that would capitalize on the strengths of the city's neighborhoods. It argued that the department had to be "reinvented," so it could form a partnership with the community that stressed crime prevention, customer service, and honest and ethical conduct. Almost half of the document focused on what had to be reinvented—ranging from officer selection to department management, training, performance evaluation, call dispatching, technology, and budgeting. The document was mailed to every member of the department, and, to help ensure that it would be read, it was included on the list of reading materials from which questions would be drawn for the next promotion exam. Its concreteness helped it become the basis for planning the eventual city-wide implementation of CAPS.

The Evolving Plan

Because of the planning model involved, it took a while before a clear outline emerged in regard to what a community-policing program for Chicago would look like. The plan described in reports by the consulting team had laid the foundation for the program, but other important elements quickly emerged, and some of the original ideas disappeared. We could discern certain aspects of the program that were actually carried out in the prototype districts only in retrospect. While myriad practical details were involved, the program had six key elements, each of which is detailed in the chapters that follow.

1. *The entire department and the city were to be involved.*
Rather than forming special units, the department was committed to changing its entire organization. Community-policing roles were

to be developed for all of the units in the organization, including the detective, tactical, gangs, and narcotics divisions, rather than just for uniformed officers who were working in the districts. Most of this had to wait until the program had proven itself in the field, however. During the first year, a few units were decentralized, so that district commanders had control over plainclothes tactical units and youth officers, and they could integrate the efforts of these special units with plans being developed at the grassroots level. The commitment to citywide involvement was reflected in the decision to use diverse districts (several of which were very high crime places) as prototypes for the new program, and to use existing personnel and leadership. In the words of one department executive, the police did not "stack the deck in favor of success." The CAPS manager knew that once the program encompassed the entire city, it would have to work with the talent that the department had. While in some cities, community policing is confined to selected districts, or utilizes volunteer officers (who often are paid overtime through special federal programs), Chicago was eventually going to have to make the program work using its existing personnel, and to stay within its budget.

2. *Officers were to have permanent beat assignments.*
Giving careful attention to the residents and specific problems of various neighborhoods required officers to know their beats, including the problems, trends, hot spots, resources, and relationships there. In order to develop partnerships with the community, they had to stay in one place long enough for residents to know them and learn to trust them, and officers had to have enough free time to engage in community work. However, the experiences of other cities made clear the importance of continuing to maintain, at the same time, acceptable levels of response to 911 calls.

The fundamental geographical building block of the new program was the beat. The city's 25 police districts were divided into 279 beats, which had an average of 10,000 residents and 4,100 households. Each district had between 9 and 15 beats, staffed with officers that were assigned to the district partly by a "weighted workload" formula that accounted for calls for service from the area. To resolve conflicts between the dual priorities of working with the public and responding promptly to calls for service, officers in each district were divided into beat teams and rapid-response units. Beat teams were to be dispatched less frequently so that they had time to work on neighborhood projects. Whenever possible, they were to be sent only to calls that originated in their beat and even then, they were to be exempted from certain classes of calls to which their turf specialization did not seem to make any contribution. The goal was to keep beat teams on their own turf— thus maintaining "beat integrity"—at least 70 percent of the time. Other calls were to be assigned to rapid-response units, tactical officers, and other teams that ranged throughout the district.

The matter of which officers served in which roles was a complicated one that was closely regulated by the city's contract with the police union. In Chicago, officers choose their district and shift through a bidding system based on seniority. (And these involved trade-offs; we knew officers with almost 20 years of seniority who had to work the midnight shift to get the district assignment of their choice.) The contract also limited the ability of the department to change the *number* of officers that could be assigned each year to each shift in each district. Thus, the general distribution of officers was effectively out of the hands of the department. Only within these parameters could district commanders decide which officers would serve in beat or rapid-response units. For the prototypes, they generally relied on their lieutenants and sergeants to negotiate the matter shift by shift—which was further complicated by the desire of most officers to remain attached to their partners. In general, officers seemed to get the assignment they wanted. Those who craved the excitement of responding to a succession of hot 911 calls jockeyed to get into a rapid-response car, while those who were interested in community-oriented work gravitated to beat teams. But the yearly rebidding process meant that they could be bumped from their position, or that they could try to improve their lot as they accumulated a bit more seniority, so that there was a steady circulation of officers through various assignments over time. The union contract thus militated against the creation of a force that might be split permanently between community and traditional policing, something that the CAPS managers, in any event, wanted to avoid. It also meant that there was somewhat more turnover in beat assignments than some community groups thought was optimal.

3. *There was to be a serious commitment to training.*
The department invested an immense amount of effort, at a critical time, in training officers and their supervisors in the skills required to identify and solve problems in conjunction with the community. Training was considered absolutely essential in promoting officer understanding and commitment to the program, and in providing

direction for officers and supervisors in their new roles. Without adequate training, they would inevitably fall back on what they knew best, which was the tried-and-true routines of traditional policing. Several other cities involved in community policing ignored the importance of training and, in effect, merely instructed their officers to "go out and do community policing." Not surprisingly, they failed to mount serious programs (Sadd and Grinc, 1993). The CAPS manager also believed that by putting a strong emphasis on training, they also would send the message to the rank and file that community policing was real and that the people downtown were committed to the program.

The training program that was developed featured several departures from the business-as-usual orientation in the department. It was planned and run by R&D, not the training academy. The sessions were cotaught by civilian trainers. The program included prototype officers of all ranks, and before the program began, at the end of April 1993, everyone received several days of training. Chapter 4 details some of the stresses and strains involved in fielding a new training effort of this magnitude in such a short time.

4. *The community was to play a significant role in the program.* At the core of CAPS lay the formation of police-community partnerships focused on identifying and solving problems at the neighborhood level. Community policing assumes that police cannot solve neighborhood problems on their own; to achieve success, it depends on the cooperation of the community and public and private agencies. In Chicago, one problem-solving role for police was to engage community resources, and to draw other city agencies into identifying and responding to local concerns. In "Together We Can," it was noted that "the Department and the rest of the community must establish new ways of actually working together. New methods must be put in place to jointly identify problems, propose solutions, and implement changes. The Department's ultimate goal should be community empowerment" (Chicago Police Department, 1994: 16).

This commitment to community involvement was operationalized in two ways. First, beat meetings began in every beat. They were regular—usually monthly—gatherings of small groups of residents and officers who actually worked the beat. These meetings were held in church basements and park buildings all over the city. Second, advisory committees were formed at the district level to meet with commanders and district staff. They were composed of community leaders, school council members, ministers, business operators, and representatives of institutions of significance in the district. The beat meetings and district advisory-committee gatherings were the principal forums for the development of joint police-citizen plans to tackle neighborhood issues. Chapter 5 examines, in detail, how well they did their jobs.

5. *Policing was to be linked to the delivery of city services.*
Community policing inevitably involved the expansion of the police department's mandate to include a broad range of concerns that previously lay outside its competence. Or, as the program's detractors put it, police were expected to be "social workers." The expansion of the police mandate was a response to several factors. Senior department managers understood that police could put a temporary lid on many crime-related problems, but that they could never fix them. They wanted to create problem-solving systems that could keep the lid on even after they had moved on. The involvement of the police in coordinating services also reflected City Hall's plan to use CAPS to inject more discipline into the city's service-delivery system. Service standards and accountability mechanisms were put in place, thereby advancing the mayor's municipal-efficiency agenda as well as supporting problem solving. The expansion of the mandate also reflected consumer demand. As chapter 5 documents, when beat officers met with neighborhood residents, the concerns that were voiced included all manner of problems, and the kinds of crimes that police are traditionally organized to tackle were often fairly low on the priority list. The CAPS managers knew that if the officers' response to community concerns was, "That's not a police matter," residents would not show up for another meeting.

From the beginning, the delivery of city services in the prototype districts was linked to community policing via special service request forms. They were to be generated by everyone, but were the special domain of beat teams. Officers' service requests triggered a prioritizing and case-tracking process that greatly increased the responsiveness of other city agencies. As chapter 6 documents, the successful integration of CAPS with a broad range of city services was one of the most important organizational successes of the first year of the program.

6. *There was to be an emphasis on crime analysis.*
From the outset, geographic analysis of crime was considered a key

component of community policing in Chicago. It was to form the knowledge base that would drive the beat problem-solving process and the tactical operations of special squads. Computer technology was to be used to speed up the collection and analysis of data so as to quickly identify crime patterns and target areas that demanded police attention. An easy-to-use crime-mapping system was to be developed for use on computers at each district station. Overnight data entry ensured that the results would be timely. Crime maps were to be routinely distributed at beat meetings and accessible to the public at each station. Other analytic tools included "beat planners," which were beat officers' notebooks filled with local information. Also, new roll-call procedures were to be developed to encourage officers on various shifts to share information about beat-level events and community resources. All of this was intended to foster problem solving at the beat level. Unlike many program elements, only a little progress was made along these fronts during the first year of the program.

Leveraging Resources

Another formidable task for City Hall and the police department was that of finding the resources necessary to support the whole endeavor. Community policing was going to take additional officers, civilian aides, equipment, and training. Consultants needed to be hired to give advice and prepare specialized training materials, and staff retreats needed to be funded. The department needed new computers and software, as well as local area networks throughout the city, to support crime analysis. Ironically, the first efforts to find these resources foundered when the mayor's political intuition failed him.

New Taxes and Threatened Take-Backs

In January 1993, the mayor dropped what was characterized by the media as a "tax bombshell" on the city council. After an arbitrator issued a ruling that settled a dispute with the union over the police contract, he asked for an $11.6 million property-tax hike in order to pay for the raises and new officers. This announcement came on the heels of a $28.7 million property-tax increase in the previous budget.

But Chicago politicians are chary about new property taxes, especially when they have not been warmed in advance to the task and provided with adequate political cover. This time, ward organizations in middle-class areas were in an uproar over the tax plan. By March, the mayor had to back down from his proposal; he could not get enough support from the aldermen, including many who were usually loyal to him. It was, gloated one of the white, bungalow-belt maverick aldermen, "a victory for the taxpayers of Chicago" (Kass, 1993). To save face, it was announced that anticipated increases in federal funding would enable the city to come up with monies to pay higher police salaries. Actually, the mayor was forced to accept an alternative tax plan, crafted by aldermen, that raised the money here and there, without a new property levy. A City Hall aide indicated that it had become quite clear that there was no support for a property-tax increase, despite the fact that if anything would get support for a tax increase, it would be efforts to fight crime. The battle that resulted over the proposed budget demonstrated that other avenues needed to be pursued.

The next tack was to try to close police stations. Each of Chicago's 25 police districts has its own station, a legacy from the days when citizens commonly ran to the nearest one to report an incident, and when there were no radios enabling headquarters to directly dispatch individual squad cars. In the consulting report of July 1992, one key cost-saving recommendation was that the city should close seven district stations and one of its five area headquarters. There was no public notice as to which neighborhoods were on the hit list, but the facilities selected for the closings were described as the oldest ones and the smallest, and this set off a flurry of rumors. A study would determine which of the eventually larger districts would absorb personnel from those that would be closed. Station closings were an integral part of the consultants' plan. The 380-odd officers that, they anticipated, would be freed from administrative matters by this action were to be poured into community policing, and these bodies went a long way toward making their calculations concerning the staffing of beat and rapid-response units add up correctly. The fact that the station-closing part of the plan was to eventually fail created severe stress within the consulting team and undermined the confidence of some of its members that their plan could be implemented.

Public outcry against the station-closing plan was immediate. As the *Chicago Tribune* (Recktenwald, 1993) described it:

> After word leaked out that the department had targeted seven of
> the oldest and smallest stations for closing, a firestorm of commu-

nity protest arose. Marches were held, petitions circulated and, in one neighborhood, blue ribbons marked nearly every home and business as a protest of the closing of the local station house.

The negative reaction was comparable among residents of high- and lower crime districts. Aldermen were also vocal in their opposition to the proposal. Police and City Hall explanations for the station consolidations were discounted. Chicagoans seemed to see their stations as symbols of police presence, at a time when crime rates were on the rise, and their disappearance signaled something ominous. One Morgan Park community activist noted, "We're usually lowest or second lowest in crime in the city. We feel the presence of the district stationhouse helps us retain that status." Another, in the Wood District, said "people are going to flee from the area." (Recktenwald and Papajohn, 1992).

Interestingly, reaction among many officers and the police union was quite nonchalant. Two Austin District officers, who were quoted in a newspaper article, made the following statements:

> A station is not like a firehouse. We don't go out on calls and come back to the station. We go out on patrol. Our calls come from 911 downtown.

> Sixty or 70 years ago, the police would wait around the station until something happened. Back then, the location of the station was very important in response time.

The union president was quick to acknowledge the community's perception that it was losing something; nonetheless, he declared:

> For the average police officer, the station is simply a place to go and pick up the squad car at the start of the shift.

A series of public hearings was held throughout the city during the fall of 1992. They were attended by a phalanx of top department brass and consultants. The superintendent emphasized that station closings would not affect police service in any community, and the consultants showed graphics that tried to prove it. To sweeten the deal, the superintendent announced the day before the first hearing that he would recommend that the districts whose stations were selected for the closings be chosen as community-policing prototypes. The meetings were large and crowded, and the bulk of the residents who attended seemed steadfast in their resolve to keep their local stations open. At a hearing we attended in the

Austin District, one speaker lamented that her community had lost its bank and its hospital; that the grammar school had just been closed; and that now its police station was threatened. By mid-January 1993, a Chicago newspaper described the mayor's plan for community policing as "stalled," and blamed it, in part, on neighborhood resistance. One week later, the superintendent announced that the station-closing plan was dead, citing community opposition and its potential harm to his community-policing program. Said the superintendent:

> I am talking about beginning an alternate policing strategy that calls for a partnership between the police and the community. If I have to start at odds with the community right off the get-go, I am going to have little opportunity for success.

One City Hall aide blamed the failure of the station closings on lack of preparation. As he saw it, Chicagoans were asked to believe that they would get better service in the future—without being given any evidence to support such a promise—in return for giving up something now. In Chicago parlance, this is a "take-back," and this time the mayor did not succeed in getting one. Instead, the station-closing effort was seen as a measure of the capacity of City Hall to push the police department around. The repeated promises of involvement by the Superintendent in community policing that were issued when residents complained made it clear that this, too, was City Hall's program, and that its roots were deeply political.

Management Efficiency

One of the jobs of the outside consulting team was to "squeeze the fat out of the department," and community policing was originally introduced as a productive way of using the officers that could be freed up through management efficiencies. Like many municipal-efficiency efforts, this proved difficult to accomplish. The consultants' spreadsheets identified 1,600 officers who could be returned to the street over a three-year period, and their second report argued that these officers would "become the resource base for the neighborhood-based strategy." Some of these newly discovered officers were to be freed by a more effective scheduling of shift times, and by reforming the department's sick-leave and absenteeism policies. Others would come through a "reduction of bureaucracy" and a "conversion of desk time to street time." The consultants caught the mayor's eye with the observation that the officers he could recapture under their plan outnumbered the entire police department of Atlanta (Booz, Allen & Hamilton, 1992: 1).

We have already noted that the department failed to consolidate its districts and save the (estimated) 348 administrative positions that this would have freed up. The city also did not succeed in significantly reducing the number of downtown top brass, or in increasing the use of one-officer cars. Also, the substantial number of uniformed personnel who could be observed answering telephones and doing clerical activity throughout police headquarters did not appear to diminish. A few specialized units were downsized, but others survived despite critical reviews. A few individual positions were civilianized. Despite its best efforts to identify bodies that actually could be moved into the districts, after 18 months the department had effectively reallocated fewer than 300 officers. This should not be surprising. Police almost everywhere are notorious for wanting to "get in" off the street. Those who are adroit enough, or who have good political connections, find their way into district or downtown administrative positions; special units with limited duties; and other daytime jobs in which they can work a normal workweek, preferably in civilian clothes. Once they are inside, it is hard to get them out again. The vacant positions in police departments are always uniformed jobs on the street.

Perhaps the most visible effect of the management review was that the department's rank of captain was abolished. There was a theoretical rationale for the action: Departments that are committed to pushing authority and responsibility down to the neighborhood and street level often find that flattening the rank structure of the department goes hand in hand with decentralization and increased organization nimbleness. The Tempe (Ariz.) department flattened its rank structure by two levels when it adopted community policing; the St. Petersburg (Fla.) department reduced it by one rank. In Chicago's case, the consultants and the department had an additional incentive: The mayor was adamant about his feeling that captains had to go. He pounded the table when he talked about them. He thought that they were overpaid and redundant; that they preened themselves as senior managers and then expected to be paid overtime to attend a meeting that did not occur during their regular shift. Not surprisingly, his consulting team agreed with his assessment. The move saved a few positions, but a lot of money; straight-time pay for captains was about $55,000 per year.

While captains who already held their civil service position were exempted from the ban, they were immediately removed from the prototype districts, in an experiment to see how it would work. Neighborhood-relations sergeants, lieutenants, and crime analysts were told to report directly to the district commander. This considerably increased the commanders' spans of control, but they could not be on duty 24 hours a day. Lieutenants, however, were on the job 24 hours a day, and there were positions for lieutenants to direct uniformed field operations, station operations, and the districts' plainclothes tactical units. In theory, the field and station operations lieutenants were to jointly share the managerial responsibilities that had once belonged to the captains who supervised each watch, but problems began to crop up between them. No one knew who had final authority over a host of practical management issues, which was a stressful issue in an organization molded along hierarchical lines.

The issue surfaced in June 1993, during a district commanders' meeting. Many situations had come up, such as handling requests for days off, for which neither the lieutenants nor their officers knew who was in charge. One commander observed, "The problem is pretty bad. On one of my watches I've got three lieutenants that do not speak." Other commanders chimed in about how bad the situation had become in their districts. R&D staffers held focus-group sessions for field-operations and watch-operations lieutenants so as to troubleshoot the matter. The focus groups confirmed that dividing responsibility among lieutenants was a problem—one that illustrated the vast gulf among the department and the collaborative, problem-solving organizations it hoped to emulate. Some of the participants noted:

> Who is steering the ship? There's gotta be a boss!

> The order is ridiculous . . . If there's a pissing contest, there's no tie breaker!

> If they choose one lieutenant to be in charge, how they gonna do it? Do we have to drop to our knees?

> It's like being a daddy. They [the officers] are like kids when they want something. They'll ask me for something, and if I say no, then they go to the watch-operations lieutenant to see if they get the answer they want. When they finally get an okay, they're gone. It's just a lousy system.

But no decision was made about who was to be in charge in every circumstance. Instead, lieutenants in the prototype districts learned to negotiate workable local solutions to the chain-of-authority problem caused by the flattening of the rank structure. In the words of the CAPS manager, they learned how to manage.

State and Federal Grants

Other efforts to generate new resources for CAPS were more successful. The state's criminal-justice agency hosted seminars for selected mid-level police managers, at which experts discussed community-policing issues. The state also provided funds for members of the department to travel to community-policing conferences in Washington, D.C., and San Diego. Many members of the exempt staff had never been exposed to operational community-policing programs, and the agency's director hoped that attending conferences and visiting other departments would help stimulate empathy for CAPS. In the spring of 1994, the department was also awarded a grant by a local foundation that supported the activities of its new strategic-planning committee.

More important, the state supported the first round of training for officers who were about to serve in the new prototype districts. The CAPS manager was convinced that the department's existing training operation could not adequately provide what was needed to prepare officers for CAPS's implementation. No one at the training academy knew anything about community policing, and he could not get the academy to prepare an acceptable curriculum. He felt that outside experts would be better suited for teaching the new concepts and methods called for in community policing. In a nontraditional move, the department applied for, and received, outside funding for the training effort, ran it independently of its in-house training program, and involved civilians as cotrainers along with sworn officers. State funding supported curriculum development and the hiring of the civilian instructors.

The department also received a number of grants that supported the development of new computer applications. The state helped again by supporting the development of a computer program which the department would use for beat-level crime analysis. The department's computer systems were extremely outdated and in need of much support. Some of this came from a $1 million grant from a coalition set up by the state's insurance industry to deal with auto thefts. The coalition's grant also supported the development of computerized crime analysis at the district level.

In February 1994, Chicago was also awarded a $4 million federal grant for use in hiring 50 new officers. The mayor announced that these officers would be hired over a three-year period, and that they would be assigned to community-policing beats.

No New Taxes, but More Police

The mayor's political instincts favored him when it came to crafting the 1994 city budget. When the 1994 preliminary budget was unveiled, the city's budget director announced he was working to avoid a property-tax increase. This was wise, in light of the lack of aldermanic support for such an increase in 1993. A few months later, on the day before the actual $3.4 billion city budget proposal was revealed, the mayor announced it included a neighborhood-renewal program to resurface residential streets, repair police and fire stations, improve sewers, and demolish vacant buildings. This budget also promised to hire 470 more police officers during the year than the department anticipated losing through normal attrition. During 1994, 25 new officers were to be added to each district, and by 1995, the average district's roster was to increase by 43 positions. The mayor also reiterated his commitment to keeping all 25 district stations open. The 1994 budget also anticipated raising $25 million via bond sales over the following five years, principally to pay for new buildings, cars, and equipment for the police department. The mayor promised this could all be done without a property-tax increase. It was to be paid for, instead, by a grab bag of special taxes and fees—the typical taxing strategy of a revenue-short city precluded from taxing either income or wealth. Community policing was to be financed through existing taxes and "revenue enhancers" like a surcharge on electric bills, an increase in the downtown parking tax, new liquor and licensing fees, and a small increase in monthly sewer fees. Despite these increases, the mayor noted that "the only thing we're raising is the quality of life in our communities." In mid-November 1993, the Chicago City Council unanimously passed the $3.4 billion 1994 budget.

Assessing the Prototyping Strategy

One of the most impressive achievements of CAPS's first year was that a substantial program was actually launched—as scheduled. In a world in which police reform efforts are frequently stillborn, or are never anything but a set of press releases, this was news. The program was far from perfect; everyone involved was openly and appropriately modest about the policing effort first put into the field. Both City Hall and department leaders understood that a more refined model needed to be developed before the program was expanded to encompass the entire city, and that the testing would be done in the prototype districts. A mayoral press release of February 2, 1993, noted, "These five districts will give us the clearest picture of how the program will work under different circumstances." The leaders said as much at press conferences, and at the public ceremonies held to celebrate the inauguration of the program in each of the five test districts. At a planning meeting that involved citizen representatives, the superintendent noted:

> This is going to take three-to-five years to implement fully. This is a serious time. We need to decide what is biteable, chewable, and digestible. I'm truly committed to your product. I many not agree with all your methods along the way, but I am committed to the product. Let's make some mistakes and get started.

The prototyping process had both strengths and weaknesses. On the plus side, the program did indeed adapt to feedback about its successes and failures in the field; prototyping was not just a planning theory. For example, one of the first edicts laid down by the CAPS manager was that each beat team had to make five friendly contacts with citizens every day. The contacts were to be recorded on a special new form. The idea behind the requirement was to get officers to communicate with the citizens on their beat. However, officers often simply went through the motions in order to meet this requirement. So surprised were citizens about these encounters that police had trouble getting people's names and addresses. The information that was collected rarely contributed to problem identification or solving; rather, the requirement led to stacks of paper that no one in the districts carefully studied or analyzed. It gradually became clear that the five-contacts requirement had little meaning for officers or citizens. It was a classic instance of "bean counting." Attempting to foster better police-citizen communication by fiat, and backing it up with more paperwork, were very much in the spirit of the old department, and not congruent with the new management model that was to be put into place. Within a few months, the rule was killed. District supervisors were told, instead, to carefully review officers' paperwork to make sure that they were in contact with citizens.

Another example was the intrateam form: The purpose of this form was to capture information on one watch that would be helpful to the officers who would serve the same beat on the next watch. The idea was central to the concept of turf responsibility, but officers swore it was redundant and unnecessary. They believed that it was simply creating more paperwork and that the same information could be captured by reworking already existing forms. The CAPS manager insisted that they stick with the form to give it a fair trial, but he did change the name of the form to indicate that it was only for emergency purposes and was not to be filled out on a daily basis. He was not convinced that the form was useless, but after several months, officers came up with suggestions for capturing the same information on already existing forms. By July 1993, the form was history.

The prototyping process put a high premium on communication and on a willingness to change gears, as required by experience. However, a drawback of the process was that it appeared, at times, to be without direction—flexibility could be confused with floundering. This concerned the CAPS comanagers a great deal, for they were keenly aware of how this process might appear to the officers on the street.

A more significant drawback was that key elements of an effective community-policing program were left on the cutting-room floor. Organizational realities and the pressure of events kept the program's managers from dealing with several significant issues.

The first of these was performance evaluation. The outside consultants knew this would be a big issue, and so did the performance-evaluation committee that labored over the problem during the fall of 1992. As in many other cities that have implemented community policing, the department's managers understood that it was critical to have in place a performance-evaluation process that promoted the values and behaviors expected of officers and supervisors. But as in other cities, they did not manage to do anything about it (Weisel, 1995).

From the outset everyone feared that if officers and their commanders were evaluated under the existing system they would appear to be doing a poor job and receive poor evaluation scores. The system in place rewarded traditional policing tasks: writing citations for moving violations (movers), making arrests (getting heads), and seizing guns; each month, the department distributes (only internally) a performance summary that ranks each district's performance on these criteria. At the outset, the CAPS manager was concerned that his prototype districts might drop to the bottom of the list because they could not sustain the effort required to "make their stats" while doing community-oriented work. With an outdated evaluation system in place, it would be difficult to get officers to focus on problem solving, or even to share information that could lead to an arrest with other officers or the community. In an attempt to forestall conflict over these competing priorities, the CAPS manager harangued his district commanders: "Don't let your sergeants reprimand or counsel officers for fewer DUIs and curfew arrests. This is unacceptable. The sergeants ain't gonna ruin this by getting all over the officers."

But attempting to alter the department's performance-evaluation system would have been a nightmare. It was fraught with legal issues—concerning the equality of performance ratings across groups—that no one wanted to confront at the moment. It was intricately associated with the labor contract and certainly could not have been changed in any significant way without opening a discussion of the issue with the union. It was deeply political, for it threatened to force the department to expain just how much it favored seemingly "soft" accomplishments as compared to traditional crime fighting. Anything that promised to raise labor costs—such as the consultants' plan to create a rank of master patrol officer, to recognize and reward good beat work—would have to pass muster with the mayor's budget analysts, and they already thought the police department was too expensive. Finally, through the period considered here, the fact that the program had not yet fully evolved had a continual impact. As one subcommittee member succinctly put it:

> Part of the problem is that we are trying to do things ass backward. I mean, how can you develop performance evaluation measures when you don't know what the job description is?

Another issue that was put on the back burner, whenever possible, was 911 and dispatching. Chicago's program was organized around the concept of "beat integrity": Beat officers were told to stay in their areas and work with residents, businesses, schools, and service agencies so as to identify and solve problems. To the extent that beat officers were pulled off their beats to respond to 911 calls, it would be difficult to get their work done.

This problem was addressed in three ways: by the formation of specialized rapid-response teams; by a capping of the frequency with which beat officers could be sent to calls that were not in their areas; and by staffing increases calculated to pick up the load removed from the shoulders of the beat teams. As the program evolved, new dispatching priorities were devised that allocated only certain classes of calls to the beat teams, rather than just controlling the frequency with which they were dispatched. But making this scheme work properly was an enormous problem. A combination of technological shortcomings and management problems in the radio-dispatching unit short-circuited early efforts to differentiate the dispatching of rapid-response cars and beat teams. There were no clear, formal rules about how dispatching should take place. Dispatchers did not understand the mechanics of the program, nor the goals, and each of the prototypes shared a radio zone with other non-prototype areas—which forced dispatchers to use different dispatch policies, depending on the origin of the call. The dispatching problem demanded a great deal of attention—first, to identify it, and then to remedy it. Management and technical issues had to be resolved; the dispatching staff required training; and a call-priority system had to be developed and approved at the highest levels of the department.

At a more strategic level, it was clear that the department needed to deemphasize 911; encourage the use of a nonemergency number for calls that did not require the immediate response of a police officer; develop procedures for holding calls and delaying response so as to efficiently deal with nonemergency cases; and to stop sending cars in response to large categories of calls. These tactics promised to free up officers, without having to hire significantly more of them; and at the time, it appeared that the staffing required to expand CAPS to encompass the entire city would call for steps of this magnitude.

However, not much happened with any of these suggestions. The charge in Houston that response to 911 calls deteriorated because police were assigned to community work had enabled its opponents to kill community policing there, and CAPS's supporters were very concerned about this issue. Encouraging the use of alternate numbers would require a massive public education campaign, with the outcomes being uncertain. Differential responses to different classes of calls also threatened to undermine the public's view that they were now getting good service from the police. To stop sending cars in response to selected calls was the most frightening idea of all. Chicago sent a car in response to about two-thirds of 911 calls—probably the highest big-city dispatching rate in the nation. This was part of an implicit contract between the police and the public, one made to help heal the breach that had been created by a terrible police corruption scandal in the late 1950s. People at City Hall and police headquarters were convinced that Chicagoans wanted cars sent when they called, and that it would be difficult, as well as politically risky, to try to wean them from that habit. Most scenarios had opposition politicians and the media labeling a reduction in the dispatching rate as a "take-away," and no one wanted to call their bluff.

The prototyping process also could not encompass strategic planning. The CAPS comanagers tried. A long-range planning group of about 30 people was convened for a while to begin to prepare the groundwork necessary for the citywide implementation of community policing. The group included the CAPS comanagers; R&D staff; a few district commanders; a generous selection of senior department executives; the head of the union; and several civilians representing different CAPS constituencies. The effort was supported by an influential local foundation, and one of its staff members participated. They held a two-day retreat in March 1994, to set their agenda, but only managed to meet three more times. At a "futures symposium," the group heard sobering presentations forecasting gloomy conditions in the city in the early twenty-first century. The group also heard a report by our evaluation team on public and officer attitudes toward CAPS, and on what was going on at beat meetings. By the third meeting, it was clear that strategic planning was very time consuming. There was a consensus that "too much planning was taking place and not enough doing was happening." More accurately, there were too many unresolved issues for the committee to consider in sufficient detail, much less resolve. The group included experienced hands and new participants who did not know much, so a great deal of time had to be spent bringing them up to date. For the R&D staff, pressure to develop and implement another new training curriculum was growing. Planning competed with a relentless implementation schedule that demanded the attention of key participants, and faced with a lack of time to keep the group moving, strategic planning died. The department released the outside consultant who had been hired to advise the planners, and the planning committee never met again. Prototyping, not planning, was the model for which Chicago seemed fated.

4

Bringing Officers
on Board

At the beginning, community policing is a battle for the hearts and minds of members of the patrol force. Their hearts and minds are indeed important, for police departments are decentralized, low-technology human-service organizations in which the motivation and skill of those delivering the services at the street level is of paramount significance. Community policing calls for meaningful changes in the way these services are delivered. This can easily lead to a battle, for inevitably police officers are resistant to change. To fail at the "Winning Hearts and Minds" (WHAM) component of organizational change "is to risk program failure due to apathy, frustration, resentment, perceived inequality, fear of change, and other factors that militate against the successful implementation of community policing" (Lurigio and Rosenbaum, 1994: 147).

This chapter examines the WHAM process in Chicago. First, it reviews some of the experiences of other cities that tried to implement community policing, for their difficulties and even their failures had, by the 1990s, become well known in policing circles. These examples illuminate some of the obstacles that Chicago's program had to overcome. Next, the chapter describes what police in Chicago thought about the new program, and about many of the tasks that constitute the practice of community policing. Officers' views were mixed about many aspects of community policing, and both stumbling blocks and bases for leveraging change could be found in their hearts and minds. The chapter then turns to the strategies used in Chicago to bring officers on board. There were several, including leadership strategies and new styles of supervision, internal communication, and structural changes in the nature of officers' jobs. But at the outset, training was the key to setting organizational change in motion at the operational level, and much of this chapter focuses on the department's training efforts. The final section examines the changes in attitudes among the patrol force that occurred as the department gained experience with this new model of policing.

Obstacles to Change

A great deal of inertia is connected with the daily work routines of individuals in any organization. Community policing requires that officers do many of their old jobs in new ways, and that they take on tasks that they never imagined would come their way. They are asked to identify and solve a broad range of problems; reach out to elements of the community that previously were outside their orbit; and put their careers at risk by taking on unfamiliar and challenging responsibilities. "The difficulty with the expectations is that they are frequently beyond the present capabilities of most officers and the traditional roles for which they were selected and trained . . ." (Lurigio and Rosenbaum, 1994: 147). Police would rather do "what they signed up for"—usually a combination of crime fighting and emergency service. In many instances, their first response to community policing is to scornfully dismiss it as "social work," and to say it is not "real police work." Former Police Chief Betsy Watson lamented what happened in Houston: "They somehow have equated neighborhood-oriented policing with social work rather than tough law enforcement—and they've missed the point" (*Law Enforcement News,* September 30, 1991: 14).

For example, in 1988, Oakland implemented a typical small-scale experiment in community-oriented policing. In one experimental area, officers were assigned to go door to door, to introduce themselves to residents. They were to inform people of the department's new emphasis on drug enforcement, give them pamphlets on crime and drug programs, and conduct brief interviews to gather information about neighborhood problems. However, they were unenthusiastic about the job. Their immediate supervisor dismissed the effort, calling it social work, and did nothing to ensure that the program—developed in the chief's office—was actually implemented. One hard-working officer saw to it that the part of the job that could be monitored—making house calls—was carried out, but none of the planned follow-up problem solving ever got done, and nothing was done with the information gathered in the doorstep interviews (Uchida, Forst, and Annan, 1990).

As this suggests, the attitudes of officers' superiors are also important. This is especially true of sergeants, who have the most direct control over what street officers do on a day-to-day basis. Rubenstein (1973) identified sergeants as most officers' "real employer"; Muir (1977) dubbed them the police organization's "cornerstone." Goldstein (1990: 157) notes, "However strongly the head of an agency may elicit a different style of policing, the quality of an officer's daily life is heavily dependent on how well the officer satisfies the expectations and demands of his or her immediate supervisor." Sergeants interpret, at the street level, the operational meaning of official policies, and let officers know if they are meeting the expectations of the organization (Van Maanen, 1983). When these policies are radically new ones, sergeants should be called on to be teachers and coaches as well as supervisors. But the roles and rules have changed. Sergeants have to learn to foster new uses of patrol time, including making informal contacts with citizens and merchants, and spending more time away from responding to radio dispatches—all of this previously fell into the goofing-off category. They also need to account for the ability of their officers to prevent things from happening in the first place, not just for their ability to drive rapidly to the scene, after the fact.

This presents several problems. First, because community policing is a new concept almost everywhere, most sergeants never did it themselves. They do not know, from their own experience, how the job should be done, or what works. Like others in the department, they have to learn new skills and roles. Observers have also noted that sergeants often have great difficulty *combining* mentoring and monitoring roles; they can train or control, but cannot do both (McElroy et al., 1993; Wycoff and Skogan, 1993; Weisburd et al., 1988). Because they are the ones who translate the policies of higher-ups into action, it is also important that at least in their behavior—what they require from their officers—that they represent organizational policies. If they actually believe in them, that would help, too. This may matter less in traditional command-and-control organizations, but community policing inevitably involves significant decentralization, pushing both authority and responsibility for decision making deeper into the organization. Sergeants therefore need to be a facilitating management layer.

However, police in many cities are skeptical about notions like "coaching," "empowerment," and other modern shop-floor buzz-words, for more typically, their agencies are run by use of punishment and fear. Although we frequently speak of the people who run police departments as "managers," in truth, too little of what they do falls into that category. Mostly, they supervise, which means they watch over the shoulders of their subordinates for violations of departmental rules and regulations, and punish them when they do not go by the book. Police supervision is essentially negative, relying primarily on sanctions for noncompliance (Weisburd et al., 1988). Among traditional police administrators, "supervision was about what an officer should not do or be caught doing, rather than what should be done competently" (Holdaway, 1995). The work of the sergeant is of the simplest kind in traditional policing. "The more routinized the work, the easier it is for the sergeant to check. The more restrictions placed on an officer, . . . the easier it is to recognize situations that suggest wrongdoing. The more emphasis placed on rank and the symbols of position, the easier it is for sergeants to rely on authority—rather than intellect and interpersonal skills—to carry out their duties" (Goldstein, 1990: 157). To a great degree, one which is hard for many outsiders to fathom, little is supposed to happen in police departments without general orders that detail how it is to be done. The working life of the organization is dominated by the need to reconstruct or redefine what actually happens in the field, so it appears to fit the model. This helps ensure that top managers downtown "don't know what really happens on the street"—a derisive charge that rolls easily off the lips of street officers and helps legitimate their resistance to strategies devised at headquarters.

It is also frequently the case that throughout transitional periods for organizations, police at all levels lack a clear understanding of the new role called for by community policing. Departments that are adopting community policing are likely, at the outset, to be uncertain or still experimental about many aspects of what they are doing, giving officers and their sergeants, at best, mixed messages. When the Vera Institute's evaluators interviewed officers in Houston who were assigned to neighborhood-oriented policing (for which they were receiving federally financed overtime pay), they frequently found the officers had no idea what the program was about, or what they should be doing differently (Sadd and Grinc, 1993).

A lack of clarity about new roles and goals also makes it difficult for transitioning departments to develop performance measures that meaningfully represent their aspirations. Like everyone else, police officers work mostly to meet the reward structure set up by their employing organization. They do what it takes to get choice assignments and days off, praise from their commanders, awards on Police Recognition Day, promotions, and more money in their pay envelopes. In addition to sheer seniority and test scores, they are usually graded by the number of arrests they make and moving violators they cite; the guns and drugs they seize; and whether they show up for work on time and with a neat haircut. Developing performance indicators that reflect either the activities or outcomes associated with community policing is a difficult task—one which few departments have successfully faced up to.

The apparent lack of role clarity also clouds officers' understanding of what they believe to be the real goals of the organization, as opposed to the paperwork involved. Police everywhere spend a great deal of time (a lot of it while on the job) debating what they think is going on amid the shifting power alliances downtown: Who are the heirs apparent, and do their views differ from the current top brass? Whose stock is rising and falling, and whose views are to be attended to or ignored? Who should they pay attention to when they get mixed messages? Evidence of divisiveness downtown over the future course of the department will be read by many as a rationale for cautious inaction until the situation is clarified. The difficulty is that divisions downtown are almost inevitable in transitioning organizations. The power of some senior managers will be undercut by decentralization and by rising reliance on on-the-spot supervisors. New management philosophies will rub salt in the wounds of those who rose to the top when the command-and-control idea was the rule of the day. In many cities, managers near the top of police organizations have mounted an effective rear-guard action against change, making life difficult for those under them who are caught in the crossfire.

Given this environment, it is not surprising that many police are cynical about newly announced initiatives. Officers usually first hear about them when programs are unveiled at downtown press conferences, and they usually feel the programs are being stuffed down their throats. At best, it looks like they will be assigned additional duties and paperwork, while still being held responsible for handling their old workload. Experienced officers have survived earlier fads in policing and may recall the acrimony that brought those down. Police are cynical about the role of politics in selecting their leaders and their missions, and anticipate that newly unveiled policies will evaporate after the next election. Chiefs and politicians also come and go, so it can seem best to just wait things out; many programs will not survive future changes at the top. Police are especially cynical about programs invented by civilians—civilian intrusion into department business touches a deep and sensitive nerve in police culture. They are resentful in cases where the community was consulted about police roles and responsibilities, but they were not. Given the command-and-control tradition of management and the state of labor-management relations in many police departments, they probably *won't* be consulted.

One avenue that officers have for voicing their disaffection is their union. States vary in the extent to which police can be represented by unions, but in most big cities, they are a force to be reckoned with (for a discussion of unions, see Bouza, 1985). In some cities, efforts to adopt a community-policing model have gotten caught in the political crossfire between labor and management and have thus become an occasion for further butting of heads. Potential acrimony is not the only relevant issue, however. Almost everywhere, contracts between cities and police unions affect the ability of department managers to make decisions about staffing. Frequently, they grant officers the right to choose assignments on the basis of seniority. This can limit the ability of department managers to determine which—and even how many—officers work in a district; what shift they will be assigned to, and perhaps their specific job assignments. For example, Minneapolis mounted a community-organizing program that was designed to include a "Cop On The Block"—an officer committed to assisting block clubs. But the civilians who conceived the plan did not understand that police there rotated between day and night shifts every few months, so that it was not possible to permanently assign an officer to assist an organization. It also proved impossible to free up enough police who could attend meetings during busy evening shifts, which is when most neighborhood residents could get together (Skogan, 1990; Pate, McPherson, and Silloway, 1987). Furthermore, contractual obligations limit the capacity of police managers to tailor assignments to (their perceptions of) the skills, backgrounds, and linguistic abilities of their officers. In addition, the federal Fair Labor Standards Act requires that officers be paid overtime if they work beyond their contractual hours, and flextime may not be allowed by the contract. This will certainly inhibit many departments from asking beat officers to attend community meetings or other events that are not conveniently scheduled. Finally, any change in the way in which officers' performance is evaluated will certainly become a labor-management issue.

Can Police Culture Change?

While the battle for the hearts and minds of the patrol force is thus a difficult one, it can be won. There are instances in which a combination of change strategies has turned around the views of tradition-laden departments. Research in cities such as San Diego, Cincinnati, Flint (Mich.), Madison (Wis.), and Edmonton (Alta.) suggests that officers who do community policing come to believe their work is more important, interesting, rewarding, and less frustrating. Evaluations have found community policing officers feel they have more independence and control over their jobs and are more likely to feel that they are functioning as part of a team; these are important determinants of job satisfaction. More community officers report knowing a great deal about their assigned turf, and they are more optimistic about the impact of their work on community problems. Finally, they tend to take a more benign and trusting view of the public than they held in their previous jobs (Lurigio and Rosenbaum, 1994; Wycoff, 1988).

In a study of Madison's decentralized management program, officers were surveyed at three points in time over a two-year period. Those assigned to an experimental district came to see themselves working as a team, believed that their efforts were being supported by their supervisors and the department, and thought that the department was really reforming itself. They became more satisfied with their job, and more strongly committed to the organization, than were officers who served in other parts of the city. They also were more customer oriented, believed more firmly in the principles of problem solving and community policing, and felt that they had a better relationship with the community. Officers throughout the department who felt they were participating in organizational decisions that affected their work life were more satisfied on a broad range of outcome measures. Department records indicated that disciplinary actions, absenteeism, tardiness, and sick days went down more in the experimental area than in the remainder of the city (Wycoff and Skogan, 1994a, b).

There is also positive—but more impressionistic—evidence from other cities that have tried community policing. In New York City, community officers reported that, when doing their new jobs, they were more exposed to the "good people" of the community and that by walking their beats, they got to know residents as people and did not deal with them just in crisis situations (McElroy, Cosgrove, and Sadd, 1993). As a result of community policing in Hayward (Calif.), officers felt that citizens had a better understanding of the role of the police, and more realistic expectations about what police could actually accomplish. Officers became more sympathetic toward problems in the community and toward residents of the neighborhoods they served. Residents, on the other hand, found that the police were receptive to change and willing to help them, rather than just coming into the neighborhood to harass them (Sadd and Grinc, 1993).

Our expectation is that meaningful shifts in these kinds of attitudes and behaviors can only follow significant changes in the way that police departments conduct their business. As we have noted, police organizations and police culture do not readily embrace change. Few departments are likely to do so without a well-conceived implementation strategy from change managers in the agency.

How Cops Viewed Community Policing in Chicago

What did rank-and-file officers in Chicago think about community policing? We examined their views at the very outset, and then again about two years later. The first round of questionnaires was completed by prototype officers of all ranks, before anyone in the organization knew anything in particular about the new program. The questionnaires were administered to 1,400 officers at the beginning of the orientation sessions that were held at the police training academy. Members of the evaluation staff described the survey to the officers and promised that their answers would be confidential. A letter from the superintendent of police endorsing the evaluation and the survey was placed on the top of each questionnaire, which took an average of 20 minutes to complete. The questionnaire probed officers' perceptions of their jobs, the organization, and the communities they served. The results provided some insight into potential impediments to organizational change, and a baseline for evaluating subsequent changes in officers' attitudes.

The officers who were to serve in the prototype districts were typical of the department as a whole. Almost 80 percent were male; nearly two-thirds were white; about one-fourth were black; and almost 10 percent were Hispanic. On average, they were 38 years old, and had been on the job for 12 years. About 60 percent were married. Many (61 percent) had completed at least some college courses, and 30 percent had a degree from a four-year college. About 15 percent of them were supervisors—sergeants and lieutenants.

What Police Look for in Their Job

The survey probed what officers were looking for in the job. High percentages of them indicated they wanted a stimulating and challenging job (86 percent said so), a job that allowed them to exercise independent thought and action (87 percent), to be creative and imaginative (86 percent), and to learn new things (89 percent). However, less than half of those surveyed felt they had a deep personal involvement in their current assignments. They were divided down the middle over whether their jobs actually gave them opportunities for independence and control over how they did their work. Less than one-third thought that the current structure of their job enabled them to actually see their work through to completion, which was something they sought. High percentages liked police work (80 percent) and liked their coworkers (74 percent), but their work was not the major source of satisfaction in their lives (only 18 percent said it was the major source). Only about one-quarter agreed that they had any influence over their job, or that their supervisors sought their opinions. Only about a third felt their supervisors let them know how well they were performing, and one-quarter felt that they could easily communicate their ideas to management. One-quarter thought that management treated its employees well, and even fewer felt that the department was open to change. On the other hand, a slim majority was loyal: 58 percent thought the department was a good organization to work for, and 50 percent thought it was one of the best in the country.

Police–Community Relations

Despite their loyalty, large numbers of officers did not think their work was appreciated by the public, and they were quite pessimistic about the state of police-community relations in Chicago. Figure 4-1 summarizes their responses to four statements that assessed this

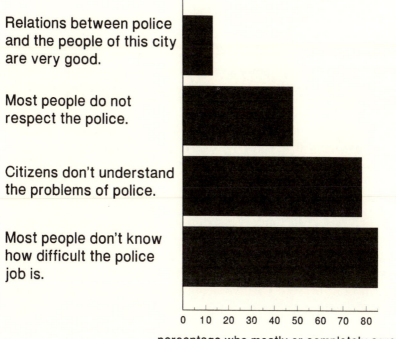

Relations between police and the people of this city are very good.

Most people do not respect the police.

Citizens don't understand the problems of police.

Most people don't know how difficult the police job is.

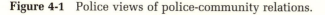

0 10 20 30 40 50 60 70 80

percentage who mostly or completely agree

Figure 4-1 Police views of police-community relations.

state of affairs; it presents the percentage of officers who either "agreed" or "agreed very much," with each statement. Responses to these four questions were also combined to produce a single index for statistical analyses (that will be discussed later). In figure 4-1, the longer each bar is, the more pessimistic police were. About half agreed that most people do not respect the police; two-thirds thought citizens did not understand their problems; and more than 80 percent believed that the public does not know how hard their job is. Almost 90 percent thought relations between police and the people of Chicago were not good. The portrait painted by these figures resemble the views of many police officers we observed. Using the same questions, the New York City Police Department found that more than 90 percent of the city's police felt the public did not understand their problems; and 75 percent thought police-community relations were bad (*Law Enforcement News,* June 30 1994: 3). Likewise, officers in Chicago who were about to embark on this new community-policing venture felt isolated and unappreciated.

Views on Community-Policing Concepts

Interviews, focus groups, and surveys of officers also indicated that in important ways, police were very ambivalent about community policing in Chicago. Some of their views were consonant with the new program, and some were not. One put it straightforwardly, and negatively:

> I'm a policeman, not a social worker. I don't have time to sit and shoot the shit. Whores, junkies, and gang bangers are my best source of information. They have a million reasons for ratting. All you have to do is be there when they want to talk, or catch them dirty and let them think you can do them some good.

Figure 4-2 documents responses to a series of statements that probed officers' orientations toward ideas and tasks often associated with community policing; the longer the bars are, the more sympathetic they were. Figure 4-2 indicates that a significant number of officers were positive about many tasks that are consonant with community policing. At the outset, there was no widespread

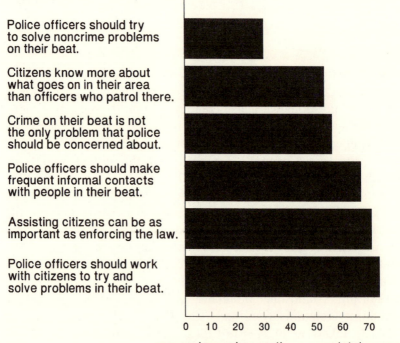

percentage who mostly or completely agree.

Figure 4-2 Orientation toward community policing.

enthusiasm for involving themselves in solving noncrime problems—only 30 percent agreed officers should be involved in that.
This did not bode well for a program that was designed to expand
the range of the police mandate and to involve officers in coordinating the delivery of city services. They did not think this was going
to work. Two officers had these comments:

> Then they devise this police program based on city services that
> we can't deliver. They tell us to tell the citizens that we can get
> the abandoned cars towed, the abandoned buildings condemned
> and demolished—they make us look like assholes.

> After all the crap I heard in training about how city services are
> there for us, I'm really furious. Citizens expect us to resolve prob-
> lems that are out of our hands.

However, a majority thought that citizens had important information to share about their beat, and that police should be concerned about problems there. Larger majorities endorsed making
frequent informal contacts with people on their beat, assisting citizens, and working with the general public to solve local problems.
Responses to these statements were combined with four responses
to others that were clustered with them, to form a single measure
(with a reliability of 0.78) of the officers' orientations toward community policing. The others included statements that endorsed
tackling the fear of crime as well as the crime rate, joint police-
citizen responsibility for crime prevention, and two questions
about the merits of foot patrols, as compared to motorized patrols,
for gathering information about the community.

Personal Capacity for Problem Solving

Officers also told us how they thought they stood in regard to their
personal capacity for identifying and solving neighborhood problems. These questions were included in the survey largely to
benchmark future change; because officers had no experience at all,
we did not expect them to recognize much of the jargon associated
with community policing. We asked them "how qualified" they felt
they were to identify neighborhood problems, use the CAPS model
to analyze them, develop solutions to problems, and evaluate those
solutions to see how well they worked. They felt most confident
about identifying problems (16 percent thought they were very
qualified to do this), but only one in ten thought they were very

qualified to develop solutions or evaluate them. Only 6 percent thought they were qualified to use the CAPS model. With regard to his officers, one prototype supervisor lamented:

> The majority are pretty uncomfortable [communicating with citizens]. They are not public speakers and some don't want to be bothered. They [citizens] don't really have problems we can help them with. They are not the typical crimes the officers are used to solving.

These survey questions formed a scale that measured officers' self-assessed capacity for problem solving, and that had a reliability of 0.84.

Despite indicators of general support for some community-policing concepts, other questions revealed that the officers who were about to take on new duties in the prototype districts were not very keen on adopting new tactics, like foot patrol, or on "marketing" their new services to the public. One prototype supervisor noted:

> What I'm supposed to do is foot patrols. I've never thought they were worth anything—it's just a public-relations ploy. We are run by the radio, like it or not. That's our job.

Views on Commitment of Resources

Another series of questions allowed officers to say how much of the department's resources they felt should be committed to each activity involved. They indicated they were willing to devote some department resources to activities such as "researching and solving problems"; "coordinating with other agencies to improve the quality of life," and "working with citizen groups to solve local problems," but only to a moderate degree. Together, responses to these questions formed a scale with a reliability of 0.83. Only 7 percent of the officers thought that foot patrol should receive a large infusion of resources. Less than a third supported similar investments in "problem solving," "helping settle family disputes," "getting to know juveniles," or "understanding problems of minority groups." They were really only interested in devoting more department resources to the most traditional concerns: responding to calls for service (52 percent), and assisting persons in emergencies (86 percent).

Anticipated Impact of CAPS

The prototype officers also did not think that the new program would have a marked impact on many important aspects of their work. They were asked if each of a number of outcomes would be more likely, or less likely, to occur as a result of the program, or if they thought things would not change. Some of the items measured their optimism about the potential impact of CAPS on *traditional* police concerns. These included the crime rate, and only 26 percent thought it would go down. As one officer put it:

> Can we affect crime? Not really. Not unless we put a cop on every corner. . . . Our biggest industry is dope. There ain't no other job. We can't control the social fabric. It can't be done.

They also did not think that CAPS would enhance their ability to make arrests (only 26 percent were positive about this); and 35 percent said that CAPS would enhance their ability to effectively use resources. They were somewhat more sanguine about the potential impact of CAPS on *community* concerns. Almost half thought it would improve their ability to make effective use of crime information and lead to the resolution of neighborhood problems, and 44 percent thought the new program would cause "greater willingness of citizens to cooperate with police." Relatively few (about one-third) thought that the new program would improve their relationship with minorities in the community. As one prototype supervisor put it:

> The Hispanics are culturally accustomed to a distance from the police. The police in their native land are corrupt and bureaucratic, so they are not used to having positive contact with them. It's not an individual thing; it's a cultural thing.

Using these and some closely related questions, we created measures of the anticipated impact of CAPS on traditional concerns (with a reliability of 0.87) and on community-oriented concerns (with a reliability of 0.85). Responses to the questions were strongly related to their orientation toward community policing and toward racial cleavages within the police department itself.

Impact on Police Autonomy. Figure 4-3 describes the extent of police pessimism—which was indeed considerable—about the potential impact of CAPS on the autonomy of police operations. One of the most striking features of police culture is its resistance to

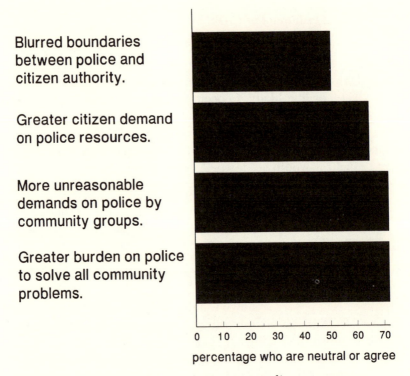

Figure 4-3 Pessimism about CAPS impact on police autonomy.

letting outsiders (e.g., civilians and, especially, politicians) control the police agenda. Police on the street gripe about "loud mouths" in the community who want the police to provide them with personal service, and about groups and organizations that want police to support or defend their economic and social interests. They complain about politicians who want them to give favor to constituent groups and award jobs or plum assignments to favored employees. Police managers worry about how the allocation of scarce resources across the city will be distorted by demands from politically powerful groups for excessive levels of patrolling in their areas; for foot patrols; and for uniformed street-crossing guards and other special-duty officers. Of all municipal service bureaucracies, the police have been the most successful at obfuscating their resource-allocation rules and maintaining the secrecy of data on their operations—partly to foil, and partly to disguise, the consequences of any intrusions into their domain.

Officers we surveyed were clearly concerned about community policing's impact on the department's autonomy, and on the nature and volume of work that would come their way as a result of the program. As one officer told us, shortly after the training period:

> There was some initial confusion, mostly because the program was not introduced to the officers. Rumors grew rampant and they grew by the hour. Cops actually thought there were going to be civilian command posts they'd have to report to.

Many of the officers we surveyed were pessimistic: 72 percent thought CAPS would generate "unreasonable demands on police by community groups," and an equal proportion thought it might dump community problems of all sorts on their shoulders. Almost two-thirds were concerned about the drain the new program might create on the department's resources, and a majority were pessimistic about "blurred boundaries" developing between police and citizen authority. Like the other attitudinal clusters described here, responses to these four questions were combined to form an index of police pessimism about the impact of CAPS on their autonomy; it has a reliability of 0.71.

Who Supported Change?

The officers who attended orientation sessions during the spring of 1993 thus had mixed views about aspects of the new program. They were pessimistic about its potential impact on their working lives, yet they thought that many specific community-oriented tasks were probably good ideas. They were willing to support a modest investment in some of these, particularly in local problem-solving efforts. The survey also revealed that, across many measures, some officers were more optimistic than others.

Ironically, our surveys indicate that many of the cleavages which divided the community over traditional policing were duplicated among the police themselves, in regard to community policing. By and large, optimism and support for community policing were more widespread within police management ranks than within the patrol force; older officers were much more likely than younger ones to be ready for change; and women were somewhat more supportive than were men. The deepest divisions, however, were along racial and ethnic lines: White officers were far more satisfied with things the way they were. And whites were more pessimistic about the potential of community policing and the adverse consequences of the effort on their workload and organizational autonomy. They were also the most pessimistic about the potential impact of CAPS on traditional- and community-policing issues. Further, white officers were less likely to think they were personally qualified to identify problems and devise solutions to them, and they were less willing than others to support diverting department resources toward the program. At the same time, they were much more likely to think that relations between police and the public were in bad shape.

The depths of some of these cleavages are illustrated in figure 4-4. It contrasts the views that officers of various races and ranks had about the potential impact of CAPS on several aspects of policing. Figure 4-4 illustrates the extent of pessimism about the program; it charts the percentages of officers who thought it would have no effect, or even a negative impact, on relations with minorities; on the willingness of citizens to cooperate with police; on the police's ability to make more effective use of information; and on the extent to which CAPS would resolve neighborhood problems. On every measure, white officers were the most pessimistic: More than three-quarters of them were pessimistic about race relations, and more than half did not think it would have a positive impact on any of these (and other related) issues. African-American officers were more optimistic (but also most gloomy about race relations), while Hispanic officers fell between the other two groups.

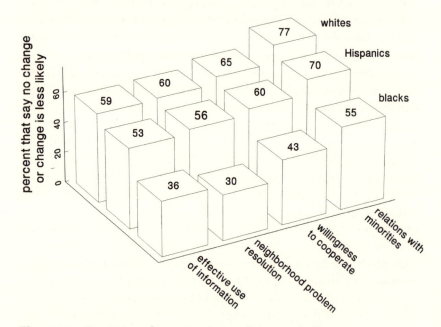

Figure 4-4 Pessimism about CAPS impact by race of officers.

Cleavages were even deeper between patrol officers and the top brass. Members of the senior command staff were optimistic on every issue, but there was a vast gulf between them and the frontline supervisors that they have to rely on to make the program really work. Sergeants and lieutenants stood closer to the troops in the field on these and other issues. More than a majority of ordinary officers were pessimistic about each of these aspects of the program.

We also conducted a detailed statistical analysis that examined the *joint* influence of the factors examined here on attitudes toward CAPS. Regression analysis is useful here because many of these factors are related to one another as well as to attitudes toward community policing. In Chicago, women officers tend to be younger; supervisors and senior staff members are older, and more likely to be white; older officers have less education; and few older officers are Hispanic. Regression analysis enables us to identify the relative importance of each of these factors, controlling for their overlap with the others.

The analysis that is summarized in table 4-1 documents the persistence of race, age, and rank differences in police views of community policing. The multivariate correlates of support for community policing (illustrated in table 4-1) are listed in descending order, on the basis of the strength of their effect. "Newer" refers to having fewer years of service. The impact of the factor listed in brackets was less statistically reliable than that of the others. In almost every case, the strongest effects were reserved for race and ethnicity. In every instance, African-American and Hispanic officers were more oriented toward community policing, and more optimistic about their relationship with the community. Being an

Table 4-1 Patterns of Support for Community Policing (CP)

Optimistic— Traditional Impact	Optimistic— Community Impact	Optimistic about Autonomy	Support CP Tasks	Support CP Resources	Public Relations— Good
black	black	black	black	black	older
older	older	college	older	older	black
hispanic	managers		managers	hispanic	managers
women	hispanic		hispanic	newer	men
	[newer]			women	

Note: Data are based on results of a multiple regression analysis of attitude scale scores. The bracketed factor was significant at $p < .10$; the remainder were significant at $p < .05$.

African-American counted the most, while differences in the views of Hispanics (who always fell between the other groups) were less pronounced. Rank was frequently influential, with support being highest at the top of the organization. Women were more likely to be optimistic about the impact of CAPS on traditional policing concerns, and they were more willing to devote department resources to the effort. Once other factors were taken into account, education did not appear to have much of an effect on attitudes. College-educated officers were more optimistic about the potential impact of CAPS on police autonomy, but otherwise, there were no discernible effects of higher education on these measures. Interestingly, in each case, the coefficients associated with age were *positive*—older officers were more optimistic and willing to support the enterprise. A detailed examination found that, among officers, more positive views began to emerge at about age 45, controlling for other factors.

This finding surprised many in the department, who assumed that younger officers would be more amenable to change. Others noted that older officers are generally less aggressive in their policing style, and many have acquired a modest view of the long-run effectiveness of what they have been doing in the past, or they are simply burned out. One individual who was of this persuasion characterized younger officers as "full of beans and hot to make arrests"; another argued that "they want to be cops, just like they see on TV."

Support for community policing was associated with other attitudes as well. Chief among them were officers' views of the state of police-community relations, their satisfaction with the organization, and their tolerance for risk. Officers who were more sanguine about how the public viewed them were more optimistic about CAPS on most measures. This did not mean that they felt police-community relations were *good;* on the contrary, in every group we examined, a majority thought these relations were bad. But clearly, the view was not that "it's broken and needs fixing," for police who, for the most part, agreed that their relationship with the people of Chicago was broken were also the most averse to fixing it—at least via community policing.

On the other hand, officers who were the most satisfied with the department were also the most supportive. Their satisfaction was registered on statements about how good the organization was as a place to work; how well management treated its employees; the reasonableness of their supervisors; and whether they thought the department was one of the best in the country. Further, the department's supporters were more optimistic about CAPS, more willing to allocate resources to its activities, more oriented toward community-policing concepts, and less pessimistic about the impact of the program on police autonomy.

Finally, the new program found some of its strongest supporters among officers who were willing to take a risk. The survey included six questions about their inclination toward new ideas and changes at work, and how irritated they got about demands for change. Officers who were tolerant of risk were the most confident about their personal capacity for doing community policing and were more optimistic about almost all aspects of CAPS.

Chicago's Change Strategy

The CAPS managers mounted a multipronged attack on the problem of capturing the support of rank-and-file officers. This concern was, in itself, a bit of a change from the business-as-usual attitude in the department, which was dominated by a very traditional, adversarial view of labor-management relations. Many of the top brass were skeptical about the motivations of the rank and file, a skepticism which was reflected in the department's command-and-control management tradition. However, it was clear to CAPS's managers that there could be no real change in the organization unless there was a change at the bottom—in the hearts and minds of the officers. One impetus for them to change involved altering the nature of their jobs, because this would encourage them to adjust their views to conform with the reality of their day-to-day tasks. The department rejected forming what was known locally as a "split force" of community officers and "real police" by avoiding forming special units. Moves were made to change and improve the quality of supervision. In Chicago's scheme, sergeants were the key management layer, and attention had to be paid to their new roles. In addition, senior department managers employed a variety of change tactics that we describe later as "providing leadership and vision." They also dealt effectively with the union. Finally, the department invested heavily in training.

Changing the Job

Jobs were changed for the officers who served each district, by dividing them into beat teams and rapid-response teams. Beat officers spent a majority of their time within their assigned geographical area. This new beat integrity—plus some freedom from answering 911 calls—was accomplished by increasing the number of officers who served in the prototype districts by about 13 percent, and by using a radio-dispatch plan that allocated only selected calls to beat teams. In their beat, officers were to work with schools, merchants, and residents to identify and solve problems, and to serve as conduits for expediting requests for services by other city agencies. An important part of their job was to attend neighborhood meetings and work with existing community organizations on a broad range of issues. Public beat meetings were held regularly, in every beat to facilitate communication between residents and beat officers. These—plus district-level advisory-committee meetings and consultations with representatives of other municipal service agencies—provided a structure which forced police to confront their expanded role definition. Over time, officers alternated between beat work and responding to 911 calls as rapid-response officers to ensure that community policing was not confined to special units within the organization.

Changing Supervision

It was also clear that the program could not become a reality until officers believed that their immediate superiors really expected them to carry it out, so the task of reshaping and strengthening the supervisory role of sergeants took on some urgency. Sergeants supervised officers who covered a sector (made up of three-to-five beats), and were responsible for how they spent their tour of duty. Supervisors were given some initial CAPS training. However, as the program unfolded, it became obvious that the role of sector sergeants was not clearly defined, and they often felt unsure about what was expected of them. They were uncertain about a number of responsibilities: maintaining officers' beat integrity; coordinating city services; satisfying the continuing demand, by other parts of the department, for success on traditional performance measures (for example, issuing traffic citations); handling differential dispatch problems; and carrying out their role with rapid-response officers who were working in their sectors. Sector sergeants had repeatedly been told that their job was to coach officers in their new community roles, but, in truth, they knew as little as the frontline force knew about what that really entailed. They were disgruntled and felt overworked. Many of these issues, particularly role confusion, were addressed in additional training for supervisors, which is described later in this chapter.

Providing Leadership and Vision

Providing leadership and vision is an important part of any organizational change strategy. Everyone in the organization—from project planners to the troops in the field—needs to know where they are headed, as well as the nuts and bolts of how to get there. A successful vision is one that is presented clearly and consistently; a successful leader is one who does not falter in this vision along the way, but, instead, finds in challenges an opportunity to clarify and expand on it.

In Chicago, the most visible pronouncement of the department's vision was found in "Together We Can." This document outlined the policing philosophy which lay behind CAPS and laid out the changes that needed to take place for it to be a successful citywide program. Partly authored and signed by the superintendent, this report became the driving force behind the citywide implementation plan, and it set the discussion agenda for the newly formed Policy and Planning Committee. It was also listed, as noted previously, among the required readings for the next exam for promotion to sergeant.

Efforts were made to communicate this vision internally. A variety of methods were employed to spread the word about CAPS to prototype-district personnel, and to receive input about how the implementation process was going. There were regularly scheduled meetings that brought together district commanders, other key prototype-district personnel, the mayor's staffers who coordinated service delivery, and CAPS's managers. R&D set up a telephone hot line so that patrol officers and their supervisors could call when they had questions or concerns. They also published a newsletter to report implementation progress and success stories. Each prototype district had a CAPS representative within R&D, who was responsible for keeping abreast of and reporting events in the district; answering questions of officers there; and collecting success stories for the newsletter. As noted previously, R&D formed focus groups that could identify and iron out implementation problems; and whenever officers gathered for training, very senior department executives turned up to conduct the question-and-answer sessions that proved so valuable during the orientation sessions. In personal interviews, many officers and supervisors remarked that these new channels allowed them to voice their opinion to the command staff for the first time. While this did not necessarily mean they felt things were going to change in ways that they favored, they were gratified that their voices were being heard.

Also, the new program was not oversold. On many occasions, the mayor and the superintendent allowed that CAPS was not a panacea for all the social ills of the city. And the CAPS program was never sold as an overnight fix for the city's crime problems. Both the mayor and the superintendent recognized that the proto-typing strategy involved trying out new ideas, and that mistakes would be made along the way. Both police and citizens were often reminded that the prototype districts were test sites, and that models of community policing would evolve from the experiences in these districts only over time. The top brass reiterated that the program could take as long as five years to implement citywide, and that everyone would have to be patient.

It was significant that Chicagoans could actually anticipate enough stability in the top leadership to believe that this admonition might be true. In fact, political and administrative instability has plagued community-policing efforts in other cities. During the decade between the mid-1980s and the mid-1990s, New York had three mayors committed to three different paradigms of policing, and five different police chiefs took turns trying to implement them. In many cities, there has been pressure for rapid implementation of, and quick results from, community policing so that incumbents can enjoy the political benefits of the program during their term of office. One way to do this is to form special units and short-change the training—strategies that Chicago wanted to avoid. Political and department leadership changes also threaten the success of community policing, as new leaders sweep out the policy debris left behind by the old ones and institute new programs in their stead. In Chicago, on the other hand, no one doubted the capacity of the incumbent mayor to hold on to his job, or to choose adminis-trators who would support his agenda. In other parts of the municipal bureaucracy, the agenda had included professionalizing, down-sizing, privatizing, and investing in efficient and labor-saving technologies. The mayor had developed a national reputation for reforming the administration of municipal government, and there-fore, many observers felt the police department should not imagine itself immune from executive oversight.

This is not to say that there were no divisions at the top of the department in regard to the move toward a community-policing model. The top brass downtown were far from uniformly supportive of CAPS, and some tried to use their power to strangle the program when it needed officers, administrative and support staff, and other department resources that they controlled. The prototyping process was probably run too long by the CAPS managers downtown, but they feared passing it down to appropriate management levels, because some of its most implacable foes dwelled there. Officers in the field, attempting to discern what was going on downtown, could spot ample evidence of internal discord. They kept asking us why they should believe in the program when their bosses did not. Those who choose to read discord near the top as evidence of a faltering commitment to the program could easily justify not sticking their neck out on its behalf too early.

Avoiding the Social-Work Image

One of the lessons the department learned from other cities was that it was risky to create special community-policing units. Almost inevitably, members of these units become marginalized within their departments, looked down on by their peers as "empty holsters" doing wave-and-smile policing. Instead, Chicago's plan was to eventually involve the entire department in the program, and eventually CAPS was to be a citywide, fully integrated program of community policing. The prototype districts that were selected to be the test bed for community policing joined the program as a unit, warts and all. The test districts were not staffed by volunteers, or by specially selected officers, supervisors, or even district commanders (two of whom never supported the program). Officers on all three shifts—not just those who were working the day watch—constituted a beat team. Unlike some cities, they received no special perks, such as selecting their own working hours or days off. (In New York, the beat officers' habit of using their flexible schedules to work just the day shift—Monday through Friday—got the program in a great deal of trouble internally and externally.) In addition, beat work was not a permanent assignment; over time, beat and rapid-response officers would rotate jobs, so that all would become involved in CAPS.

The program successfully avoided developing a "soft" image. The top brass constantly reiterated the message that traditional police work would continue and would be rewarded. They stressed that officers would not become social workers; rather, they would be referral specialists for many problems at the neighborhood level, and there would be a new effort at City Hall to see to it that other city agencies kept up their end of the bargain. There were many discussions between CAPS's managers and the command staff about continuing to put a strong emphasis on arrests where appropriate.

Dealing with the Union

Employee organizations were major players in department policy making and city politics. Chief among them was the Fraternal Order of Police (FOP), which represented police officers at the bargaining table. There were also unions that represented the department's civilian employees, and staff associations that spoke separately for sergeants, lieutenants, and captains, who were not allowed to form unions.

From the outset, it was clear that the program had to be consistent with the union contract. As noted in chapter 3, officers' district assignments were made on the basis of seniority, and they were all renewed at the end of each year through a complex bidding process. Within districts, shift choices were made on the basis of bidding by seniority. Only assignments to specific functional tasks—for instance, either to beat teams or to rapid-response cars—lay within the discretionary authority of district commanders. As a result, it was impossible for downtown managers to do any detailed tinkering with the matching of officer's skills to varying district conditions. Nor could they commit the organization to keeping the same officers in any job or beat for more than a year. The labor agreement also obligated the department to pay overtime wages to officers who staffed important components of the program. As we shall note in the next chapter, one of these components involved a commitment that officers from all three shifts would attend each regular community beat meeting in order to meet with local residents. This entailed extra pay for officers not assigned to the evening shift, when most of these meetings were held. Likewise, the cross-shift team meetings of all beat officers and sergeants, which were to be held quarterly, went on the overtime bill.

The FOP remained tolerant of CAPS through its formative years. The union president took a few swings at selected parts of the second management report presented by the mayor's consulting team, objecting particularly to the recommendation that more use should be made of one-officer cars. But the union's real attention stayed firmly focused on the substance of the first report, which examined health care, sick leave, pensions, and other bread-and-butter issues. Perhaps the most critical juncture for the program occurred during the bitterly contested campaign for the election of a new FOP president, during CAPS's first year. Neither side in the contest chose to make an issue of the new program. Both the old union president and the new one told us that they would occasionally receive inquiries from officers about CAPS, and their position was that the union remained neutral toward the effort. After the election, the new union president was included on a policy-planning committee formed by the department for the purpose of thinking strategically about the future of policing in the city. He was widely consulted, as were representatives of the department's civilian employees' unions. Later, at the end of 1995, the FOP's executive committee actually endorsed the program, lauding the way it returned the quality of service delivered by individual police officers to center stage in the department.

Training for Community Policing

If change processes were to be set in motion within the organization, training had to be one of the most important mechanisms for getting them under way. Training for the rank and file and their immediate supervisors was one way that they were to be brought on board. Even if their hearts had been won over, police, in the absence of a comprehensive training program, would be forced in their minds to fall back on what they already knew how to do. If this happened, problem solving would inevitably focus on old, familiar problems, and the strategies that officers chose to deal with them would be those they had always employed: conducting visible patrol, issuing summonses, and making arrests.

Officers would be particularly frustrated if their superiors told them to do things they did not understand, so the practical information content of their training was important. But in addition, community policing calls for autonomous, creative action by officers, so it was also important that they be thoroughly conversant with the underlying values and principles that were to guide their action in particular circumstances. Officers work alone in the night, rarely under the watchful eye of a supervisor; policing is one of the few organizations of the industrial age in which discretion increases as one goes down the formal hierarchy. Street policing involves making many decisions that are based on subtle situational criteria as well as general legal principles, and those are highly discretionary. Line officers need to customize laws and department policies to fit specific situations—on the spot. This will work best if they are working almost instinctively from a set of internalized general principles. "The more effective an organization's training, the less there is a need for restrictive, detailed and cumbersome organizational rules and procedures" (Silverman and Solis, 1994: 8). This is why both their minds and their hearts were important.

The CAPS managers also believed that, by putting a strong emphasis on training, they would send a message to the rank and file: that community policing in Chicago was going to be a real, rather than a paper, program. Some cities involved in community policing have ignored the importance of training and simply instructed their officers to "go out and do it." In Houston, Vera Institute researchers found federally funded INOP (Innovative Neighborhood Oriented Police) officers received neither training nor even a briefing. One noted, "I remember them just saying that they had money for overtime" (Sadd and Grinc, 1994: 36). Their review of INOP in eight cities found that officers' ignorance of what they were about "could be traced in every instance to inadequate efforts on the part of police administrators to communicate the philosophy, goals and tactics of community policing to their officers" (1994: 36).

The first round of CAPS training had two components: an initial orientation and follow-up skill-building sessions. The key actors involved in the development and implementation of the training effort included staff from the department's administrative and R&D divisions; consultants; and civilians drawn from community organizations, who were interested in CAPS or hired to participate as trainers. Staffers from the department's training division made some early suggestions, but later they were excluded from the process. The core group devised a training schedule that could be completed before the inauguration of CAPS: 24 orientation sessions were held, involving almost 1,800 patrol officers, sergeants, and lieutenants. Three-day skill-building sessions were then conducted, during two shifts each day, at a large Park District building, and a total of 1,500 police personnel of all ranks were trained. A few focus-group sessions were held along the way to discern if training was being effectively delivered, but once training was under way, the accelerated time schedule did not allow for significant changes in the curriculum.

The orientation sessions opened (following our questionnaire) with a videotaped welcome from the superintendent of police, who made clear his commitment to the program. There were two-hour-long descriptions of community policing in general, and of the CAPS model, which were separated by a discussion of how community policing differed from the traditional variety. There was also a description of some of the paperwork requirements the new program would impose, and of the role of the community in the plan. At the end of each session, there was a question-and-answer period, conducted on almost every occasion by the CAPS project manager. Perhaps the most dramatic segment, it offered most officers their first opportunity to dialogue freely with a member of the senior command staff (a "gold star," named for the special color of their badges) over department issues. These issues frequently had little to do with community policing, and the Q&A sessions quickly became the place for officers to vent their frustrations about a wide range of issues. Later this venting was viewed as an important contribution to the orientation sessions, and Q&As became a routine part of the CAPS training programs.

Skill-building sessions lasted three days. They involved mixed teams of sworn and civilian trainers, and the classes were relatively small. The purpose of the sessions was to allow trainees to develop the decision-making and interpersonal skills believed to be essential to CAPS' success. The curriculum covered five topics: communications, problem solving, alliances, goal setting, and ethics. Questions that came up about the program were written down and reviewed later, and they took up a significant amount of time.

Several aspects of this training effort represented startling departures from business-as-usual in the department. The training materials were developed, and the entire program was planned and conducted, outside the control of the department's training division. The skill-building sessions were held away from the training academy, and police attended in civilian clothes and were trained in mixed-rank groups. Most strikingly, civilians were involved in training police.

Our evaluation suggested that the accelerated pace of the preparations for training created problems. The CAPS implementation schedule was being driven by City Hall, and it was clear that the program would be kicked off on time, and that some sort of training had to be completed on schedule. The fact that a training program that involved a large number of officers actually took place, and was conducted in a professional manner, was in itself a noteworthy achievement. However, the planners could not find much useful training material from sources around the country, nor any evaluations of community-policing training, so everything had to be developed from scratch and without assurance that it would be effective. The rapidly shrinking time frame for training shrank everyone's expectations about what could be accomplished. During the planning process, orientation evolved from a week-long, indepth program to one-day lectures. Sufficient time was not available for planning, evaluating, and revising the curriculum, so that comments and recommendations gathered along the way could not easily be incorporated into the materials used. The hectic pace of preparation was also detrimental to the trainers: They did not have adequate time to internalize the CAPS philosophy, which led to inconsistencies in their presentation of crucial material. Nevertheless, an impressive package of training materials was developed, and during the entire process, a significant degree of cooperation, coordination, and professionalism was exhibited by department staff and civilian consultants and trainers.

Unity was not always evident behind the scenes, however. Many of the sworn trainers resented the fact that their early curriculum recommendations appeared to be ignored by the CAPS managers. They expressed hostility toward a curriculum that they believed was imposed by a civilian consulting firm, although in fact there was a great deal of input into its formulation by department staffers who were not members of the training division. The experience left hostile feelings among police trainers, who felt that their expertise was not being utilized (although we observed that they were fairly young). They were also upset because the civilian trainers did not understand police operations. They thought the civilians were naive, and that they came up with unrealistic examples of key points. There was behind-the-scenes animosity toward the civilian trainers, which grew as the civilians demonstrated their lack of understanding of police culture and department operations. As one trainer noted:

> Initially, I thought it was a good idea that we were working with civilians, because I thought they must be really strong in their areas of expertise. But after a while, we all saw that they didn't have any experience. . . . I guess they were all very nice. But the next thing we know, one of them says, "What's a beat?"

It was not clear to us that the problem was entirely one of civilian naïveté, however. The sworn personnel used in training were young and relatively inexperienced, as well as being new to community policing themselves; and they themselves had a distance to go before accepting that civilians would be active partners in the CAPS program.

The CAPS training program was supposed to be a departure from traditional training practices. However, for the most part, trainees were mostly lectured to, and they were seldom involved in the sessions as active learners. A concept from the field of adult education, active learning draws on the experiences of students and encourages them to participate in discussions, problem-solving groups, and role-playing exercises. However, despite the fact that the officers being trained were all experienced, the curriculum was not organized around confronting and developing new understandings of the issues that they believed they already understood very clearly. They were never required to take responsibility for note taking, to respond during class discussions, or to read the materials. There were no tests. For their part, many officers we interviewed dismissed the curriculum as being too abstract to provide much guidance. They wanted to know what to *do.* One trainee noted: "It wasn't relevant. It taught skills that we could not apply. What they tried to teach us was just not the way it is on the street." Another said, "The role playing and problem solving were somewhat interesting, but cops just want to learn what we are supposed to do." And a third person noted, "You can't bullshit a bullshitter. That's what the training was. Bullshitting the cops."

Other concerns officers brought into training were not addressed, including the very widespread conviction that the experiences of other cities had already shown that "community policing doesn't work." They disliked the civilian trainers even more than did the sworn trainers. Participants generally liked the fact that they could appear in civilian clothes, and that the sessions were held in a relaxed, civilian setting. However, senior managers in other parts of the department felt that this just encouraged trainees to goof off and drink at lunch. Also, lieutenants and captains who were included in mixed-rank training groups grumbled about the indignities this inflicted. Many did not like to be debated or corrected by their underlings, and they also did not like the casual give-and-take that was encouraged by the dress code and the setting of the training. One lieutenant noted: "Some idiot thought it was a great idea to put us with the patrolmen and sergeants. Well, you can't be buddy-buddy and then lead the patrolmen on the street."

The notable lack of involvement by the department's training division in this effort was a harbinger of future conflicts. CAPS managers did not like the plans that trainers brought forward for the skill-building sessions, and in ensuing months, they rejected the division's proposed CAPS modules for rookie training. In their view, the academy planned to marginalize CAPS, rather than build it into every component of the training effort. They also did not think that academy staffers understood the program. On their end, training staffers thought their good ideas were not respected, and that curricula put together by civilian consultants were stuffed down their throats. As one put it:

> We really worked hard on it. And we came up with a good curriculum. It was sent down to City Hall for revisions, and the whole thing was ignored. The Booz, Allen people [the consulting firm] came up with the curriculum that was used. We couldn't believe it when we saw it.

Virtually every sworn trainer we interviewed spoke negatively about the three-day skill-building sessions, which lay at the heart of the department's first venture into community policing.

These conflicts came to a head after the CAPS managers planned and conducted two further extensive rounds of training, without the support of the training division. Following a shift in the power structure of the department, they gained control of the academy; purged it of many of its personnel; and brought in a new director, who was more attuned to the program.

In the months following the first round of CAPS training, the department developed a completely new set of training materials. Two experienced consultants—one the acting director of a big-city police training academy—played a major role in developing early drafts of the new materials. The redesign team conducted nine focus-group sessions that explored the link between the training that officers received and their actual jobs, the information that they retained, and what they thought about the instruction. The redesign people met with the director of our training evaluation team to discuss changes in the curriculum. They concluded that the initial curriculum had too much emphasis on concepts, and lacked clear guidance for officers and supervisors who were anxious about nuts-and-bolts issues. Instead, they needed to begin with material that had reassuring clarity and specificity, and to move, later, to the concepts that lay behind the procedures and expectations that were outlined. They also decided that, henceforth, they would not mix ranks in the classroom, and that they would use only sworn trainers. The next time they conducted training for officers, they also announced that there would be a test at the end that participants had to pass; if they didn't, they would repeat the course. This appeared to have a salutary effect on their attentiveness.

New Roles for Supervisors

The first beneficiaries of this evolving training plan were supervisors. Not convinced of the effectiveness of their initial efforts to train prototype supervisors, and mindful that the program would soon become a citywide one, a new round of training was conducted from March through May of 1994 for sergeants, lieutenants, and captains from all over the department. Captains and lieutenants received two days of training, while sergeants completed a four-day session. Our evaluation team examined the nature of the training, the performance of trainers, and the participants' views of their jobs.

The purpose of the training was to hone the participants' leadership skills, explain their management responsibilities under CAPS, familiarize supervisors with the jobs they would be assigning to their officers, and give them some direction about how to get started in the nonprototype districts. The training was meant to teach supervisors how to do more than give orders and sign forms. It was to encourage them to become teachers, coaches, and mentors; these were all new roles in the department.

The training curriculum consisted of nine modules. The opening section described the critical elements of CAPS. A leadership module emphasized, in very concrete terms, how supervisors' different styles and approaches to management problems, would influence their interactions with subordinates and affect their ability to handle CAPS-related assignments. The segment, which was very thought provoking, encouraged participants to explore their own leadership styles. A session on building partnerships focused on how to run a beat meeting, and help citizens assume responsibility for problems that they can solve themselves. The partnerships segment used videotaped segments of actual beat meetings to illustrate how to perform this activity competently. It provided very graphic examples of scenarios that the trainees could identify with and understand. A discussion of beat integrity reviewed the department's dispatch policy; another, on beat profiling, explained how officers should collect and share CAPS-related information. The problem-solving segment offered a dynamic model for solving the problems of crime and disorder in the community. A module on team building examined supervisors' specific roles and responsibilities in implementing CAPS; they learned about team development, information flow, time management, and team-performance assessment. The course concluded with a Q&A session conducted by senior command staff members. Our observers reported that the most effective modules worked because not only did they tell supervisors how to do something, but they also showed them how to do it. They also drew participants into the training sessions by helping them envision themselves in realistic situations.

In general, the trainees were very attentive and cooperative during these classes. They seemed to grasp the material, and most were willing to participate in exercises and to share their questions and concerns about CAPS during open forums. A sergeant we interviewed noted that past CAPS training was "a little abstract. The problem last year was that they asked questions like, 'Would you rather be a tree or a forest?' " Similarly, another sergeant indicated that "last year, it was just theory. I mean the program hadn't started, so you couldn't really make it too practical." Another said, "They finally gave us something we could sink our teeth into. I guess this time they were careful in their selection of instructors. They asked for a lot of input, and we had the freedom to say what we wanted. We were free to criticize."

Most important, the lieutenants and sergeants felt that the trainers knew about supervisors' jobs, which one lieutenant observed, "was the real difference between last year's [CAPS training] and this year's training. Last year, they ate the civilians alive. They took exception to everything the [civilian] trainers said." Many of the supervisors we interviewed indicated their preference for sworn trainers over civilian trainers. One noted, "At least they were cops. We tend to like our own. We can be a pretty tough audience otherwise." Another observed that many trainers were selected from the districts: "Yeah, they had street guys, not empty holsters. I gotta give them credit this time for doing that." They also reported that the trainers were not condescending, as they perceived previous CAPS trainers to be. "Last year [it] was like for kiddies," said one lieutenant.

One advantage was that this time, in the discussion, the trainers could involve participants who were serving in the prototype districts, which enhanced the training sessions for everyone. The involvement of trainees from the prototype districts in communicating information about CAPS made them feel like an integral part of the training, and they had a chance to share their direct CAPS experiences with other officers. They provided examples of how CAPS was actually carried out, shared their triumphs and tribulations in implementing the program, and helped allay trainees' anxiety about CAPS. In the words of a nonprototype sergeant, "We learned from the prototype people who were there. We heard about their mistakes." The prototype trainees also corroborated many of the trainers' comments and provided object lessons to illustrate the trainers' points. According to a lieutenant from a prototype district, "I was called on quite a bit to explain things because I'd already been through it. We all had name cards sitting in front of us that listed our district, so the instructors knew who to ask." The prototype trainees' cooperation in the sessions seemed pivotal in helping the trainers make the program seem like a real one. One prototype lieutenant reported, "I enjoyed talking about CAPS to the nonprototype people and seeing the attitude change as the training went on." Another noted:

> There were people who had their doubts, but those of us who were involved [in CAPS] the first year told them that we had the same doubts, but that they'd like it. We all pretty much want the same thing, but I guess we differ on how we'll get there. It wasn't like there was fighting or anything. It's just that they don't know the program like we do. We told them to give it a chance. After they try it, they'll see that it's certainly no worse than they have it now.

Compared to the initial round of CAPS training, there were also very few instances in which trainers denigrated the program. In these sessions, attacks on CAPS were relatively mild and subtly communicated through trainees' attitudes, nonverbal cues, and references to traditional policing and the department's culture. Nonetheless, many of the trainees we interviewed in person were still dubious about the department's ability and willingness to institute the massive organizational changes required to implement CAPS. One trainee said:

> Those of us from the prototypes know that it [CAPS] is not perfect and that we can't do anything if there's no support from above. It's real bogus to tell us to change if there is no change from above. The command structure needs to change, but let me tell you, we have to wait for those guys to die.

Roll-Call Training

Following the completion of supervisor training, in the spring of 1994, many aspects of the CAPS implementation effort ground to a halt. Summer in Chicago signals the onslaught of an immense number of neighborhood and ethnic festivals, a 50-percent increase in reported crimes and other incidents, and a round of vacations for police personnel. These make it difficult to free officers' time for training or other events, but the CAPS managers did not want to lose the momentum they had built up during the winter. They were also aware that the program was soon to become a citywide one, and they had not yet trained officers who were serving in 20 of the city's police districts.

Their solution was to experiment with a new form of instruction—roll-call training—which was to be conducted at station houses citywide during the summer of 1994. Roll calls at the start of each shift usually involved uniform and shoeshine inspections, and announcements about recent crime trends or hot spots in the district. The purpose of the new roll-call training was to provide all beat and rapid-response officers with an initial orientation to CAPS. The training was administered by their own sergeants and covered nine topics: the rationale for change, the definition of CAPS and the description of its organization, beat integrity, beat meetings, the role of city services, beat profiling, problem solving, and team building. We observed that officers in the nonprototype districts appeared to benefit more from the information. Sergeants who instructed there gave more attention to the details of the program, and more officers asked questions about the material. On the other hand, in the prototype districts, much of the material appeared to be redundant.

A later survey found that, overall, 40 percent of those who recalled receiving roll-call training thought the information they received was useful; and 40 percent believed the training gave them enough information to start filling out city service-request forms. Furthermore, 35 percent thought they learned enough about attending beat meetings. When asked if more training should be provided through the roll-call effort and training bulletins, 52 percent agreed, 34 percent were neutral about the idea, and only 13 percent disagreed with it. Older officers more often thought that roll-call training was useful, and that they had learned enough about beat meetings and service requests. Older officers were also more apt to call for further training. White officers were much less sympathetic toward the training effort than were black or Hispanic officers.

Changes in Police Attitudes

By the end of 1994, the Chicago Alternative Policing Strategy had become the official posture of all 25 police districts. Patrol units had been divided into beat or rapid-response teams; the units were being differentially dispatched to calls; and community beat meetings and district advisory meetings were being held on a regular basis all over the city. However, except for the roll-call sessions, officers in the 20 districts that had just been converted to the program had not yet been trained. Downtown managers believed that the bulk of officers in the field had not yet "got the message" or committed themselves to the program in a significant way, and that there was very little alternative policing really going on in most districts. Our follow-up surveys of officers confirmed that this was largely the case, and that even in the prototype districts, support for the program was still tepid. On the other hand, there was some evidence of movement toward increased optimism about CAPS among those who actually had experience with the program.

As noted previously, in 1993, we gathered baseline survey data from 1,200 police officers and from 200 of their immediate supervisors when they were summoned to orientation sessions for the new program they were about to implement. At that time, we surveyed, separately, 335 police officers who were serving in five other districts that would not be affected by the program, but that were closely matched to the prototype districts in terms of their demographic composition and rates of crime. Later, we were able to gather new data to assess the extent to which the views of police who were serving in the districts may have changed over time. During January–May of 1995, we surveyed almost 7,000 police officers who were serving in all 25 districts. Among this group, 1,056 were serving in the five prototype districts, and their views could be compared with those of the officers who had served there 20 months before.

These surveys enabled us to make two kinds of gross comparisons that helped clarify the extent to which officers came on board as a result of their training and experience. The first involved contrasting the views of officers who were serving in prototype districts with those of officers in nonprototype districts, at two points in time—before CAPS was implemented; and then some time after it was launched. Of greatest interest in this comparison were differences in the change (or the stability) in the views of officers in the prototype districts as compared to possible changes in the views of officers who were serving elsewhere. This was the most useful approach, and we employed it when we posed questions consistently, across time, to sufficiently large groups of police officers. The other approach was to simply contrast the views of police who were serving in prototype and nonprototype districts in early 1995—20 months after the inauguration of CAPS, and before many changes actually began to take place in the new districts. In both cases, it was also possible to use statistical controls to account for how the officers differed demographically, before we made these comparisons. This was important because in no case were we able to directly assess how individuals' views changed. Each of these surveys was independently administered, and it was impossible to link the responses of individuals over time or by changes in assignments. However, in the 1995 survey, 72 percent of the officers who were then serving in the prototypes had already been there in the spring of 1993, and they had been surveyed at the initial orientation sessions. As a result, comparisons of the views of prototype-district officers in 1993 and 1995 offer fairly strong evidence of attitude changes.

Changes among Officers

The 1993 and 1995 surveys of police officers in prototype and non-prototype districts uncovered evidence of modest opinion shifts in the department toward more optimism about community policing. The results of analyses that examined over-time changes among groups of officers who were serving in prototype and nonprototype districts are presented in the second column of table 4-2. Statistically, the most visible shift was that officers' fears about the potential impact of the program on their working life had been allayed. Indeed, in 1995, prototype-district officers were less concerned about the loss of their autonomy than they were in 1993, while those serving in other districts were more concerned than in the past. For example, 50 percent of prototype-district officers, when they were first interviewed, thought a blurring of authority loomed on the horizon, but only 38 percent of the officers who were serving in the prototypes 20 months later felt the same way. At the same time, the percentage that felt this way increased from 38 percent to 42 percent among officers serving in other districts. A statistical

Table 4-2   Changing Views of Officers in Regard to CAPS

Multi-Item Attitude Scales	Changes Among Officers in Prototype and Nonprototype Districts, 1993–95
Optimistic about impact on traditional police concerns	Those in prototypes became more optimistic.
Optimistic about impact on the community	Both groups became more optimistic.
Oriented toward community-policing concepts	Both groups became more so.
Personal capacity for problem solving	Those in prototypes improved.
Willing to devote resources to CAPS	No change
Optimistic about impact of CAPS on police autonomy	Prototypes up, others down
Satisfied with the department as an organization	Prototypes up, others down
Think relationship with the public is good	Both up insignificantly

Note: Data are based on comparisons of the statistical significance of 1993–1995 changes in scale scores for prototype and nonprototype districts. Analyses are controlled for race, age, sex, and education of officers.

analysis of a four-question measure of officer pessimism (the results of which are summarized in table 4-2) found that service in a prototype district was very significantly related to lower levels of concern about police autonomy, an effect that was second in magnitude to the effect of race.

Likewise, prototype-district officers became more optimistic about the impact of CAPS on traditional policing concerns, while the views of other officers did not change much at all. Compared to the others, more prototype-district officers interviewed in 1995 thought that CAPS might reduce crime and lead to the more effective use of police resources, and would enable them to respond more effectively to calls for service. In terms of their personal capacity for problem solving, officers who had served in a prototype were significantly more likely to report that they could identify and analyze problems, but they were not more confident about their ability to solve them. There were no changes at all in the self-assessments of officers serving in other districts. Other questions found that, compared to officers surveyed in 1993, the prototype-district officers in 1995 were more likely to report using community meetings and surveys, and information from other city agencies, to identify problems in their areas.

At the same time, officers' satisfaction with the police department went up a bit in the prototypes, and down a bit in the remainder of the department. For example, in 1993, 22 percent of prototype-district officers agreed with the statement "Management in general treats its employees quite well," while 27 percent agreed in 1995; 26 percent of those serving in other districts agreed in 1993, but only 22 percent agreed in 1995.

Other changes between 1993 and 1995 were not specifically linked to experience with CAPS in the prototypes, but represented more general shifts in department opinion. As a whole, officers grew more optimistic about the impact of CAPS on the community: The percentage that thought CAPS would make it more likely that citizens would be willing to cooperate with the police went up by six points in both prototype and nonprototype districts. There were 5- to 10-percent increases in the proportions that thought that police-community relations would improve, and that there would be more frequent resolution of neighborhood problems. The largest shift was related to problem solving: The percentage of prototype officers that endorsed the idea that CAPS would lead to more effective use of crime information went up by 13 percentage points (to 59 percent), and among officers serving elsewhere, it went up 14 percent (to 54 percent). Racial cleavages between police and the community remained a sticky point, however; there were no changes in either group in the percentage that thought CAPS would improve police relations with minorities.

Comparisons across time also pointed to modest but general increases in officers' orientation toward community-policing concepts. For example, positive responses to foot patrol went up by 7 percentage points in prototype areas, and 9 percentage points elsewhere. The percentage of officers in the prototypes that agreed that it was important to make frequent informal contacts with residents went from 62 percent to 69 percent, and this figure was up a little in other areas as well. Of all the measures in this cluster, only enthusiasm for solving noncrime problems did not go up at least a bit. There was no statistically reliable figure to indicate a change in officers' views of the level of support they were getting from the community. However, across four other measures, officers in both prototype and other districts were a bit more optimistic on these points. Across the board, the percentages that thought that most people do not respect the police and that they do not understand the problems of police went down.

What Chicago Did—and Didn't—Accomplish

During the first two years of CAPS, a great deal was accomplished to move rank-and-file officers closer to the community-policing model. We found that most of the key ideas for making change in the hearts and minds of officers were carried out in some fashion. Officers' jobs were changed, so that they had time and a responsibility to stay on their beat, learn about neighborhood problems, attend community meetings, and work with residents. There was an attempt to reshape the department's management style, to more fully engage first-line supervisors in the program and involve them in team building and management. The department's top executives supplied more than a little leadership and vision. Their message was not always consistent during the first year, as the program's managers tried first one tactic and then another, but officers were warned that the program was being developed iteratively and that the top brass were not necessarily wedded to every new idea it tried. They worked cooperatively with the union and tackled the "social work" problem head-on—and neither became a problem.

They did not tackle the issue of performance evaluation. It was apparent to everyone involved that new ways were needed to monitor officer and team performance. Performance in community-policing assignments needs to be recognized; and performance measures need to be developed that enable managers to give their line workers routine feedback about how well they are doing, and to convey to the department, and to the general public, the reality of the agency's new values and expectations (Wycoff and Oettmeir, 1994). They could also assist in identifying promising innovations and documenting the benefits of sometimes costly—because they are labor intensive—community programs. A department working group actively investigated the performance-evaluation issue as early as the fall of 1992. However, they did not make any headway. The chicken-and-egg problem of trying to generate change without a clear idea of the organization's destination had been cleared up by the end of 1994, when the need to develop very specific officer and supervisor training materials had driven the CAPS managers to develop clear task definitions. However, they did not revisit the performance-evaluation issue as a consequence.

5

Citizen Involvement

The success of CAPS' depended on accomplishing a discouragingly long list of goals, one of which was the formation of police-community partnerships that would identify and solve neighborhood problems: The CAPS model of community policing called for building bridges between police and community members. As individuals, beat officers were encouraged to establish working relationships with residents of their beats. The program's plans for organized police-citizen interaction were probably more important, however. At the grassroots level, police were to meet on a regular, frequent, and well-publicized basis with beat residents. At these so-called beat meetings, they were to exchange information, identify and prioritize local problems, develop strategies to address them, and begin the process of identifying police and community resources that could be mobilized to support problem solving. As a department training bulletin noted, "Beat meetings ensure community input in the problem-solving process" (Chicago Police Department, 1994: 1). At the district level, commanders were to form new advisory committees that would be broadly representative of interests in the community. They were to advise the commanders about matters of concern to the community, and help them evaluate the effectiveness of projects in the districts.

However, while the community side of community policing is as critical as any, many cities have experienced great difficulty in getting neighborhood residents involved. Like police officers, the residents too must be brought on board, and they often do not prove readily cooperative. The Vera Institute's study of community policing in eight cities found "all eight . . . sites experienced extreme difficulty in establishing a solid community infrastructure on which to build their community policing programs" (Grinc, 1994: 442). The study concluded (1994: 437) that, of all the implementation problems these programs faced, "the most perplexing . . . was the inability of the police departments to organize and maintain active community involvement in their projects." This could be as difficult as involving police officers, and the list of potential problems in sustaining community involvement in policing is just as long as that on the police side of the equation.

Above all, the two groups do not have a history of getting along. Especially in poor and disenfranchised neighborhoods, residents often have a history of antagonistic relationships with the police. The police may be perceived as arrogant, brutal, and uncaring, and not as potential partners. Residents may fear that more intensive policing could generate new problems with harassment, indiscriminate searches, and conflicts between them and the police. In chapter 2, we documented the gulf that existed between the races in Chicago in the months before CAPS began. Hispanics and African-Americans were almost three times as likely as whites to think that police who were serving their neighborhoods were impolite, and more than twice as likely to think they treated people unfairly. About 35 percent of Hispanics felt police were not concerned about the problems that people in their neighborhoods faced; 25 percent of African-Americans, but only 15 percent of whites, also felt this way.

Organizations that represent the interests of community members also may not have a track record of cooperating with police. Poor and high-crime areas are often not well endowed with an infrastructure of organizations ready to become involved. Since their constituents often fear the police, groups that represent poor and minority areas can be more interested in monitoring police misconduct and pressing for greater police accountability to civilians than in being involved in coordinated action with them. Research on participation in organized crime-prevention programs also finds that it is not easily initiated or sustained in poorer neighborhoods. Crime and fear stimulate a withdrawal from community life, not an involvement in it. In crime-ridden neighborhoods, mutual distrust and hostility are often rampant. Residents tend to view each other with suspicion rather than neighborliness, thereby undermining their capacity for forging collective responses to local problems. They fear retaliation by drug dealers and neighborhood toughs, so programs requiring social contact, neighborly cooperation, or public involvement are less often successful in areas with high levels of fear (Hope, 1995; Austin, 1991; Skogan, 1986).

The problem may be compounded when program boundaries imposed by the police department link diverse communities. Suspicion and fear may then divide the area along race, class, and lifestyle lines, leaving residents and the organizations that represent them at odds with one another. They will almost inevitably point fingers at one another, in deciding who causes what problems, and there will be pressure for the police to choose sides. Groups that contend over access to housing, municipal services, infrastructure maintenance, and public-sector jobs and contracts may also find themselves battling one another for policing priorities and the ear of the district commander (Skogan, 1988).

It is also difficult to get out community policing's message. Nothing in the past has really prepared residents for this new mission. They are unlikely to understand the new goals and tactics involved in community policing. Vera Institute researchers found that none of the cities they studied had recognized the need to train residents in their appropriate roles. They concluded, "Any potential for the success of community policing will be limited if major commitments to community education and training are not forthcoming" (Grinc, 1994: 455).

Finally, there may be no reason for residents of crime-ridden neighborhoods to think anything about community policing except, "Here today, gone tomorrow." Too often, their past is strewn with broken promises, and with programs that flowered, but then wilted when the funding dried up or the newspapers looked the other way. They are rightly skeptical about whether it will be any different this time, especially when they discern that the police officers they deal with hope for the same end result.

This chapter examines how community involvement developed during Chicago's first 18 months of community policing, from the start of the program late in April 1993 through October 1994. It examines how the beat meetings worked—who identified problems, and who took charge of implementing solutions to them. It also charts the progress made by each district toward adopting the CAPS model. In fact, not much progress was made during the first 18 months, even in the best districts, for it proved difficult for both police and neighborhood residents to adapt to their new roles. This chapter then examines the role of neighborhood organizations in CAPS. Even before the program began, some groups were jockeying for influence over its operation, for it promised to be a valuable resource for advancing their agendas. However, not every district was honeycombed with organizations that were prepared to make use of the program, so the contribution that neighborhood groups could make to community policing varied considerably from one neighborhood to another. Finally, this chapter examines the operations of the citizen committees set up to advise the district commanders, who were struggling to find their role in community policing. These committees provided a voice for some of the community's vested interests, and those that stuck closest to local issues, using local solutions, probably were the most successful.

Involvement in Beat Meetings

Beat meetings were one of the most unique and visible features of Chicago's new program. Around the country, many cities have held occasional public meetings to kick off community policing or publicize major events. In Chicago, beat meetings were held regularly, in church basements and schoolrooms all over the city. The police who came were those who patrolled the neighborhood. The meetings served a variety of functions. They were occasions to exchange information. Participants learned about police procedures, including when to call 911 rather than a list of alternate nonemergency numbers, while police learned something about residents' priorities. Beat meetings engaged citizens in the CAPS program by generating requests for city services. In bringing residents and officers together, some of the meetings helped to build a sense of familiarity, and even trust and a working relationship, between the parties. At best—but not frequently—these regular gatherings helped officers and residents to collaborate in identifying and solving problems, and even to evaluate the success of their troubleshooting efforts.

Making beat meetings work was hard. Police officers offered resistance to this new routine and to spending time away from tasks that they believed to be real police work. Often, not very many people came to the meetings, and when they did, police fretted about how unrepresentative they were of the community as a whole. There was profound distrust between some police and some district residents. Some residents also feared retaliation by gangs if they took part in beat meetings. The limited training and experience of police in regard to problem solving, and the limited understanding of CAPS that civilian participants brought to the meetings, also undermined the utility of many beat meetings. Too many unraveled into "911 sessions" in which residents complained about specific problems without viewing them collectively or analytically, and without moving toward devising strategies for dealing with them. Police, by taking charge of too many meetings, undermined the goal of developing residents' participation and initiative, although in fairness, most of these seemed to lack civilian leadership. And too much responsibility fell into the hands of specialized neighborhood-relations officers, rather than the beat officers who actually worked the streets of the community.

A Typical Beat Meeting

What was a typical beat meeting like? During the first 18 months of CAPS, our observers attended 146 beat meetings in the five prototype districts. A total of 679 beat meetings were held during this period, so our sample of observations covered just over one-fifth of all the gatherings. All of the beat meetings visited by our observers were held in the evening. Half took place in local churches, and another quarter were held at park buildings in the districts. The remainder took place at schools, banks, city government buildings, and police stations. Most of the meetings involved relatively small groups of people: a median of 22 residents and five police officers. Although most residents who attended a typical meeting were middle-aged or older, participants appeared, otherwise, to be representative of the racial, ethnic, and class breakdown of residents of the beat area. Typically, the highest ranking police officer present was a sergeant, and the police delegation included a mix of beat officers and neighborhood-relations staffers. If the meeting was held in Austin, it was attended by a representative (or two) from community-service and nonprofit organizations, along with a professional community organizer; otherwise, it was just police and residents.

The typical beat meeting lasted for about an hour and a half. It was run informally by a police officer, who acted mostly as a facilitator of discussion. There was no formal agenda, nor any handouts—just frank talk. The typical discussion had an even balance of the views of officers and residents, although it was not unheard of for citizens to dominate the discussion—especially in Rogers Park—or for officers to spend much of the time lecturing residents, as often happened in Morgan Park.

At some point in the meeting, officers brought up their expectations for public involvement in CAPS, especially stressing the need for residents to identify neighborhood problems so that police could begin working on them. Residents were frequently reminded of the importance of organizing themselves into block clubs, watches, and patrols. Citizens rarely talked about what the police ought to be doing as part of CAPS; when they did, the main themes were the responsibilities of police in reducing crime and disorder; working on crime prevention; and keeping residents informed about criminal activity on the beat. While police were frequently reminded of this last role it was very unusual for crime or arrest reports to be distributed or discussed by police at a beat meeting.

At typical meetings, most of the time was devoted to open discussions of neighborhood issues, and residents were especially encouraged to make officers aware of local problems. Most of their exchanges dealt with drug, gang, and youth problems, and with the quality-of-life problems posed by abandoned buildings, vacant lots, graffiti, and trash on the streets. When problems were brought up by residents, police officers usually suggested solutions to them. Sometimes, these solutions involved community action, but they were defined mostly as police business. While this kind of back-and-forth discussion would continue throughout the meeting, it was rare for participants to report about actions they had actually taken, or to mention whether solutions suggested at previous meetings had been put into practice.

The style of interaction between citizens and police at a typical meeting depended on the district in which it was being held. In Englewood and Austin, police and residents tended to talk as if they were partners. In Rogers Park, there was also talk about working together as members of one team in order to coordinate efforts and influence the neighborhood in a positive way. In Morgan Park, however, police and residents typically behaved as though they had similar goals but separate agendas. Police there stressed some neighborhood problems; citizens emphasized different ones; and both acted as though their efforts were independent of one another. A different pattern emerged in Marquette, where police representatives normally took charge of organizing citizens and developing plans for them to implement. Regardless of the district in which the meetings took place, the tone of the average discussion was cooperative and cordial. Nevertheless, officers and residents would rarely mingle informally before or after the meeting.

Who Showed Up?

Police involvement in beat meetings was similar from place to place because there was an established department policy on the matter. The sergeant on duty at the time typically headed the police contingent at beat meetings. The official policy was that beat officers from each watch should be present, so evening-shift beat officers were joined by off-duty police, who were given overtime pay to attend. Our observers found that at least one beat officer attended nearly every meeting held in Englewood, Austin, and Morgan Park, but beat officers were absent at about 15 percent of the meetings held in Rogers Park and Marquette.

Attending in their stead were neighborhood-relations officers, who played an important and controversial role in CAPS. Each district had a neighborhood-relations unit, which was headed by a sergeant and staffed by four other officers. Prior to CAPS, these units conducted mostly "Officer Friendly" public-relations programs of dubious effectiveness; but under this new policing strategy, their role was redefined, and more officers were assigned to neighborhood relations so that they could provide staff support for the program during the daytime and early-evening watches. These officers had some skill in handling the public, while our experience showed that many beat officers could be less diplomatic. For instance, when citizens at one beat meeting complained that not enough was being done about late-night loud music, a beat sergeant's response was, "What kind of punishment do you want, five days in the electric chair?" The plan downtown was to use the skills of neighborhood-relations officers to cushion the transition period during which regular officers were acquiring new skills and confidence in dealing with audiences, and were gaining an understanding of their new roles in the CAPS program. That being accomplished, neighborhood-relations officers were to withdraw from leadership and defer to members of the beat team, who actually worked in the area. We found that neighborhood-relations officers attended nearly every Morgan Park meeting and that they participated in two-thirds to three-quarters or more of the meetings in the other districts. But their role did not diminish as anticipated downtown (which is an issue we will return to later).

In addition to showcasing the police, beat meetings also presented an opportunity for local nonprofit and grassroots groups to make an appearance and demonstrate their involvement in the program. Austin had more involvement from public and private agencies, and politicians or their staff members, than any other prototype district; more than two-thirds of the meetings there included at least one agency or political-representative. Organizational representatives were present at about half of the meetings in Englewood and a third of those in Rogers Park. Morgan Park and Marquette had the lowest agency and politician turnout among the prototype districts; these groups were represented in only 20 percent of the meetings in those districts.

The number of residents that attended meetings varied greatly among the prototype districts. On average, 27 residents came to Morgan Park beat meetings, compared to 24 in Rogers Park, 20 in Marquette, and 17 in both Austin and Englewood. Sometimes, the numbers were discouragingly low. Overall, 10 percent of the meetings drew fewer than 6 residents, and 30 percent drew fewer than 10.

Was There Bias in the Turnout?

Was CAPS successful in involving residents throughout the city? Were beat meetings characterized by the same low turnouts that plague other community crime-prevention efforts. To answer these questions, our observers provided quantitative data on the extent of involvement by neighborhood residents. They noted the number of residents at each meeting and described what they looked like. The 54 prototype beats varied widely in population because their boundaries were drawn so as to equalize the workload they generated via 911. As a result, whites and homeowners lived in bigger beats. We therefore examined per capita rates of beat-meeting attendance in order to control for this disparity.

By this measure, attendance rates were actually highest in African-American beats, and they were marginally higher in poorer areas. Chicago is highly segregated by race, so there were few mixed-race beats in the prototypes. Attendance in largely black beats averaged 25 residents per 10,000, while in areas where other groups predominated, the average was 16 (the correlation between the two measures was +.23). Attendance in the poorest beat areas (measured by the percentage of households that were headed by women) averaged 23 residents per 10,000, while in the wealthiest areas, it averaged 14 (the correlation was +.12). Another factor that drove up attendance was crime. In the highest crime beats attendance averaged 24 residents per 10,000, while in the lowest crime areas, it was 16.

Attendance was also associated with housing styles. Attendance was lower in beats dominated by larger apartment buildings (10 or more units), where it was 20 residents per 10,000, than in areas with mostly single-family homes or small rental buildings (where the rate was 26). Home renting, rather than ownership, had a correlation of −.16 with attendance rates. Another factor that was consistently related to low attendance rates was the proportion of the beat that was Hispanic. Attendance at meetings in the most heavily Hispanic beats averaged 17 residents per 10,000, while in the least Hispanic areas, the average was 23 (the correlation between the two measures was −.21). This being Chicago, attendance also went down during the winter: It averaged 24 residents per 10,000 in the summer, and 13 from December to February (the correlation was −.25).

In short, there were contrary social forces at work, and attendance rates were not sharply and consistently divided along the rich-poor cleavages predicted by research on participation. Taking into account the size of the beats, turnout in African-American areas and the poorest districts looked pretty good.

The down side of this finding is that it seemed, in part, driven by the crime factor. As we have noted, crime rates were significantly higher in black and poor areas of Chicago. To examine the separate influence of these factors, table 5-1 presents the results of a multivariate analysis of the correlates of meeting turnout. This takes into account the overlapping of key indicators that were related to each other as well as to turnout. Because many of them were skewed in high or low directions, all of the variables were logged. Statistically, the most important determinants of turnout were race, crime, lifestyle, and housing patterns. This is indicated by the ordering of the explanatory variables presented in table 5-1, which are ranked by the size of the standardized regression coefficients associated with each. The data were drawn from the 1990 census and from police department data on recorded crime. Turnout was lowest in heavily Hispanic and (only when other factors were taken into account) poor beats. Turnout was strongly higher in high-crime areas. There was also a significant tendency for residents of family-oriented areas, where most people lived in smaller, low-rise buildings, to get involved more frequently. Controlling for other factors, such as crime, residents of African-American areas

Table 5-1   Correlates of Beat-Meeting Attendance

(Logged) Independent Variable	Standardized Coefficient	Statistical Significance
Race		
% Hispanic	−.61	.00
% black	−.22	.08
Poverty		
% female-headed families	−.50	.01
Crime		
total crime rate	.48	.00
Lifestyle		
% families	.37	.04
Housing style		
% big buildings	−.33	.00
Season		
winter months	−.25	.00
R-squared: .32 No. of cases: 143		

Note: The dependent variable is the log of meeting attendance per 10,000 residents. All independent variables except winter are logged.

were somewhat less likely to get involved, but the effect of that factor was one of the weakest on the list. Meetings held during the winter months were consistently more sparsely attended.

We were also able to compare the complexion of the meetings with the demographic composition of the beats in which they were held. The observers estimated the percentage of civilians at each meeting who were white, Hispanic, and African-American. When their attendance observations were compared to census data, each measure broadly fit its counterpart. For Hispanics, the correlation between the percentages of those at the meetings and their percentages of the population in their beat areas was +.84; for whites, it was +.88; and for African-Americans, it was +.95. There were still important patterns in the data, however. Few Hispanics turned out for beat meetings in areas where they made up less than about 75 percent of the population; in areas where they were more than 75 percent, they predominated at meetings. Whites, on the other hand, were overrepresented at meetings in areas where they made up less than about 50 percent of the population. Because Chicago's African-American community is highly segregated, there were relatively few beat meetings where they constituted anything but the extremes— more than 90 percent of participants or less than 25 percent.

What Was Discussed?

In the CAPS model, beat meetings were to be the forum for exchanging information among residents and police, and a place for them to develop and report on joint problem-solving strategies. It turned out that the roles adopted by police officers and residents were among the most important aspects of what actually took place at beat meetings. The side that took the initiative at each stage of the problem-solving process left its distinctive mark on the range of problems and solutions brought up for consideration. The problems mentioned largely reflected residents' concerns, and these shaped the discussion agenda at the meetings. However, suggested solutions reflected the distinctive viewpoints of the police officers who were present, and they determined the action agenda at the meetings.

Nearly all of the problems brought up for discussion at CAPS beat meetings were suggested by beat residents. Police officers brought up only 6 percent of all problems discussed, and attendees from organizations and agencies, and local elected officials, identified another 2 percent. There was little variation across districts when it came to those who identified problems: Residents named 88 percent of the problems in Marquette and Austin, and as much as 96 percent in Morgan Park. Marquette had the most police input, with officers bringing up 11 percent of the problems for discussion. Thus, the beat meeting was a successful mechanism for residents to communicate their concerns to police officers.

Discussions about Neighborhood Problems. Our evaluation team observed a total of 1,079 problems being discussed during these meetings. We sorted them into 113 problem categories, along with 36 types of solutions to the problems that we heard discussed. Of the 113 problem types recorded in our observations, only 21 were mentioned in at least a tenth of all beat meetings. Figure 5-1 depicts the most common topics: Half involved drugs, gangs, and social-disorder issues such as noise, curfew violations, and troublemaking youths. Complaints about police performance made up another quarter of these issues, including two of the top four problems (these will be detailed in a later section). Another fifth of the top issues concerned the decay of the physical environment, including such problems as graffiti, litter, and abandoned cars and buildings. Interestingly, the kinds of core problems around which policing is traditionally organized—represented here by complaints

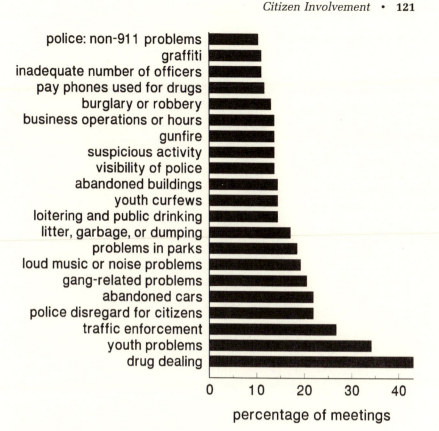

Figure 5-1 Top problems at beat meetings.

about either burglary or robbery—ranked only seventeenth on the list, and they were brought up in only 12 percent of all meetings.

To gain a more comprehensive picture of the sorts of problems brought up for discussion, see table 5-2, which sorts each of the 1,079 problems we observed being discussed into 10 categories:

- Physical decay of the neighborhood—problems with abandoned cars and buildings, litter in alleys, graffiti, vandalism, vacant lots, and problems with street lighting and street cleaning.

- Drug problems—drug use or sale; use of pay phones.

- Social disorder in the neighborhood—problems that range from gang problems to public drunkenness, disturbances, truancy, gunfire, prostitution, and alcohol sales to minors; gang problems are included because, separately, they accounted for only 3 percent of all problems.

Table 5-2 Problems Discussed at Beat Meetings

Issue Classification	Englewood	Marquette	Austin	Morgan Park	Rogers Park	Total
Physical decay	33%	21%	34%	13%	24%	23%
Drugs	11	12	15	8	8	11
Gangs and social disorder	24	31	18	32	30	28
Predatory and property crime	4	6	5	3	7	5
Fear of crime	4	2	0	3	0	2
Police performance	12	14	9	21	15	15
Police-citizen communication	2	3	4	5	2	4
CAPS program	1	0	1	1	3	1
Getting organized	1	2	0	1	3	2
Other and miscellaneous	8	8	11	12	7	10
Number of issues	133	242	206	350	148	1,079

Note: Columns sum to 100 percent, except for rounding.

- Predatory and property crimes—robbery, assault, rape, scams and con games, stolen cars, break-ins, bike thefts, fire bombings, and other such crimes.

- Fear of crime—general concerns about personal safety, particularly in traveling to and from CAPS meetings, and, more broadly, any general dissatisfaction with the amount of neighborhood crime.

- Police performance—police harassment of residents, response time to 911 calls, insensitive police personnel, traffic stops, and patrols of the neighborhood.

- Police-citizen communication—use of 911 and nonemergency numbers, anonymous calls to police, informing police of neighborhood concerns, getting information on arrests made, and other related issues.

- Problems with the CAPS program—issues relating to public anticrime gatherings, use of ideas from other successful programs, the court-advocacy program, and the location of CAPS meetings.

- Problems in getting organized; getting people to meetings; distributing materials; and problems with citizens not getting involved.

- Miscellaneous—topics and issues that were mentioned in too few instances to merit a separate category, including complaints about the judicial system or elected officials.

Overall, as indicated in the rightmost column of table 5-2, the most frequently discussed topics of concern (28 percent of problems discussed) were gangs and social disorder. Next came neighborhood decay, at 23 percent. The third most talked-about subject was police performance, which accounted for 15 percent of issues discussed; this was followed by drug problems, at 11 percent. Together, these four categories of problems comprised more than 75 percent of all topics brought up for discussion at beat meetings. Many conventional crimes were not mentioned very often, including a long list of violent and predatory offenses and property crimes.

It is important to note that there were clear differences between the (relatively few) problems identified by police and those identified by residents. Police mentioned predatory and violent crime four times more often than residents did (these accounted for 14 percent of the issues cited by police, versus 3 percent of the issues that residents mentioned). Police mentioned property crime almost eight times more frequently. On the other hand, police were less likely than residents to identify social-disorder problems. Almost 40 percent of residents' issues, and 49 percent of issues raised by organization representatives, were devoted to social-disorder problems, but only 31 percent of problems identified by police had to do with social disorder. The traditional crime-fighting concerns of officers were somewhat at odds with the issues brought up by beat residents.

Discussions about Police Conduct. Beat meetings provided residents with an opportunity to voice complaints about police performance, and we monitored each meeting for such discussions. At about a third of all the meetings, residents took the opportunity to express concern about the quality of police service. Complaints about police performance and procedures also rose as the CAPS program unfolded. Some of this could be attributed to frustrated residents, who expected CAPS to spark rapid changes in police behavior, but found that such changes were slow in coming. There were complaints about police inattention to open-air drug sites; their apparent disinterest in information that residents attempted to give them about problems in the area; their disregard for victims; their abusive language; and their unwillingness to stop when citizens attempted to wave them down for assistance. The following dialogue took place at one beat meeting:

FIRST RESIDENT: On [a certain street] at 2 a.m. some guy grabbed me. An officer was driving by. I tried to wave him down but he just kept on going.

SECOND RESIDENT: On the top of each car there is a number. If you have a complaint get the number.

FIRST NEIGHBORHOOD-RELATIONS OFFICER: Call 911. Ask for a supervisor.

SECOND NEIGHBORHOOD-RELATIONS OFFICER: I'm not defending them, but . . . they're working in another world. You may think they are ignoring you, but they are not. Everyone here has a police story, a beef. There is time to bash later on in the agenda.

Grievances expressed about the police were most widespread in Marquette and Morgan Park, while the residents of Austin and Rogers Park lodged the fewest complaints. Complaints about police service came up in half of the meetings in Morgan Park and Marquette, compared to just 8 percent of Rogers Park meetings. Early in the program, there was little mention of police conduct at beat meetings in Englewood, Marquette, and Austin. But by the first winter, the subject accounted for an increasingly significant portion of all issues raised at beat meetings. While during the first six months of the program, not a single voice complained about police in Englewood, Austin, and Rogers Park, after about a year, these grievances were raised at half of Englewood's meetings, a quarter of those in Austin, and 10 percent of those in Rogers Park. At nearly half of meetings held during the first six months, and at more than two-thirds of meetings in the following summer, residents of Morgan Park were critical of police performance.

Complaints about the operation of the department's 911 dispatching operation followed a similar pattern, and there were many of them. There were frequent complaints about slow 911 response times and about the fact that even when complainants requested anonymity, responding officers would come to their door or shine lights on their homes, identifying them to onlookers as those who had made the call. During the first autumn, there were no criticisms of the 911 system in three of the districts, but by the following summer, the percentage of meetings where complaints were made rose to 38 percent in Englewood, 55 percent in Marquette, and 13 percent in Austin. The system was widely criticized at Morgan Park meetings, and after about a year, 911 grievances were mentioned in 55 percent of the meetings held there.

Solutions for Neighborhood Problems

Solutions were proposed for 76 percent of the problems cited at beat meetings, and most of these were suggested by police officers. From the discussions, we identified seven general classes of solutions to neighborhood problems—very few of these resembled the problem-solving tactics recommended by the CAPS model of community policing:

- *Let's talk:* The most common suggested solutions entailed improvements in how residents and police communicate with one another; this category made up one-quarter of all proposed solutions.

- *We're working on it:* The second most common solution (21 percent) was an announcement by police or agency representatives that they were working on a problem. This served to end the discussion, and—as we shall note later—there was almost never any other feedback about their efforts.

- *Call the City:* Another popular solution was for someone to suggest that residents contact city service agencies or ward offices; this came in response to 10 percent of problems.

- *Let's act on it:* Specific, proactive action by citizens and neighborhood groups was proposed 7 percent of the time, and more frequently in Austin than in the other districts.

- *Let's prevent it:* General problem-prevention strategies were stressed in Rogers Park, but, otherwise, came up only 6 percent of the time.

- *We need to get organized:* Organizing efforts—but not specific activities—were suggested for 3 percent of problems.

- *We need more cops:* Getting more police officers assigned to an area was suggested for 1 percent of problems.

When it came to proposing solutions to problems, residents had very little to suggest. Indeed, police and citizen roles were reversed: Whereas problems were identified largely by residents, police officers suggested nearly 9 out of 10 possible solutions to them. The Austin District differed from the overall pattern because of the large role played there by professional community organizers and representatives of neighborhood organizations; 29 percent of the solutions discussed there were contributed by them, compared to 66 percent by police and 5 percent by residents. Rogers Park residents presented more solutions (17 percent) than residents in any other district. In general, residents almost always looked to officers to take the lead in developing solutions for neighborhood problems.

There were very telling differences between the types of solutions proposed by police and those suggested by residents. Citizens tended to put greater emphasis on the need for neighborhoods to get organized, and for acting themselves on local problems, rather than depending on outside help; self-help ideas encompassed 41 percent of solutions offered by residents, compared to 8 percent of those proposed by police. Conversely, police put more emphasis on solving problems by improving communication. Officers also focused on traditional solutions that emphasized police action, rather than on nontraditional solutions that emphasized community participation. For example, in response to a complaint that police were not taking drug dealing in one beat seriously, a neighborhood-relations officer noted:

> This is kind of insulting. Drug trafficking is not going to cease even if we make some arrests. And we are arresting. This year we have arrested over a thousand people. Just recently, we had a sting operation when we arrested 63 people. Things are being done around here.

When physical-decay problems were discussed, 29 percent of the proposed solutions involved residents contacting city services, while only 7 percent called for citizens to get organized or take action themselves. Discussions of social disorder also emphasized the need for citizens to contact police (30 percent of solutions) and for action by police or city departments (20 percent of responses); action by neighborhood residents was called for only 18 percent of the time. The most common response to problems that involved predatory or property crime also emphasized the reactive role of police in dealing with these matters.

Lack of Action on Neighborhood Problems

Of the 1,079 problems heard by our observers during discussions, there were reports of actions taken in only 49 cases. Our observers found that police had dominated when there was any discussion of action that had been taken: When actions were reported on neighborhood problems, police officers were responsible for acting in three cases out of four. In only 8 percent of cases was action taken jointly by residents and police, and residents took independent action another 12 percent of the time. Residents of Austin were *never* associated with action on neighborhood problems: Police were responsible for 93 percent of cases where action was taken in Austin, while agency representatives that were present at meetings took credit for the remainder. No independent action was attributed to Englewood residents, but citizens there worked jointly with police in one-third of cases in which action was taken. Residents in Marquette were top-ranked—they took independent action 14 percent of the time; and 21 percent of the time, joint action was taken by officers and residents. Morgan Park residents took action in 14 percent of cases, while Rogers Park residents acted in 27 percent of cases.

However, we do not think that the infrequent discussion of problem-solving efforts at beat meetings meant that little was happening in the prototype districts. Independently, we heard about a great deal of problem-solving activity, some of which is described in the next chapter. Rather, it appears that police and residents were not making effective use of beat meetings as a forum for reporting on their activities. A significant portion of the frustration we heard the public express about the CAPS program arose either because police did not appear to be responding to problems brought up at previous meetings or because residents were upset that so little seemed to be getting accomplished. The frustrations of many residents were voiced by one block-club president, who asked:

> How do we know what the cops are doing? We need a secretary. Need a report from the police. We want to know what you did about our last meeting's complaints. We come every month and get general information—the same thing every month.

The following dialogue took place at another meeting:

> FIRST RESIDENT: Why are we, then, always here, complaining of the same things?
>
> NEIGHBORHOOD-RELATIONS OFFICER: All I know is arrests are being made.
>
> FIRST RESIDENT: The community knows very well [that] nothing is happening.
>
> SECOND RESIDENT: What we are tired of is rehashing the same everything. We call ten times, you make them move from block to block; nothing happens, no results. This upsets us.

The effectiveness of the program depends on the developing of feedback—a direct linkage between the discussions of problems at beat meetings and the subsequent reports on interim problem-solving efforts. This would increase the visible utility of attending the meetings, speaking out, and stepping forward to act. In the long term, developing these forums could be central to the problem of sustaining residents' involvement and police commitment to the usefulness of the effort.

There were other impediments to problem solving. One was that some of what passed for problem solving failed to address neighborhood concerns in a systematic way. The following exchange was a typical example:

RESIDENT: At [a certain address], they are selling drugs. They were gone and now they are back.

BEAT OFFICER: This is what I will do. I'll go on my half-hour lunch and buy a big coke and get a burger and sit in the car at the intersection where they are selling drugs. It won't eliminate the problem and I know it's just a band-aid, but it acts as a deterrent. For a half hour, they can't sell and they may stay away for longer. I'm watching.

Despite the officer's commendable desire to help, the solution he offered was (as he recognized) not likely to affect the problem. Our observations suggest that when residents looked to the police to solve their problems, officers tended to respond by offering to do more of what they had always done: patrolling and enforcement.

A second impediment to problem solving was the format of beat meetings, which often precluded in-depth discussion about a particular problem or topic. With few exceptions, meeting leaders tended to make sure that all those attending had an opportunity to state their concerns. This egalitarian atmosphere discouraged participants from lingering on one issue. Consider, for instance, the following discussion:

RESIDENT: How can we get the city to change the curfew law?

SERGEANT: We *have* a curfew.

RESIDENT: I mean enforce it.

SERGEANT: We *do* enforce it. [Turning to police officers seated nearby]: What are the curfew laws?

BEAT OFFICER: Sunday night through Thursday night: 10:30 P.M. to 6 in the morning. Friday night and Saturday night, it's 11:30 to 6. We pick up kids all the time, take them home; the parents don't do nothin' about it.

SERGEANT: We can't rely on the government to raise our children. *[Residents applaud]*. We're all in agreement. What do we do? It's an open forum.

Despite agreement over the need to deal with youth problems, no one there that night responded to the sergeant's invitation, and the discussion quickly turned to problems that involved pay phones.

A third impediment to problem solving was that the repertoire of solutions available to beat officers was constrained by their role in the police department. Beat officers retained a very traditional role vis-à-vis detectives in Chicago's community-policing model. Virtually every case in which oficers did not make an arrest at the scene was immediately handed over to detectives. All case follow-up efforts, information gathering, victim recontacts, crime analysis, and the like were therefore in the hands of detectives. But detectives were neither organized by district nor responsible to district commanders; they reported to officials further up a separate chain of command, and neither the public nor many patrol officers learned what ultimately happened to cases that were taken over by detectives. One resident brought up this complaint about police performance: "Last year, my son was robbed, and they called and said they were going to come and get him to identify him; and they never did." The only response came from a beat officer who said, "We cannot do anything about the follow-up investigation. That's [the work of] the detectives." The fact that nothing more could be done by beat officers pointed to a difficulty in relying on them to address many issues that came up in beat meetings.

The general lack of organized problem-solving efforts at beat meetings contributed to a widespread sense of frustration among residents who were regular beat-meeting participants. They increasingly verbalized this at meetings during CAPS's second summer. At beat meetings, residents commented:

> I've only missed one CAPS meeting in 14 months. I come here and I see the same faces and they have the same problems. It's not working.

> In one and a half years, there has been no problem solving going on.

> They [the police] don't want to dialogue.

> Folks don't feel CAPS is on the case.

> You [beat officers] all ask for our help and we give it to you and nothing gets done.

In many cases, nothing got done because, after 18 months, residents in most beat areas were still poorly organized, despite the fact that many residents recognized the importance of organizing blocks and neighborhoods:

> We need to band together—a group of men walking up to a group of drug dealers. Take it [the neighborhood] back. Communities with low crime rates, they don't tolerate it. . . . The community has totally changed because we sat back. How well can we organize? We love to talk and point a finger and do nothing.

> People need to support what the police are doing. We need to be proactive. I remember when community members set up lemonade stands on the drug corners for three days in a row. The drug dealers were forced not to sell. Positive energy eliminates negative energy.

While the barriers to mobilizing and consolidating the resources of residents were many, some organizing efforts did take place at beat meetings. For instance, volunteers were called for, or sign-up sheets were passed around, at 22 percent of the meetings. The frequency with which this was done varied by district—from as many as 31 percent of meetings in Marquette and Rogers Park, to just 7 percent in Austin. In Rogers Park (only), residents also discussed the need to raise funds to support CAPS-related activities.

Who Took Charge?

To understand the inability of CAPS to ignite joint problem-solving efforts among police and prototype-district residents, we examined how closely the meetings corresponded to the CAPS model. We watched how leadership emerged at the meetings; how police and citizens' roles were defined; and how well officers and residents worked together.

The CAPS beat-meeting model emphasized shared leadership responsibilities between police and community members. However, during the program's first 18 months, many meetings failed to meet this standard. Leadership responsibilities were shared by police, citizens, or community organizers at only 1 in 10 meetings, while nearly two-thirds of the meetings were run principally by the police. About one-third were conducted by beat officers and another 30 percent by neighborhood-relations personnel. Community organizers ran 17 percent; residents ran 11 percent; and in 9 percent of meetings, there was shared leadership among officers, organizers, and residents. The proportion of meetings led by police dropped somewhat over time, and the number of meetings run by citizens and organizers increased from 25 percent during the first summer and fall to 33 percent during the following summer. These were not big changes, but they were in the right direction.

Police leadership did not mean that most beat meetings were dominated by officers. Discussion at these meetings was generally balanced between residents and police personnel. At close to 60 percent of all meetings, the discussion was roughly equally divided (i.e., it was at least a 60 percent–40 percent breakdown) between police and citizens, with the remainder being split evenly between meetings dominated by officers and those dominated by citizens. Some districts were more unbalanced than others: Police in Englewood, Marquette, and Morgan Park dominated the discussion at a quarter to a third of meetings, while citizens dominated the discussion at about half the meetings held in Austin and Rogers Park.

Changes over time in the way groups dominated discussions indicated that beat meetings were gradually moving toward a community-policing model. Three districts demonstrated a trend toward increasing equality in the amount of discussion between citizens and police. By the end of our evaluation period, 83 percent of Englewood's meetings had a roughly equal give-and-take between groups, as did 91 percent of meetings in Marquette and 67 percent in Rogers Park. In Austin, on the other hand, an increasing number of meetings were dominated by police, although at the end of our observations, most discussions still involved civilians. Morgan Park was the most alarming exception to the general pattern—its beat-meeting discussions were more balanced when CAPS was first introduced than they were 18 months later: When the program began, discussions at more than three-quarters of Morgan Park's beat meetings were evenly balanced between police and citizens. But by the end of the evaluation period, nearly two-thirds of meetings there were dominated by police, with discussions at the remaining third being evenly balanced between the groups.

Which group took charge had consequences. One involved the clarity of purpose at the meetings. Our observations indicated that leadership by the police was often exercised very casually. Most of the time, there was no clear agenda for the meeting: only 16 percent of all meetings had a written agenda, and clear verbal agendas were articulated in only another 5 percent of meetings. When neighborhood-relations officers were in charge, 85 percent of meetings had no clear agenda. When beat officers were in charge, 99 percent of meetings had no clear written or announced agenda.

But when citizens were in charge, 54 percent of meetings had an agenda that was announced in advance, and 46 percent of meetings run by community organizers had clear agendas. Civilian-led meetings also more frequently included calls for volunteers for various tasks and the circulation of sign-up sheets.

A more equitable distribution of leadership responsibilities, and a balanced pattern of give-and-take at the meetings, were desirable for several reasons. The more dependent that beat residents were on police leadership, the less likely they were to independently take initiative or act outside the bounds of responsibilities assigned them by police officers. Our observations documented that police in all of the districts, except Rogers Park, downplayed the adoption of nontraditional roles by beat residents, and it seems unlikely that citizens dependent on police leadership will successfully adopt these new responsibilities on their own. Effective community policing requires the support and unique perspectives of civilian leaders. CAPS would have benefited from a focus on strategies for encouraging beat residents to share in leadership responsibilities.

The Role of Beat-Team Officers

In the CAPS model, beat officers were to take leadership roles at the meetings. However, the proportion of meetings run by neighborhood-relations officers rather than by members of beat teams rose. Relying on neighborhood-relations officers to represent the police at beat meetings put this responsibility in the hands of people who had no daily involvement with beat residents and their concerns. Chicago's community-policing model emphasized the need for close coordination between beat officers and residents. However, the proportion of meetings run by beat officers declined from 46 percent, in the fall of 1993, to 30 percent in the summer of 1994. At the same time, the proportion run by neighborhood-relations personnel increased from 21 percent to 32 percent.

The increased leadership role taken by neighborhood-relations officers was concentrated in Englewood, Austin, and Morgan Park. The most dramatic shift occurred in Morgan Park, where leadership by beat officers dropped from 77 percent of meetings during the first six months to just 27 percent of meetings during the next summer. At the same time, leadership by neighborhood-relations officers rose from 15 percent to 64 percent. This sharp move toward leadership by neighborhood-relations officers was a very unpromising development.

Marquette and Rogers Park went the other way. Beat officers ran 21 percent of Marquette's winter meetings and 46 percent of its meetings the following summer, while leadership by neighborhood-relations personnel declined. In Rogers Park, leadership by neighborhood-relations specialists dropped from 40 percent of the meetings in the winter, to just 10 percent of those the following summer.

Indeed, the trend in three districts toward leadership of beat meetings by neighborhood-relations officers was a serious issue for CAPS, for it ran squarely in the face of the articulated policy of the program's managers. In their view, neighborhood-relations officers should have been withdrawing from leadership positions, and they were not happy when we discovered that this was not occurring. When neighborhood-relations specialists took charge of beat meetings at the expense of either line officers or community residents, the meetings were subverting the CAPS model in terms of developing successful police-community partnerships.

Police-and-Citizen-Partnership Roles

Another important feature of the beat meeting was how officers and residents perceived their roles. We examined the dominant style of interaction between police and residents at each meeting. Four types of relationships emerged:

- Police as leaders—when police set the agenda and residents follow.
- Police and residents as partners—when officers and citizens have a balanced and cooperative relationship that closely follows the community-policing model.
- Police and residents as independent operators—when each sees the other as having different functions and agendas.
- Police and residents as adversaries—when each takes on an uneasy relationship characterized by conflicting goals and methods.

In the aggregate, each of the first three styles characterized about one-third of the meetings, while residents and officers adopted adversarial roles in only 6 percent of the meetings.

Police As Leaders. Police officers adopted a leadership role in their dealings with residents in just under one-third of the meetings we observed. This role was tied to the impression by both police and residents that the goal of CAPS was to support traditional law enforcement. For instance, one beat officer explained the CAPS program as, "Police working with people. You get involved. You call and report crime." A sergeant described the CAPS program to residents by telling them, "You're the eyes and ears. . . . But we do need the whole body. We are the hand and feet. We are the ones who chase them and arrest them." This "eyes and ears" metaphor for was a hallmark of the "police as leaders" style of interaction. As another sergeant put it, "We need your input and information about felons, drug corners. We need you here every month."

This relationship characterized nearly half of the meetings in Marquette, around a third of meetings in Englewood and Morgan Park, and just under a fifth of meetings in Austin. Rogers Park had the lowest incidence of this type of relationship; there, police took on a leadership role in only 9 percent of meetings. Over time there were fewer meetings in which the police took on a leadership role, down from almost 46 percent of all meetings during the first summer and fall to 27 percent the next summer. In Rogers Park, there were none during the second summer.

Partners and Independent Operators. In the CAPS model, partnership is the preferred mode of police-citizen interaction. Discussing citizen complaints about city services, one sergeant took this stance: "[the Department of] Streets and Sanitation needs to be addressing these problems. At the next meeting I will try to have a Streets and Sanitation person here to try and talk to you. You and your block club need to get an answer." A partnership attitude was also demonstrated by residents, including one who remarked, "The beat officers here are doing a good job, but we need to help them. We have to control our fear. We can't just sit back and let the others take over."

Residents and police acted as partners in a little less than one-third of the meetings. Nearly three-quarters of Rogers Park meetings were characterized by a partner relationship, compared to just over two-fifths of meetings in Englewood and Austin, less than one-fifth in Marquette, and just one in twenty of Morgan Park's meetings. Over the span of our observations, the proportion of meetings where police and citizens acted as partners grew from a low of 14 percent to a high of 39 percent. But in Morgan Park, none of the meetings we observed in the fall of 1993 or summer of 1994 could be characterized as partnerships, and only 11 percent of winter meetings could be characterized as such.

If police and citizens were unable to adopt a partnership relationship, the next best mode of interaction probably was as independent operators. This style was characterized by a clear division of functions between police and residents, and it frequently signaled resistance by officers to adopting new responsibilities. For instance, one beat officer responded to citizen complaints about abandoned buildings by saying, "That is not really police responsibility. It only is through CAPS that it has become one. You've got to make choices. Police fight crime or check buildings." Another beat officer put it this way to residents: "We are here to assist you in helping yourself with community matters. The police still deal with illegal matters. That's what CAPS is all about." In another instance, when told that there was an abandoned car problem on a block, the beat officer advised, "Call Streets and Sanitation and bitch, bitch, bitch."

Like the partnership style, police and citizens followed an independent operator model of activism in just under a third of all meetings. This was the dominant relationship in Morgan Park meetings, where more than half of all meetings were characterized by a lack of overlap between citizen and police efforts. Around a quarter of meetings in Marquette and Austin could be characterized in this way, as could just less than one-fifth of meetings in Rogers Park and Englewood.

Police and Residents as Adversaries. The emergence of adversarial conflicts between officers and beat residents was clearly an obstacle to successful community policing. However, they became adversaries during only 6 percent of the beat meetings we observed. The meetings that took on an adversarial style were concentrated in the three poorest districts (Englewood, Marquette, and Austin), the districts where our surveys revealed that citizen expectations about the police initially were the least favorable. In these three districts, as many as one in ten meetings took on an adversarial flavor. Our observation data show that adversarial relationships began to emerge in beat meetings in January 1994, fully eight months after CAPS began. The only district to be apparently free of rancor was Rogers Park. The proportion of adversarial beat meetings increased dramatically in Englewood, from zero to 29 percent over the period we observed.

While the sudden rise in adversarial styles of interaction was cause for concern, the general trend was for police leadership of beat meetings to be eclipsed over time by independent operator and partnership approaches. By the end of the evaluation period, the proportion of meetings exhibiting partnership styles of interaction began to decline somewhat as independent entity approaches became more widespread. Whether the emergence of rancor in the beat meetings will persist as CAPS becomes more deeply rooted in the community remains an open question.

Progress Toward the CAPS Model

We have seen that the five prototype districts varied considerably in their evolution during 1993 and 1994. Figure 5-2 captures some of this progress by identifying the percentage of beat meetings in each district that matched the CAPS model.

The left side of figure 5-2 presents the percentage of beat meetings that were conducted in a CAPS-like manner. These were meetings during which citizens took or shared a leadership role; police adopted a partnership stance; discussion was evenly balanced between police and beat residents; and a cooperative atmosphere prevailed. Figure 5-2 indicates the fraction of meetings in each district that met three or four of these criteria; we gave those a "passing" grade. But many meetings failed our test. Morgan Park failed on most of the criteria: Police there dominated beat meetings while acting as independent operators or leaders rather than as partners,

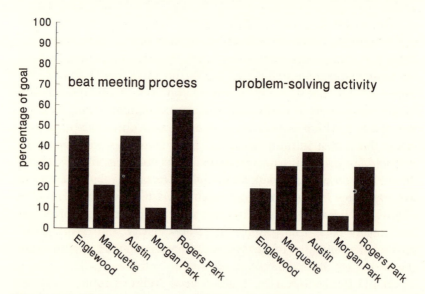

Figure 5-2 District progress toward the CAPS model.

and there was also an adversarial flavor to some beat meetings. Rogers Park stood out on most criteria, especially when it came to police who adopted partnership roles, and residents who took an active role in beat meetings. Austin and Englewood were not far behind, but Englewood's meetings were almost always led by police; and professional organizers dominated much of the discussion in Austin. Marquette's meetings were dominated by police; there were few discussions of partner relationships; and police and residents there engaged each other cooperatively at only about 60 percent of meetings.

Figure 5-2 also presents a summary of how much problem solving went on at beat meetings. The meetings were scored along four problem-solving dimensions—to determine whether either police or residents identified a problem; whether any solutions were proposed; whether any reports were made about ongoing problem-solving efforts; and whether the results (positive or negative) of any problem-solving efforts were discussed. Problems were identified at 97 percent of all meetings, and solutions were discussed at 93 percent of them. However, feedback was given about ongoing efforts at only 24 percent of meetings, and the results of problem-solving efforts were mentioned at only 23 percent. Figure 5-2 shows the percentage of meetings in each district that received a score of three or four on this measure, which indicated that ongoing activities or their results were discussed. Austin's high score reflected frequent reporting on the results of problem-solving efforts in this district—feedback that was provided mostly by community organizers who attended the sessions there in large numbers. Police officers in Marquette frequently suggested solutions, reported on their activities, and discussed the results of their past efforts; so this district received a high problem-solving rating, even though its beat meeting process did not score well because police dominated problem solving there. Beat meetings in Morgan Park were also dominated by police, but by neighborhood-relations specialists rather than by beat officers. Perhaps as a result, only 7 percent of the beat meetings observed in Morgan Park featured discussions of problem-solving efforts, and reports were made about their effectiveness at only 5 percent of meetings. Rogers Park did well on all dimensions, with much more civilian leadership and with police adopting partnership roles. However, it was clear that after 15 months, little problem solving was going on at the majority of beat meetings, even in the best of districts.

Involvement of Neighborhood Organizations

While community policing was a new concept in Chicago, community organizations had prepared for its arrival far in advance of the formal announcement of CAPS. A citywide federation of community organizations (CANS—the Chicago Alliance for Neighborhood Safety) agitated for community policing for several years. CANS's representatives had visited other cities to observe active programs; they wrote reports and held press conferences that demanded police reform. The Citywide Task Force on Community Policing, which represented 70 organizations who were pressing for the program, soon joined the chorus. Local foundations funded organizations to help get them involved in community policing. Once the program was announced, the next struggle was over the question of which districts would be named CAPS prototypes. Then local organizations began jockeying for influence over its operation. They played several important roles, one of which was to provide support for the beat-meeting and problem-solving processes.

To explore the involvement of community organizations in community policing, we interviewed hundreds of informants about the roles their groups played in Chicago's program. One goal of our study was to document the extent of organization activity that developed around CAPS in the five prototype districts. Anticipating that this would vary considerably from place to place, we also captured information about the organizations that might explain why support from some districts was more extensively mobilized for the program.

We found that groups were very involved in supporting the beat-meeting process. Across the prototypes, more than 70 percent of groups sent representatives to CAPS-related meetings, encouraged turnout at beat meetings, and worked with beat officers. Two-thirds encouraged people to request special CAPS city services, and almost half held meetings and distributed flyers in support of the program.

We also found that the involvement of organizations in community policing was explained, to a large extent, by the kinds of organizations they were—by their goals; by how they were organized to meet them; the extent of their territorial involvement; and their relationships with other organizations. Districts with the right mix of organizations were heavily mobilized around CAPS. However, these organizational mixes were themselves rooted in the race and class constituencies that they served. Different constituencies had different needs, and community policing did not seem to speak to many of them. As a result, organizations that served better-off and white constituents invested heavily in CAPS, while those serving African-Americans and (especially) Hispanics were less committed to the program.

Our working definition of an organization required that they have a name. To be included, they also had to be turf-based; that is, they had to at least partly define themselves geographically. In the end, we examined the activities of 253 named, turf-based organizations. This definition encompassed a wide variety of groups. In Chicago parlance, the most basic organizational unit in a residential neighborhood is a *block club.* These clubs encompass a small expanse of turf—typically three to four square blocks—and usually are named after streets or intersections, or have adopted local neighborhood names. Next, there are many *community organizations* that have storefront offices and are professionally staffed. They are supported by membership dues, foundation grants, and government grants and contracts. *Umbrella organizations* are federations of organizations, mostly block groups. While they are often sparked by individual activists, their membership base consists primarily of members of other organizations. We also identified a large number of *client-serving* organizations active in the districts. Supported by contracts or fees for services, they were service-providing organizations rather than membership-based ones. *Churches* fell within our net, and many were engaged in political, social, and economic-development activities. In addition, we included local *merchants' associations,* which typically represent small businesses clustered at the intersection of major arterials or spread along four-to-five-block arterial strips.

Interviews were conducted with knowledgeable informants who represented the organizations. A variety of approaches were used to develop a sample of organizations and informants that was as diverse and inclusive as possible. The names of organizations and contact people were contributed by other researchers, local knowledgeable people, police commanders, and neighborhood-relations officers. We listed the contacts we made at a host of community meetings, and each time we conducted an interview with an organizational informant, we asked about other organizations that the person had run across. We also culled data from local news articles and newsletters to locate additional organizations and named contacts that we could add to the list. It is unlikely that we overlooked any important organizations that were active in the prototype districts. Whenever possible, data were gathered from two respondents from each organization. Altogether, 476 interviews were conducted by telephone; for 223 organizations, two respondents were interviewed, while for 30 organizations, only one respondent could be interviewed. The responses of multiple informants were combined to characterize their organizations. The interviews were conducted at the end of the first prototype year, during the spring and summer of 1994. The study included from 43 to 59 organizations per prototype district. (For a complete description of the study's methodology, see Lovig and Van Stedum [1995]).

Mobilization for CAPS

One of the issues explored in the survey was what community organizations were doing to support the beat-meeting process. This part of the study included responses to seven questions about CAPS involvement. These identified organizations that encouraged people to make CAPS service requests, hosted or encouraged attendance at CAPS-related meetings, sent representatives to meetings, worked with beat officers, and distributed CAPS-related newsletters or flyers. The frequency of these efforts is summarized in table 5-3. The most frequent activities were as follows: attending meetings (in the five districts, an average of 75 percent of organizations attended meetings); encouraging people to attend meetings (71 percent of organizations did so); and working directly with beat officers (70 percent of organizations). Activities in this category took advantage of the newly created CAPS infrastructure, but CAPS, in turn, depended heavily on this kind of organizational support. Police had only a limited capacity for getting residents to turn out for beat meetings. Groups were needed to create and distribute flyers, and announcements of meetings, and to list them in their newsletters. Block groups met to identify service-request needs. During the first 18 months of the program, half of all beat meetings were held in churches.

We found a number of factors that systematically affected levels of CAPS involvement, and these factors differed across districts. Prominent among them were the goals that these organizations pursued and how they were organized to achieve them.

Organizational Mission. Each informant was asked to describe his or her organization's mission. This produced a variety of re-

Table 5-3 Percentage of Organizations Involved in Support of CAPS, by District

CAPS-Related Activity	Marquette	Austin	Englewood	Morgan Park	Roger Park
Hosting CAPS-related meetings	24%	33%	24%	29%	52%
Distributing newsletters or flyers	8	42	45	64	64
Holding general-public meetings	28	42	51	53	56
Encouraging people to make service requests	49	54	64	84	75
Working directly with beat officers	49	67	74	87	75
Encouraging people to attend meetings	51	67	72	87	81
Having group representatives at meetings	59	65	74	89	88
Number of organizations	53	43	53	45	59

sponses that were often closely intertwined with descriptions of the organizations' major programmatic activities; in people's minds, what the organizations do is their mission. We organized people's answers into six general categories. Even at this general level, these organizations frequently pursued more than one mission, so they fell into overlapping, rather than exclusive, categories. An average of 2.7 general missions was mentioned for each organization. Because organizations are purposive bodies, it is not surprising that their mission was the factor that was most strongly related to the extent of their involvement in CAPS. Our six mission categories were as follows:

1. *Crime-Prevention Mission.* Organizations that reported promoting programs or activities that were specifically geared to preventing crime were grouped together in this category. Also included here were organizations that mentioned their goal was to foster anticrime patrols and neighborhood watches, as well as those that cited crime-prevention programs for youths, anti-gang-related youth programs, and substance-abuse education programs for youths. There were 66 organizations in this category, or 26 percent of the total.

2. *Cultural and/or Religious Mission.* This category encompassed organizations that served or promoted ethnic or general spiritual needs. The missions in this category ranged from providing services targeted only at specific ethnic groups (e.g., immigration counseling for Hispanics), to promoting church, religious, or spiritual development. There were 42 organizations in this category—17 percent of the total.

3. *Economic Mission.* This category encompassed organizations that reported they wanted to promote business or economic development. Included in this category were stated goals like "advertising the area," or missions that involved promoting chambers of commerce or merchants' associations. There were 31 organizations in this category, or 12 percent of the organizations.

4. *Family Mission.* This category primarily featured organizations that offered family- or child-oriented services or programs. Included in this category were references to parenting skills, child development, family health, youth services, and youth education. There were 74 organizations in this category—30 percent of the total.

5. *Neighborhood Mission.* This category encompassed organizations interested in improving their immediate community, or those developing neighborhood-based activities. The largest portion of organizations in this category described efforts to improve the quality of neighborhood life. The category also included missions that ranged from holding block parties or other social activities to cleaning up the community, dealing with vacant buildings, or fighting discrimination in the awarding of local housing loans or insurance. There were 143 organizations in this category, or 57 percent of the organizations we examined.

6. *Service Mission.* This category included organizations that reported they provided services for individuals. The specific services they supplied were diverse: Frequently mentioned were adult-education programs, drug-treatment programs, programs for low-income individuals, and job-referral programs. Other organizations included here provided mental-health counseling, services for victims of domestic violence, youth employment counseling, legal advice, programs for senior citizens, referral programs of diverse types, and support for ex-offenders. Some described their role as

one of helping individuals find services appropriate to their particular problems. There were 125 organizations in this category, or 50 percent of the total.

Some of these missions were strongly related to organizational involvement in CAPS. To examine this, we developed a summary score that measured the extent to which each organization was involved. Each organization was scored according to the percentage of the seven activities, listed in table 5-3, that they were involved in. For example, an organization that was involved in all seven CAPS support activities received a score of 100 (41 actually did), while organizations that did not do any of them received a zero (36 fell in this category).

Figure 5-3 depicts the extent of organization participation in support of CAPS. Organizations that pursued crime-prevention goals were involved in an average of 63 percent of the support activities; there was a 70-percent participation rate among those interested in economic development, and a 69-percent rate among those committed to neighborhood improvement. The high level of activism among organizations that reported a crime-prevention mission reflected the close fit of CAPS with their goals. Economic-development organizations (often involving area merchants and property owners) were also extremely concerned about crime,

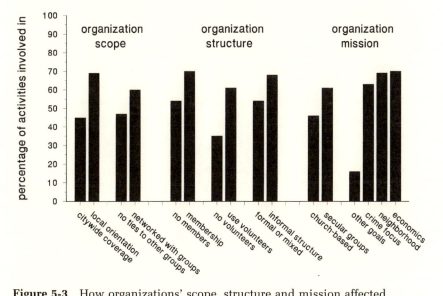

Figure 5-3 How organizations' scope, structure and mission affected CAPS involvement.

which erodes the value of their real estate and threatens their customer base. CAPS's turf-based approach to policing, and the avenues for participation in problem solving that beat meetings created at the neighborhood level, appealed to organizations with a strong neighborhood focus.

Organizational Structure. Figure 5-3 indicates that other organizational factors were linked to CAPS involvement as well. One set of factors included structural features of the organizations—the extent to which they were formally organized; whether they were formed around a membership base or a client base, and whether they used volunteers to carry out their mission.

The formalness of each organization's structure was represented by whether or not it had external funding, office space, its own telephone number, any part-time paid staff, and any full-time paid staff. For example, one formal organization we examined was the Boys and Girls Club of Chicago, active in the Marquette area. It reported receiving gifts and external funding from private foundations and government agencies; it had office space and phone lines; and it employed both full-time and part-time staff. The formalness score broke down easily into three categories: 25 percent of the organizations were quite informally organized; 51 percent were very formal; and 24 percent were mixed in character. As figure 5-3 indicates, the biggest difference was that between informal organizations (they were involved in an average of 68 percent of the CAPS support activities) and the others (54 percent).

Another structural feature of these organizations was their relationship with the public. The survey allowed us to classify them as client based (138 organizations, or 58 percent of the total), membership based (24 percent), or involving both clients and members (18 percent). Groups with individual members had a median of 55 of them. Client-based organizations typically fell into service-providing mission categories, while membership organizations more typically served neighborhoods. Groups with a membership base participated in 70 percent of the activities that supported CAPS; and they were also much more likely to have promoted CAPS and to be involved in turf-based activities.

The third structural feature of these organizations was whether or not they used volunteers. Most did—overall, 90 percent of the organizations we surveyed used volunteers, and at the median they had 18 of them. Organizations in this group were involved in 61 percent of the activities that supported CAPS, as compared to 35 percent among the organizations that did not use volunteers.

Organizational Scope. Organizations also varied in the extent to which they were linked to others active in the community, and in the expanse of the area that they served. There were big differences between organizations that had a local or neighborhood focus (these were 54 percent of the total) and those that served the city as a whole, the county, or the nation. As figure 5-3 indicates, locally oriented organizations were involved in an average of 69 percent of the support activities, compared to 45 percent among the remainder.

Linkages between organizations were also important. These were measured by asking informants if their organization had any close affiliations with other community groups. Fully 85 percent indicated that they did. Organizations that were networked to others were also more likely to participate in CAPS than were those working in relative isolation (the figures in this regard were 60 percent as compared to 45 percent).

Churches. Churches constituted a separate analytic focus because of the deep involvement of religious organizations in the life of several of the prototype districts. For example, in Englewood, the pastors' subcommittee of the district advisory committee claimed the participation of more than 50 churches. The church category also included affiliated organizations that had been founded by, and remained closely tied to, individual churches. In our sample there were a total of 52 organizations in this category, or 21 percent of all the organizations we examined. All indicated that they had religious goals, but 96 percent had another mission as well. Indeed, churches were involved in providing services (65 percent), targeting neighborhood problems (53 percent), or pursuing family-oriented missions (35 percent). Fewer than 10 percent had a crime-prevention mission. And, as figure 5-3 indicates, secular organizations were involved in 61 percent of the activities that supported CAPS, while the many church-related groups in our sample reported participating in an average of 46 percent of them.

CAPS involvement, then, was highest among locally oriented organizations that were networked with others; among those with an informal, membership, and volunteer structure; and among secular organizations that pursued crime prevention, neighborhood improvement, and economic-development goals. Groups with other missions were significantly less involved—in particular, groups with a cultural or spiritual mission, and those that specialized in delivering a variety of services to individual clients, had little to do with community policing in Chicago's prototype districts.

The Effects of Race and Class on Involvement in CAPS

The difficulty was that most of the above factors were linked to the race and class of the constituencies that the organizations served. One of the hypotheses that originally guided this research was that fewer organizations in poorer, African-American, and Hispanic areas of the city would be involved in community policing. Our surveys of Chicagoans found that residents of poor and minority neighborhoods too often felt they and their neighbors received unfair and impolite treatment. Since their constituents often mistrusted the police, we anticipated that groups in poor and minority areas would be less enthusiastic about getting involved in coordinated action with police than groups that represented white homeowners.

We measured constituency factors by asking informants to characterize the clients or members of their organizations. We asked them to give us a racial breakdown and to estimate the approximate incomes of their constituents, using categories that we presented to them. We found that the effects of race and class on involvement in CAPS were strong ones, but that they were indirect. That is, we found that the principal causal connection was that race and class were linked to the kinds of organizations that people were involved in. Organizations that served white and better-off constituents were more likely to be locally oriented, informally organized, membership based, and not in the business of providing services to individual clients. On the other hand, there were virtually no membership-based groups that served Hispanic constituents, and less than 5 percent of those serving the poor fell into this category. Organizations serving the poor were more often directed toward family, cultural, religious, and service-providing missions. And the poor were significantly less likely to be served by organizations that pursued neighborhood or economic-development goals. Both Hispanics and African-Americans were much more likely to be the clients of service-providing organizations.

These factors were in turn linked, as we have noted, to organization involvement in CAPS. Organizations that served largely white constituencies were the kinds of organizations that were particularly likely to be heavily involved in CAPS. Those serving African-Americans and (especially) Hispanics were the kinds of organizations that were less likely to be involved in the program. The most consistent relationships, however, were between organizational factors and poverty: Groups that served the poor were, almost across the board, the kinds of organizations that were least likely to be involved in community policing.

Key District Variations

In sum, our examination of the role that organizations played in CAPS found that it varied considerably in each district. Organizations active in Morgan Park and Rogers Park were very involved in supporting beat meetings, while those in Marquette and Austin were much less active. Englewood stood somewhere in between.

We also found that the five prototype districts featured varying mixes of organizational life, and that these mixes facilitated or inhibited involvement in CAPS. Districts that were endowed with an organizational life that meshed with the structure and mission of CAPS got on the bandwagon. In those areas, organizations found it easy to support the program and took advantage of its initial visibility and credibility in the community. This was most clearly the case in Morgan Park and Rogers Park, where CAPS involvement was highest. There, many more organizations were membership based; locally oriented; networked to others; informally organized; secular in their roots; and focused on crime, neighborhood, or economic-development issues.

On the other hand, the organizational milieu in Englewood, Austin, and Marquette did not mesh quite so easily with the new policing program. Organizations there had other agendas. They served clients, rather than a citizen membership base. They provided them with services and were often supported by grants and contracts from foundations and government agencies. They pursued cultural or religious goals, especially if they had Hispanic constituents. As a consequence, they were more often formally organized, blessed with staff members and office space. However, CAPS seemed relatively irrelevant to many of these organizations, and as a consequence, levels of participation in the program were much lower among them.

District Advisory Committees

District advisory committees were another vehicle that fostered police-citizen collaboration in the prototype districts. They met with district commanders on a monthly basis to discuss conditions in their district and ways of attacking those that were problems. They helped the commanders identify community resources that could be mobilized for district problem solving, and they helped evaluate the effectiveness of these efforts.

A police department special order issued in April 1993 included sections that described the new district advisory committees. As detailed in the order, the committees were to "appoint subcommittees to identify and address the needs and problems of the community and advise the district commander of possible solutions and strategies; advise the district commander of the current matters of concern to the community; and assess the effectiveness of implemented solutions and strategies and inform the district commander of the progress or lack thereof of the solutions and strategies."

Because this directive was a broad one, each of the commanders formed committees and devised meeting formats that seemed appropriate to the district. The composition of the advisory committees was determined by the commanders; they chose the members on the basis of their standing in the community, previous service, willingness to participate, and ethnic and geographical representation. In some districts, personnel from the park district and city and state government agencies were also named to the committees, but later, the CAPS management team ruled that they could serve only in an ex-officio capacity. The new order also gave the prototypes direction on topics about which there had been some confusion—such as how the committees should select officers—and on term limits and voting rights. The order required that each district form a court-advocacy subcommittee—a group of district residents that identifies cases of concern to the community and follows them through the court process. Finally, the new order noted: "The Committee is an independent extension of the City of Chicago Department of Police. Committee members work closely with the district and other police personnel but do not have direct control over police operations."

To observe the committees in action, we attended virtually every prototype advisory-committee meeting that took place during the evaluation period—a total of 22 meetings in 1993 and 43 during

1994. During this period, they devised bylaws, and either elected officers or paved the way for elections. Several wrote grant proposals, and some planned fund-raising efforts and applied for drug forfeiture assets. During the formative months, these efforts were directed by the district commanders. However, a 1994 directive ruled that civilian chairpersons be chosen, and control of the meetings was then handed over to them.

Englewood

Englewood's advisory committee met monthly. The commander encouraged members of the subcommittees to take part in the general monthly meeting, so as many as 70 attended on several occasions. Englewood's advisory committee meetings were quite spirited and spiritual. They generally began and ended with a prayer, occasionally with everyone holding hands. Attendees, signaling their agreement with the proceedings, shouted, "Amen" or "Praise God." The meetings had a very informal, grassroots atmosphere and were quite positive in tone. Committee members seemed to feel that if people worked together, they could effect real change in the community. A very trusting and cooperative spirit was obvious among the police and the citizens at these meetings.

Another significant contributor to the mood of these meetings was the district commander. He made game-show-host entrances and was an exuberant master of ceremonies. The chairperson of the advisory committee was a local religious leader, and her enthusiasm and capacity for stirring up the assemblage got things moving when they threatened to bog down. Englewood's meetings provided an opportunity for showcasing positive efforts that were taking place in the area. Descriptions of many fairs, marches, and programs were offered, most of which were sponsored by area churches. Youth programs were high on this district's agenda, and often youths made presentations or gave performances. This was the only prototype district where young people consistently attended meetings of the advisory committee.

The chairwoman started a typical meeting with a general update on recent events that affected the district, and then the heads of the seven subcommittees delivered their reports. Special guests were often introduced, and they generally provided an overview of their role in, and impact on, CAPS. These guests included the commander of the gang-crimes unit, the City Hall CAPS liaison, an attorney who provided pro bono legal services, and a banking executive who described services available to the community. There was little talk about specific crime problems, in sharp contrast to some other districts. Rather, the meetings featured reports on the progress of the ambitious social projects that each subcommittee was planning.

In Englewood, the subcommittees focused on social and economic problems rather than on strictly crime-related issues. Police there joined with the citizens in numerous long-term civic and social programs. These projects included a complete survey of properties in the district, an effort that supported the commander's agenda of dealing with the large number of abandoned buildings that plagued the district. The committee was also involved in developing a section of the city's proposal to create a federal Enterprise Zone; although Englewood was not selected to participate, the enthusiasm that the effort generated led to the creation of a local redevelopment project. The committee also sponsored several self-help workshops and programs for first- and second-time offenders, and it was involved in getting an automated teller machine installed in the lobby of the police station (see chapter 6).

Some shorter-term issues that were identified and addressed by the committee were the cleaning up of an abandoned bus garage that posed environmental hazards; the demolition of a shuttered YMCA whose swimming pool loomed as a danger for children; participation in decisions about the renovation and reopening of stations on the elevated transit line that runs through the district; and the shortage of supermarkets in the Englewood community. The committee dealt with these issues by lobbying city agencies that could deal with abandoned buildings, by gaining representation at transit-authority hearings, and by negotiating with a supermarket chain about setting up an outlet in Englewood. However, by the end of 1994, court advocacy had still not taken off there.

Marquette

In Marquette, usually only members and special guests were present at advisory-committee meetings. The committee was made up of beat representatives and subcommittee heads. The meetings were held in the auditorium of a local hospital. Guests frequently appeared to make presentations about their activities. Maps that showed crime occurrences by area and arrest figures generally were distributed to committee members, and a variety of printed materials about upcoming events and city services were usually available.

Reflecting the district as a whole, this advisory committee had to deal with recurring tension between its Hispanic and African-American members. The atmosphere of the meetings was business-like, but when the meeting room was arranged in rows divided by a center aisle, African-American committee members generally sat on one side of the room while Hispanic members sat on the other. African-American neighborhood-relations officers generally spoke to and for their ethnic group, as did Hispanic officers for theirs. The committee's ethnic schism became increasingly evident early in 1994 when one of the caucuses held a closed meeting to elect advisory-committee officers. The election was nullified when the entire committee convened at the next regular meeting. There were ongoing linguistic problems as well. A significant amount of dis-cussion at the meetings was carried out in Spanish, with translation provided by an officer assigned to the neighborhood-relations staff. On at least one occasion, an African-American committee member, observing the intensity of a Hispanic committee member's reaction to her statements, voiced concern that something she said was not translated accurately. The two ethnic groups that were joined on this committee had not otherwise worked with one another, and committee members felt that any progress they made toward build-ing bridges between the two communities was a significant accom-plishment.

Perhaps one reason why building interethnic bridges seemed so difficult is that this committee received little guidance from the dis-trict commander. He rarely attended meetings and, when he did, seemed unfamiliar with many of the matters under discussion. He also appeared to fall asleep during some meetings. Furthermore, many of the meetings were dominated by members of the district's neighborhood-relations unit; they were very attentive and apparently very involved in both CAPS and the advisory committee. But clear civilian leadership did not emerge on this committee during our eval-uation period; only at the end of the evaluation period did committee members begin to take turns as moderators on a rotating basis. At the same time, however, the practice of hearing problem reports from the beat representatives was discontinued. Often, these reports were a detailed listing of specific problems that were more appropriately aired at beat meetings, but the decision to terminate beat reports ap-peared to be a unilateral one by the police. By the end of 1994, several beat representatives expressed frustration over the restriction, ar-guing that they found it helpful to compare their problems and solu-tions with those from other parts of the district.

Issues that were identified by the committee included slow 911 response and a shortage of Spanish-speaking 911 operators; drug dealing; gang intimidation; public drinking associated with the large number of liquor stores and taverns in the district; and simmering after-school gang unrest at a public transit stop. Little could be done about the 911 situation, but gang problems and drug dealing were aggressively addressed. Area residents stepped forward to act as informants, and police carried out reverse sting operations. The committee looked into voting to make precincts dry in order to control public drunkenness, but it found that demanding liquor-commission hearings on individual locations could be a better alternative. However, in spite of identifying this problem-solving tactic, fear of retaliation by tavern owners kept members from actually participating in many hearings. To deal with volatile after-school gang unrest, committee members met with police, the alderman, and city transit representatives, and they arranged new bus routes so that rival gangs would not cross paths after school.

Marquette's advisory committee was among the first to investigate the possibility of seeking not-for-profit status in order to be eligible to receive drug forfeiture assets; and, with the help of training officers at the academy, it devised and executed a problem-solving workshop. However, the committee's bid for nonprofit status was disallowed downtown, and the problem-solving workshop was dominated by a tug-of-war between the district and CAPS's managers, who disapproved of it and wanted more control over training. In addition, the district's required court-advocacy subcommittee never made any headway.

Austin

The Austin advisory committee held its meetings during the day, largely for safety reasons. Throughout the evaluation period, the group met in the roll-call room of the station; as a result, there was a constant bustle of activity all around, and district personnel wandered in and out of the meeting. Later, the committee moved to a local branch library, and its meetings became more dignified and focused.

Austin's meetings began and ended with a prayer, and a number of the community members were ministers. There was a grassroots atmosphere at the meetings, but also, a greater presence of police officers than at meetings in any of the other prototype districts. In Austin, beat officers and tactical-team members were often called on to provide details about their recent missions or projects

that were under way. Updates on the efforts of the four subcommittees were not a regular part of the advisory-committee meetings,
and it was difficult to discern whether any of the subcommittees
were doing much. On the other hand, Austin did not waste much
time writing its bylaws—a set was devised by a member of the
neighborhood-relations staff and was promptly adopted.

Austin's commander was very involved with the advisory committee, and until the election of a chairman toward the end of 1994,
he carefully orchestrated its meetings. He called on police officers
to speak to the assembly, decided how long certain subjects would
be discussed, and determined exactly when and how advisory-
committee officers would be elected. He did relinquish control
when a civilian chairperson was elected; however, this action was
so abrupt and uncharacteristic that the new chairperson was
stunned that he was suddenly running the meeting.

A distinguishing feature of Austin's advisory committee was
that it was considered by many to be a titular one—real CAPS work
was carried out by a separate group of beat facilitators that met on
a biweekly basis. The facilitator group was made up of residents
and professional community organizers, and its meetings were not
open to the public, or to us.

Two successful efforts undertaken by the advisory committee
were the implementation of the local component of the city's
Youthnet Project, which promised to bring programs and services
to Austin's young people, and its role in shaping the city's proposal
to the Federal government to create an Enterprise Zone. Austin was
in line to receive a great deal of money as a result of the successful
proposal. Other efforts that were vaguely connected to the advisory
committee included a positive-alternatives program that focused on
youth empowerment; a program in which adults escorted children
to and from school to ensure their safety; and the development of
several grant proposals. The court-advocacy subcommittee in Austin was quite active and believed it successfully affected the outcome of several cases that were important to the community. There
was a problem with the proliferation of drug-recovery houses and
facilities for newly released convicts in the community, and the
committee traced their ownership to a single individual. The continuous presence of court-advocacy activists at court hearings relating to his properties had positive effects. Another case pursued by
the subcommittee involved a resident of the Austin YMCA who
was dealing drugs from his room. He was eventually evicted by
court order—in large part, because of the group's persistence.

Morgan Park

Morgan Park's advisory committee was well connected to City Hall and other influentials downtown, and many of its members had worked together for years on issues that faced the better-off parts of the district. The committee's opportunity to leverage new resources with the advent of the CAPS program encouraged it to expand its scope to encompass the African-American parts of the Morgan Park district. In addition, a number of committee members were acquainted with influential people in city government and were adept at drawing attention to their concerns. This was reflected in their capacity for getting the district named as a CAPS prototype in the first place. Their political clout was also reflected in the fact that more police officers and city employees resided in this district than in any other prototype district and, possibly, any other police district in the city. A criminal-court judge who lived in the district attended committee meetings on a fairly regular basis, and he proved to be helpful to the court-advocacy subcommittee. City council members attended this district's advisory-committee meetings more consistently than in any other prototype district, and they were often active participants. Each of them contributed to a gathering that celebrated the first-year anniversary of CAPS in Morgan Park.

The district commander, who was determined that his district was to be the most successful CAPS prototype, provided strong leadership for the advisory committee. He was quite comfortable with the members, and he was obviously admired by them. The commander was a resident of the district and had worked with many of the committee members for years. He was knowledgeable about most of the efforts of the advisory committee, and he was reputed to be very accessible to residents of the district. Furthermore, Morgan Park was the first district to have a civilian chair to run the meetings. She represented the most powerful community organization in the area.

Like the others, the Morgan Park advisory committee grappled over its bylaws for several months. Painstaking deliberation occurred over the structure of the body, voting rights, and reporting responsibilities. In spite of the substantial amount of time devoted to procedural matters, the committee did identify several key issues that affected the district and took action to address them. Among the core issues were slow police response time on the main business strip, youth crime, low participation in beat meetings, and the lack of a lockup in the district stationhouse. The group was also very concerned about the complex and user-unfriendly computer system installed in the district station for crime analysis—another mark of its sophistication.

Because business owners were concerned that their 911 calls were not producing timely responses to emergencies, the advisory committee convinced the telephone company to donate pagers for the beat officers assigned to the business area. Business proprietors we interviewed who participated in the pager program reported decreased response time and a resulting feeling of greater security. To address the youth-crime issue, the committee encouraged the prosecutor's office to set up an alternative-consequences program that assigned youthful offenders to community service in the district. (For more details about these two efforts, see chapter 6.) The beat-meeting participation problem was addressed by organizing rallies and launching an aggressive local marketing campaign. The committee demanded meetings with the department's data systems division in order to explore why the district's computer system was unmanageable. The district's interest in court advocacy predated CAPS, and grew to include representation from each beat in the district. Representatives of the community attended proceedings of cases that were being tracked; the subcommittee was a highly organized operation.

Rogers Park

At the outset, Rogers Park was considered by many to be the "safest bet" when it came to citizen participation in community policing. The area was already honeycombed with feisty community organizations, and the district's residents were more educated and politically involved than many. Some of the area's key organizational players became members of the advisory committee. Its meetings were generally amicable, and there was a good working relationship between the committee and the district's dedicated and effective neighborhood-relations team. Nonetheless, there was often an undercurrent of tension and verbal sparring among the various blocs represented on the committee—reflecting conflicts and alliances among them that predated CAPS.

Rogers Park's committee was one of the first to get under way, but from the outset, it faced a leadership problem. The difficulty was that the district commander was unenthusiastic about community policing, and—nearing retirement—he was not willing to put much energy into the program. Little actually happened in the district during the nine months it took this commander to announce his retirement, and he was replaced by a dynamic new commander only late in our evaluation period. During the initial period, the committee focused largely on internal matters. The sophistication and experience of its members led many observers to expect a great deal from them; instead, initially, these factors served to complicate and draw out decision-making processes. Deliberations about seating arrangements, which in this district were correlated with status, took them several months. A written statement that prohibited political candidates from participating in advisory-committee activities also took several months to be formulated, due to jockeying over who should write and distribute the text. (This was not an idle concern; one board member later ran against the incumbent alderman, on the strength of her activism in policing matters.) Developing the committee's bylaws took three-quarters of a year.

Conflict also arose over who could attend and vote at meetings. The committee originally included elected officials as well as representatives from city agencies (none of whom were permitted to vote), and a number of citizens. The committee's bylaws also forbade the district commander to vote—a naive attempt to limit his influence on the proceedings. However, there was continuous agitation from beat activists to include a formal role for beat representatives at the table, and at the end of our evaluation period, they were added to the advisory committee, which then numbered 47 people. A very concrete challenge the committee did not address effectively was the fact that it was composed almost entirely of whites—and this was one of the city's most ethnically diverse districts.

In the committee's view, the key issues in the district included panhandling, public drinking, robberies in a commercial area, decrepit buildings, and irresponsible landlords. The committee was most involved in efforts to clean up or board up unsafe buildings, while court cases that involved negligent landlords were aggressively tracked and observed by the court-advocacy subcommittee. The committee also held a daylong problem-solving retreat to learn how to grapple with local issues. The beat subcommittee held training sessions to prepare the community to take an active role in CAPS, and the court-advocacy subcommittee sponsored a mock trial involving an actual judge and court personnel in order to educate the community about court proceedings.

Representative Consultation

If beat meetings were the vehicle through which neighborhood residents expressed their concerns and participated in police and citizen problem-solving efforts, district-advisory committees were the vehicle through which significant local interests, the representatives of influential public agencies and private organizations, and politicians voiced their priorities. Which interests were represented around the table varied somewhat from district to district. In Englewood and Austin, where churches provided much of the social infrastructure of the community, pastors were heavily involved with the committee. Businesses and professionally led community organizations were well represented in Morgan Park and Rogers Park. Activities in Austin were heavily influenced by professional community organizers. In Morgan Park, well-organized white and African-American communities were both represented at the table, while in Rogers Park—known for its multiethnic population—membership on the advisory committee remained largely white. The most pervasive cleavage in Marquette involved race: The two predominant culture groups there were well represented. However, they functioned independently, with members of one group often weighing the attention and service that the other group received against their own. While significant organizations were active in the district, none were formally represented on the advisory committee. Marquette's was also the only advisory committee that could not settle on a committee chair by the end of 1994.

The purpose of the committees was broadly stated, and thus each of them could point to some successes. All had a core of active members who met with the commanders. Some of the committees were adept at identifying local issues, although agreeing on priorities and taking action proved to be more daunting. The advisory committees that seemed to be the most successful at these efforts were those in which citizens developed a consensus about the most important issues in the district, and identified discrete and potentially obtainable short-term goals. This was one of Englewood's shortcomings, as its advisory committee chose to tackle some of the most fundamental social and economic problems in their community—targets that probably were beyond their reach. On the other hand, Morgan Park's committee focused on a few quite feasible projects—including the pagers (we mentioned previously) and the creation of a special community service program for youthful offenders—and saw them through to completion.

After an initial honeymoon period, the advisory committees grew restless as they realized that they were organizationally adrift. Some set about writing mission statements, and finally a set of guidelines was issued by the CAPS managers that identified their formal purpose, membership and terms of office, attendance requirements, and the like. The guidelines also referred to bylaws, which, to this point, were nonexistent. The advisory committees then had a common goal, and crafting these regulations became a time-consuming (if sometimes spirited and divisive) focus for their energies.

The leadership provided by the commanders was also clearly important. Where they were indifferent (as in Marquette, and during the first year in Rogers Park) the committees focused on internal issues and were sidetracked by their preexisting internal divisions—one of these involved race, notably in Marquette. Where commanders were strong and supported citizen involvement, the committees focused more of their energy on community issues, and an upbeat mood generally characterized their proceedings.

Did All Chicagoans Get Involved?

Was CAPS successful in involving all Chicagoans in community policing? We indicated previously that initiating and sustaining citizen participation in this new venture is not an easy task. Many cities have found it difficult to foster extensive involvement, for the same reasons that it could be hard to capture the attention of the organizations that represent citizens.

Chicago faced the same problems and made some limited headway against them. There was trouble getting beat meetings started off right. Community-relations specialists dominated too many meetings, and did not back out of their leadership role in the way that downtown brass had anticipated. In most districts, beat officers did not step forward, and when they did, they were not very good at running meetings. Residents identified a wide range of problems, but police came up with most of the proposed solutions, and they stuck mostly to familiar, enforcement-oriented tactics. They promised to intensify their patrol efforts and make arrests, and they asked residents to be their "eyes and ears" and keep them informed via 911. Specific proactive action by citizens was proposed for only 7 percent of the problems that were identified, and in another 6 percent of cases, there was talk about the community taking future preventive action.

The middle-class bias that generally pervades public and private programs that rely on voluntary citizen participation also affected CAPS, but this influence was a subtle one. During the first 18 months, beat meetings in the poor and African-American parts of town were relatively well attended, considering the small size of beats there. However, this attendance rate was driven in large measure by crime, which was higher there as well. This meant, at least, that meeting attendance in Chicago was highest where, by an important measure, it was most needed, but this was not good news to those who turned out. In other cities, middle-class biases in voluntary turnout have been so large that turnout was highest in lower-crime areas (see Skogan, 1990). In Chicago, controlling for other factors or not, Hispanics simply did not turn out in expected numbers, except in the relatively few beats where they made up a very large fraction of the population.

We did not discover any district-level factors that made a difference in beat-meeting participation. In addition to the beat-level demographic and crime data described previously, we also looked for district differences in turnout that might have been related to the effectiveness of the district advisory committees. We found none—all the explainable variance seemed to lie at the beat level.

It was also difficult to mobilize the support of community organizations in some areas. CAPS's problem-solving model called for the community—not just the city—to bring resources to the table, and organizations had to play a big role in this effort. Another goal of the program was to foster autonomous problem solving by the groups, so that police did not always have to spearhead the process. Resident groups also played an important role in making beat meetings work. In the most active districts, they created, duplicated, and distributed flyers door to door to advertise the meetings; saw to it that area newsletters and church bulletins featured the meetings and detailed their locations; and activated block-level networks of neighbors to drum up attendance.

However, we found that only the better-off districts were endowed with organizations that meshed with the structure and mission of CAPS. Organizations there found it easy to support the program and got involved early in beat meetings and problem solving. Organizations active in poor and minority areas had different agendas—providing clients with services, or pursuing cultural and religious goals. More of them were directed by professional staffs, and few had the kind of grassroots membership base that attached itself to CAPS. In their district advisory committees, they pressed for action against fundamental social problems, while their business and community-based counterparts focused on resolving specific issues. As a result, in the poorer districts, there was less organized community involvement. Fewer groups serving African-Americans and (especially) Hispanics held CAPS meetings or rallies; worked to turn people out for beat meetings; or tried to use CAPS resources to advance their agendas.

In sum, it appears that CAPS beat meetings created important opportunities for participation that were relatively uniform across the city; were brand new in disadvantaged areas; and probably would not have been initiated by indigenous groups in many areas. If the 20 percent of meetings that we observed were a fair representation of the other 80 percent, people turned up on almost 15,000 occasions to discuss local problems with the police. Because they were a regular feature of the program, these occasions presented themselves everywhere, every month. Research on naturally-occurring, organized anticrime activity indicates it is least common where it is most needed—in low-income, heterogeneous, deteriorated areas. Ironically, self-starting community organizations that focus on crime issues are more common in better-off neighborhoods. People can participate only where there are opportunities to do so; so by creating relatively uniform opportunities for participation, CAPS took the first step toward mobilizing wider participation among all segments of the community.

6

The Program in Action

This chapter examines the program in action. First, it looks at how the service-delivery component of CAPS actually worked. By the 1990s, local officials had absorbed the idea that crime—and especially fear of crime—was intimately linked to both casual social disorder and the physical decay of the city's neighborhoods. They were therefore not surprised when our first survey found that building abandonment was among the most bothersome problems in high-crime Englewood; the district commander already had a list of more than 600 abandoned buildings in his desk drawer. Like researchers (Spelman, 1993), he knew that they were a haven for drug dealers, purse snatchers, prostitutes, and squatters; that they presented a constant threat of fire; and that they were a nagging eyesore that undermined the commitment of property owners who were struggling to maintain their own buildings. Policymakers also knew that the public, when given the opportunity to speak out, would queue up to demand that something be done about neighborhood disorder as well as about crime. They created a vehicle for responding—the CAPS service request—and handed it over to the police department to make it work.

The remainder of this chapter examines the roles of the police and the public in neighborhood problem solving. Some of these efforts made use of the new service-coordination responsibility of the police; they also involved local businesses, established community organizations, and informal groups of irate residents. In every case, the community attempted to form some kind of partnership with the police so as to tackle an issue. The problems they focused on varied widely, and there was considerable variation in how successful they were at solving them—some of these problem-solving efforts were spectacularly successful, but others flopped. After reviewing these efforts, we discuss some general principles about how problems were identified and how solutions to them were developed; about the roles of organizations, city agencies, businesses, and the police in sustaining these efforts; and about the ability of neighborhood residents to get involved. The latter turned out to be among the most problematic elements of the CAPS model, and the difficulties residents faced in sustaining their involvement highlighted the importance of the participation of organizations and institutions in the process.

Forming Interagency Partnerships

From the beginning, it was clear that Chicago's new program had to be closely linked to other city agencies; community policing could not be just the police department's responsibility. Around the country, police departments have found that an inevitable consequence of opening themselves up to citizens' input is that they become involved in a broad range of neighborhood problems, including issues that they traditionally did not consider police problems. Community policing indeed implies a significant expansion of the police mandate. As we noted in chapter 5, the issues raised at Chicago's beat meetings did not often fall into traditional crime categories: Citizens called for action against abandoned buildings and cars, garbage-strewn vacant lots, loitering youths, and loud music more frequently than they demanded that police do something about burglaries or robberies. If the response of the police present was that these were "not police matters," no one would come to the next meeting. Regardless of who actually did the problem solving—police, neighborhood organizations, or other city agencies—it was apparent that police would at least have to be the coordinator of these efforts, and that they would be held responsible for seeing to it that something got done.

However, many cities have found it difficult to get municipal service agencies involved in their community-policing efforts. A report by the Vera Institute on the implementation of community policing in eight cities concluded that "interagency involvement is probably the least discussed and perhaps the least well implemented component of community policing" (Sadd and Grinc, 1993: 82). It is easy to understand why the issue was overlooked in the eight cities studied, for most cities have seen community policing as the police department's program. However, it is clear that the involvement of other city service agencies is important. Expanding the scope of the police mandate and involving police and the community in identifying and solving the problems that appear on their turf require that police rely on other organizations to actually do a significant proportion of the work. While officers and residents may identify the problems, many tasks—such as repairing darkened street lights, towing abandoned cars, boarding up abandoned buildings, filling potholes, silencing barking dogs, and keeping truants in school—have to be accomplished by other agencies.

One challenge for the police is that this is not always clear to residents. Citizens call the police because they have a problem, and they do not necessarily understand the bureaucratic complexities involved in responding to their needs. The challenge grows bigger when departments declare themselves open for new forms of business, perhaps by fostering community meetings which generate diverse new requests for service. In doing so, the *police* have made these "police problems," and the public can reasonably hold them responsible for delivering on their promises. When coupled with service needs identified by community-policing officers, the resulting flood of service demands can strain relationships between them and other agencies.

While delivering on their promises is very important, it surely does not mean that coordinating agency responses to demands for service is easy, or even possible, to accomplish. The eight-city evaluation (cited above) found that plans to involve other city agencies in the effort floundered in seven of them. In Newark (N.J.), police labored for more than a year to get the school system to open gymnasiums for an evening sports program, but never succeeded (Skogan, 1990).

The reasons for this will be familiar to anyone who has ever attempted to coordinate the efforts of several organizations. They have different agendas. They almost speak different languages, for each is bound up in separate service technologies, professional associations, and jargon. They have already established procedures for identifying their priorities, and have built those into their budgets. They have different seasonal, and perhaps even staffing, cycles, and may not be able to respond to unanticipated service requests. They may view agencies making too many of these requests as making a grab for their pocketbook. Agencies have different definitions of who constitutes relevant "communities": property developers loom large in the building-inspection world; chain store managers, among the weights-and-measures set; and restaurant owners, with health inspectors. They have different ideas about the roles of these communities in setting agency priorities, and about the kinds of information that should remain confidential. Many are strikingly unresponsive to service demands that do not come through established channels; they probably do not have a special "window" open for police officers to queue up for service, and it could be difficult to open one. Every agency fights a running battle with its own red tape, and it is easy to strangle outsiders with it (Crawford and Jones, 1995; Gilling, 1994).

The only Vera-evaluated city that succeeded in forming a partnership between the police and other agencies was Norfolk (Va.). The key there was executive leadership—from the beginning, the mayor and the city manager made it clear to every department head that they were part of the program. Staff members from every city agency were involved in community-policing training, and monthly interagency coordination meetings confronted and resolved service-delivery problems.

On the other hand, service agencies in other cities were more fragmented; this was particularly the case in municipalities with weak political institutions. In the absence of executive leadership, the police attempted to call agencies together, but they did not have the clout to bring agency managers to the table. Service agencies saw the police making demands on them, without having much to offer in return. In an era of budget cuts, rather than one of predictable increases, this was not a welcome contribution. Community policing was not their problem, and they were not interested in bailing the police department out of its difficulties. The police had taken on a responsibility without ensuring that they had the resources to deliver on their commitment.

Of course, interagency involvement is a two-way street. Not only must other agencies be brought on board, but police officers must adopt new ways of thinking about problems and the solutions that will involve the services. Left to their own devices, officers will easily fall back on the usual tools of their trade, including issuing warnings and making arrests. But many of the quality-of-life issues that plague urban neighborhoods cannot be solved by traditional police methods, nor by departments that act on their own.

Officers need to know enough about the organization and the mandate of various agencies to make responsible judgments about where problems should be taken, and about what kinds of responsive action they can realistically expect. Before they can explain to neighborhood residents just what can be done about an apparent building-code violation, they may have to master arcane bits of the municipal code. However, "for community poilicing to be successful, it must incorporate problem-solving policing into its design, and no police department can do effective and efficient problem solving without the active involvement of other city agencies" (Sadd and Grinc, 1993: 82).

Interagency Coordination

From the beginning, Chicago planned that the delivery of city services would be an integral part of community policing, and that the prototype districts would receive priority attention from all city departments. This decision had major implications for these agencies; for the officers who were to be involved in the prototype districts; and for the Mayor's Office of Inquiry and Information (MOII), which was charged with coordinating city service support for CAPS.

The centerpiece of the process was the CAPS service request form. Officers completed this single-sided sheet, which gathered information about the specific service that was requested; called for a description and the address of the location involved; recorded information about the requesting officer; and included space for a narrative description of the problem. Completed forms were funneled through the district neighborhood-relations offices. They indicated which cases were emergencies, and then forwarded a copy of the form to MOII. At MOII, the form was prioritized, given a tracking number, entered into a case-tracking system, and then delegated to the proper city agency. Neighborhood-relations officers could also call in high-priority cases, receive a tracking number over the telephone, and then fax the precoded form to MOII. Problems identified through this process were often the work of officers on routine patrol in their beat, but many were filled out as a result of discussions at beat meetings or of informal contacts between beat officers and individual citizens. Residents could also directly contact district neighborhood-relations offices about problems, and they in turn could generate service requests.

The mayor's first contribution to making the process work was to bring together the heads of the city's service agencies and let them know that if their departments did not cooperate in prioritizing prototype-district service delivery, they would be held personally responsible; they held their positions at the sufferance of the mayor, so they took notice. This was a dramatic move, but it reflected the fact that the mayor actually was pursuing two agendas at the same time. First, he wanted the new community-policing effort to make a visible mark in the prototypes during the first year. This would send a message to residents that the program was indeed in operation. Just as important, it would also signal rank-and-file police officers that City Hall was firmly committed to the program. When prototype-district officers were presented with the service-delivery component of the program at their initial orientation sessions, they were very skeptical that the city's cumbersome bureaucracies would ever be brought into line. It helped a bit that some of the most important agency heads were personally on hand to brief the rank and file about their plans, but most officers took a wait-and-see stance. As one prototype-district officer noted,

> What's going to happen when we keep promising things [city services] that can't get done? If we promise to have the garbage picked up and the truck don't come, what are we gonna do? How long are we gonna be the friend of the people then?

The city service component of CAPS also reflected the mayor's long-standing concern about enhancing municipal efficiency. The management and accountability system that was created to ensure the effective delivery of city services in the prototype districts promised to be a useful tool for bludgeoning them into becoming more responsive and effective all over the city.

Several mechanisms were put in place to ensure adequate cooperation and communication between police and the agencies needed to deliver services in the prototypes. The mayor formed an interagency task force that involved all city departments. The task force was to develop procedures for focusing the city's resources on problem solving in the prototypes, rather than pigeonholing them into different administrative categories. For example, in one prototype, a neighborhood tavern was the source of noise and teen drinking on weekends. Neighbors complained on several occasions, and the police would come in response to specific calls, but the problems always reappeared the following week. Finally, a savvy community group and a beat officer gathered evidence that the tavern had a rodent problem and was violating several provisions of the building code. They then launched a multiagency attack on the tavern, involving the health department, the building department, and the liquor commission. They shut the tavern down temporarily, and sent a strong message to the owner that he could not continue to conduct business this way.

To systematically track service requests, MOII set up a computer system that logged in, and kept track of, all incoming service-request forms, and that recorded the final disposition made by the relevant city agencies. The computer generated regular reports for each district that enabled it to watch the progress of specific problem-solving efforts. It took several trys before these reports became user friendly; nevertheless, the final product was highly useful for both beat officers and citizens who were monitoring problems in their neighborhoods. These summary reports could be made available to citizens at beat meetings, and they were presented to the district's advisory boards. When representatives of city agencies addressed these groups, residents could ask them about the status of specific cases that were still listed as pending and could receive a status update. Citizens could also telephone or come to their district station to check the status of a particular problem through the neighborhood-relations office.

In the beginning, weekly meetings were held with district commanders, their staffs, and high-level representatives (and often the heads) of various city departments, in order to iron out service-request and interagency-communication problems. A City Hall staffer who was responsible for overseeing the entire process also attended these meetings. These troubleshooting meetings proved to be highly useful, enabling district commanders to give those on the service-delivery side concrete and immediate feedback on how the service-request process was progressing.

For example, an early problem was that MOII's case-status reports used administrative codes that were impenetrable to lay readers, including police officers. Another was that service-request identification numbers were not being assigned quickly enough for district personnel to check on recently reported problems. The reports issued by MOII were cumulative, and as time went by, they became too cumbersome to be useful for spotting current problems. In addition, problems came up that were clearly emergencies, but there was no special process for closely tracking their progress. These problems were tackled, and many new service procedures were developed and standardized at the weekly meetings. The code names on the reports became more meaningful; case tracking numbers were faxed to the districts to expedite the process of checking on the status of problems; the size of the report became manageable; and a special process was created for tracking the status of emergency situations.

During the prototyping period, a great deal of personal commitment to dealing with service-delivery crises was evident in the meetings. Top MOII staffers slept beside their pagers. At one meeting, the head of a city department noted, "Any commander can call me directly if [he has] a problem. I'll get out of bed in the middle of the night if I have to." Department heads gave commanders the numbers of the telephones that rang at their desks; they designated troubleshooters to work directly with district personnel; and they showed up at beat meetings and at district advisory-committee meetings. Agency managers and MOII staffers went through the police department's standard officer training curriculum so that they understood what the other side was expecting from them, and why they needed the help.

The district commanders were very vocal at their meetings with the agencies. For example, the Englewood commander pressed his view that too many street signs in his district were torn down or were so defaced that they could not be read. This created hazardous situations, particularly at rush hour. As a result, the entire district was surveyed and new signs were put up throughout. The commanders also complained about how long it took to get a dangerous abandoned building torn down, and as a result of their persistence, MOII spearheaded the development of a fast-track demolition process. This program required that owners of targeted buildings show progress in resolving problems in these buildings within 30 days, or the city would demolish the buildings or ask the court to award them to the city for resale. A demolition coordinator noted that it once "took up to two years to accomplish what fast-track demolition can handle in five months' time."

Troubleshooting CAPS service-delivery problems also led to new city policies with regard to towing cars. This was critical, because in almost every part of the city abandoned cars were rated a significant problem. Local (unverifiable) folk wisdom indicated that more than 10,000 abandoned cars clogged the city's streets and alleys at the start of the city's community-policing program. However, abandoned-automobile tows proved to be one of the slower services to come on-line. The city's original towing ordinance specified that apparently abandoned cars had to be tagged and then left in place for seven days and that if they were moved at all during this period, they could not be towed. After much complaining by the commanders, the law was changed. Under the new ordinance, if nothing was done to change the status that had justified tagging the car (e.g., an outdated license plate, or the lack of a city vehicle stickers), after seven days, it could be towed away even if it had been rolled from place to place. In addition, any vehicle that officers identified as posing a hazard could be towed immediately, and they were encouraged to make this assessment whenever possible.

One of the most visible new city services developed during this period involved the so-called Graffiti Blasters. These teams used baking soda, combined with high-pressure water, to remove graffiti from brick, stone, cement, and metal surfaces. The service was free, but to receive it, a building's owner or manager had to sign a waiver form obtainable from beat officers, block clubs, community agencies, and city offices. Groups were encouraged to organize block-wide cleanup visits by the Graffitti Blasters.

Our surveys and observations confirmed the widespread nature of many kinds of physical decay and related problems that demanded the attention of the city's service agencies. The survey that we conducted prior to the implementation of the program asked respondents to report on the extent of environmental and regulatory problems likely to come to the attention of CAPS officers. They were asked to rate a list of conditions in terms of how big these problems were in their neighborhoods. The survey found that these were cited as "big" problems relatively frequently. Abandoned cars were rated a big neighborhood problem by 16 percent of those interviewed; 18 percent reported that liquor sales to minors were a problem in their area; 21 percent thought abandoned buildings and liquor establishments that attracted troublemakers were big local problems; and 23 percent thought that graffiti and trash-filled vacant lots were nearby problems.

We also assessed the extent of city service needs by observing the prototype districts and systematically noting the extent of observable dilapidation. Teams of observers were dispatched to random samples of block faces—both sides of a street, from intersection to intersection. They observed conditions on each parcel of land. They also noted the presence of seemingly abandoned cars, and they peered down each intersecting alley for signs of loose garbage and other trash accumulations there. They found that 5 percent of the sample blocks featured seemingly abandoned cars. However, garbage-strewn alleys were more common. About 46 percent of alleys that adjoined the sample blocks had loose garbage. Observers also noted the presence of graffiti, litter, garbage dumping, empty liquor bottles or cans, and other signs of vandalism in each individual parcel of land. About 70 percent of the blocks we observed had one or more of these problems. Observers noted some evidence of physical decay in 20 percent of residential parcels, but in 41 percent of parking lots, 38 percent of commercial parcels, and 69 percent of vacant lots.

By the end of the first year, the city had towed 2,200 autos from the prototype districts; Graffiti-Blaster teams had removed graffiti from 538 prototype-district buildings; and 322 streetlights had been repaired. Except for the complaints about abandoned buildings—a problem that continued to raise cumbersome legal issues—MOII staffers calculated that they had fulfilled 91 percent of all CAPS service requests.

The extent to which CAPS service requests were logged in by district officers varied considerably. Table 6-1 presents the number of service requests reported to MOII. They are presented as a rate (requests per 10,000 residents) in order to control for significant differences in the population of the various districts (which ranged from 64,000 to 138,000); both the total rate of service requests and rates for several high-volume subcategories of these totals are presented. It is apparent that abandoned buildings and abandoned cars were the most frequent sources of registered complaints, followed by graffiti, requests for traffic signs, and complaints about potholes. Two districts—Austin and Englewood—stood out as sources of the highest rates of CAPS service requests, while Rogers Park produced by far the fewest service requests relative to its population.

It does not appear that the rates at which CAPS service requests were registered were entirely a function of the level of actual problems in these areas. Table 6-2 presents the results of our survey of

Table 6-1   CAPS Service Requests per 10,000 Residents of Each District

Problem That Led to Service Request	Englewood	Marquette	Austin	Morgan Park	Rogers Park
Sewers and water	9	3	11	7	4
Potholes	8	4	58	9	4
Traffic signs	12	6	20	13	7
Graffiti	10	22	19	20	3
Abandoned buildings	106	19	81	14	1
Abandoned autos	107	46	95	41	44
Total	321	112	382	140	63

Note: Total includes other scattered categories of requests. The service-request data are for the period April 1993–May 1994.

Table 6-2 Service Requests and Perceived Service Problems

Problem	Englewood	Marquette	Austin	Morgan Park	Rogers Park
Abandoned autos					
problem	21	28	18	2	4
requests	107	46	95	41	44
ratio	5.1:1	1.6:1	5.2:1	20.5:1	11:1
Abandoned buildings					
problem	41	28	23	4	3
requests	106	19	81	14	1
ratio	2.6:1	0.7:1	3.5:1	3.5:1	0.3:1
Graffiti					
problem	20	51	17	3	21
requests	10	22	19	20	3
ratio	0.5:1	0.5:1	1.1:1	6.6:1	0.1:1

Note: Table gives the percentage reporting each as a "big problem," and CAPS service requests per 10,000 residents. The service-request data are for the period April 1993–May 1994.

the perceived levels of three problems—abandoned cars, abandoned buildings, and graffiti. It compares them to the rates at which these problems were logged in by MOII. To facilitate the comparison, table 6-2 also presents the ratio of problems to service requests. Except for abandoned buildings, where MOII could complete action on only 74 percent of cases, referral was virtually a measure of problem solving during the first year of CAPS. Table 6-2 indicates there were some clear differences in the success of the districts in completing action on cases.

Based on this comparison, the relative frequency of service requests was quite low for the Marquette District, in light of the magnitude of problems there. A full 51 percent of Marquette residents reported graffiti was a big problem (in fact, according to our survey, this was the second biggest problem in the area); MOII logged in 22 service requests for every 10,000 people. On the other hand, while only 3 percent of Morgan Park residents thought graffiti was a big problem in their neighborhood, they made 20 service requests per 10,000 residents, a rate virtually identical with the Marquette rate. Similar observations can be made concerning abandoned buildings and abandoned automobiles, for which Marquette stood at or near the bottom. Rogers Park registered a low rate of service referrals for two of the three problems—abandoned buildings and graffiti—but a relatively high rate of requests for tows of abandoned cars. The clear winner in this regard was Morgan Park, which combined a very low level of problems (as measured by the surveys) with a robust level of service requests. Morgan Park made particularly aggressive use of abandoned auto tows and graffiti-removal programs. On the basis of the problem-to-service ratios in table 6-2, Austin and Englewood came in second and third respectively on all measures.

Did all of MOII's efforts pay off? Did neighborhoods that made better use of the CAPS service-request process look better as a result? The results of our analysis of the impact of CAPS in the prototype districts are presented in the next chapter. We note there that the service-delivery component of Chicago's community-policing effort was one of its most successful elements during the first year. Compared to matched to comparison areas, physical decay, in general, was down significantly in the three worst prototype districts. When we examined trends in regard to the most important neighborhood problems, we found that Englewood made significant gains against both building-abandonment and trash problems, and that graffiti problems declined in Marquette.

Examples of Problem-Solving Efforts

In the course of our evaluation, we encountered numerous examples of police and citizen problem-solving initiatives at the grassroots level. This section presents some examples of CAPS efforts in each of the five prototype districts; we then discuss some general lessons about problem solving in Chicago. It is based on detailed case studies that were developed from personal interviews with key informants; observations of neighborhood meetings and court cases; observations of the area under study; and newspaper and other media sources. (The detailed case studies are described in Whelan [1995].) The studies illustrate some of the kinds of problems that were addressed by CAPS, as well as the alternative avenues for solving them that were developed by police and citizens. The cases demonstrate how partnerships were formed among police, neighborhood residents, community organizations, and city agencies. Not all of these problem-solving efforts were particularly successful; a number foundered because of the inability of residents to sustain involvement in the face of very adverse conditions. But even these cases contribute to the general lessons that we discuss at the end of this chapter, and they help illustrate how the new program really functioned during its first year in the field.

Operation Beat Feet

In April 1994, 60 residents of a beat in Rogers Park joined forces with district police and the ward alderman's office to launch Operation Beat Feet. The project featured organized marching and "positive loitering" by residents. Armed only with flashlights, cellular phones, and notepads, residents of the beat staged nightly walks that ranged from one to three hours in duration. The walks took them along a busy commercial artery as well as surrounding residential streets. They thought they achieved a quick success: Within six months, police reported a 33 percent decrease in five key crimes, compared to the previous year. The residents cut down on the frequency of their walks during the winter months, but returned to the streets every night the next spring.

Residents of the beat began to organize when CAPS was in its infancy. Their initial targets were panhandlers, loiterers, and gang members who threatened to take over the commercial strip, creating problems for businesses and residents around the elevated train station in the center of the beat. The group's goals were to help residents get to know their neighbors, to create an atmosphere of safety in the center of the beat, and to reclaim control of the street. The nightly walks were designed to encourage people to repopulate the area, and to announce that there were limits to the behavior that would be tolerated in the neighborhood. The group did not refer to itself as a "patrol," shying away from the confrontational connotations of the term. It preferred to think of the walks as establishing a "people presence." While they did not wish to be confrontational, the walkers were active, and they maintained regular contact with the evening foot-patrol officer serving the area. They took notes and used their cellular phones when they encountered problems, and they were not afraid of being recognized while they walked along the streets of their neighborhood.

A key to implementing the program was establishing a reliable group of walkers. A core group was quickly established because the walks were only one expression of the efforts of well-established community organizations in the area. Block organizations, beat-meeting activists, and a business-led beautification group lent support. Together, they were able to establish strong links with local service agencies, including the area's principal community organization; a nonprofit economic-development corporation; the ward alderman's office; and district police. The continued commitment of these activists led to the formation of a particularly close relationship between activists and the district's neighborhood-relations office. The walkers coordinated their efforts with foot-patrol officers to ensure a visible community presence at court hearings for panhandlers, loiterers, and gang members who were arrested in the area. The group's building committee established close ties with the alderman's office to ensure that irresponsible landlords were closely monitored. The group received citywide attention when the telephone company recognized its efforts by donating cellular phones to the group.

Marching against Drugs

In the spring of 1993, a group of Englewood's community activists decided to make a proactive move against the gang loitering and drug dealing on their streets, by engaging in anti-drug marches and "positive loitering" at street corners known for being heavily populated by troublemakers. These efforts were organized by a local minister and the police as a response to the complaints citizens made at beat meetings. Englewood presented a tougher target than Rogers Park. During the prototyping period, crime rates in Englewood ranked among the highest in the city. Decay and disorder abounded, and the drug trade was flourishing in Englewood, strengthening its large and well-organized gangs. Marching there proved much more difficult than in Rogers Park.

The goal of the marchers was to hit every drug site in the beat until the dealers left the area. More than 60 residents of all ages participated in the first effort, dubbed the March for Peace. During the march, the minister used a megaphone to preach about the evils of drugs, and he led the marchers in chants. Gang members watched from their corners, and laughed as the chanting marchers passed by.

Because of the large turnout for this event, local hopes were high that this indication of strength and community intolerance could be sustained in subsequent marches. The second event presented a stark contrast to the first, however. Fewer people participated, and those that did were mainly older residents. When participants came back from the second march, they were more pessimistic, feeling that they had been successful in halting the drug trade for only a few minutes. And, while the marchers had police protection, many residents pointed to fear of retaliation as one of the major factors that explained the low turnout. In general, residents of Englewood had mixed feelings about the success of the marches. Many believed they were only pushing the drug dealers into the alleys, while others feared retaliation, and still others only hoped that they could divert the drug trade to some other area.

In retrospect, several things became clear to them. First, they realized that clergy from the district's other 244 churches had to get involved in the problem; one reverend's work would have to be supplemented by others. According to district police, the community needed to organize across a wider area in order to tackle the drug dealing in the streets. If areas as small as that targeted by the marchers continued to be their focus, the battle could not be won. While the idea for the peace marches originated at a beat meeting, and it received the support of district police, the surrounding community needed to become committed for the project to have a lasting impact. Finally, the members realized that the participation of the community's youth was necessary to the success of the marches, but they could not get them to turn out.

Tackling a Bad Building

Housing quality was a recurring concern in Rogers Park, for the eastern portion of the district consisted predominantly of older rental apartment buildings. As a result of community pressure, one of these buildings was identified as a priority by district police. It stood at the center of an alarming concentration of criminal activity, and in 1993, residents and beat officers determined that it was the area's number-one problem.

The building was managed and owned by someone who owned a number of other problem buildings in the area, and by the end of the episode, the main goal of beat residents and police was to take him to housing court on criminal charges—a rare and dramatic move. The building in question was a four-story structure with commercial space on the ground floor and apartments above, located on an otherwise adequately maintained street. Problems with the building surfaced in 1993, when residents complained that an unhealthy mix of gang members, prostitutes, and unsupervised children were living in the building. At the time, it was still half occupied by rent-paying tenants, but they were leaving, and the building was quickly being taken over by squatters. Community concern escalated when the collapse of a portion of a ceiling on one resident revealed deep structural problems in the building; and later, when a woman who was not a tenant was found dead in an apartment.

According to community activists, the building "went bad" when the landlord began renting apartments to drug dealers. This drove out other responsible tenants, and as the number of vacant apartments in the building rose, the owner was unable to choose his tenants selectively. Then he converted the building into Section 8 housing, enabling low-income residents to live there with federal rent assistance. Soon after the conversion, the owner abandoned the building because he still could not make a profit from it. Nonetheless, he remained the legal owner of the building, and residents decided they would take action against him. Both the district commander and the ward alderman took a personal interest in the case because of community pressure and the extent of criminal activity in and around the building.

The community's initial attempts to informally negotiate with the owner were unsuccessful. Then the prosecutor's office approached him with a list of improvements the building needed, but he ignored these concerns. Community activists learned that it was necessary for the landlord to be cited for three instances of "reckless conduct" in order to be charged under the state's criminal housing-management statute. A sustained effort by the community and the police eventually generated evidence that supported these charges. Throughout, police and community residents attended court hearings concerning the building. After more than a year of effort, the involvement of the community and the police paid off when the owner was fined $1,000 and ordered to perform 200 hours of community service, after being found guilty of three counts of criminal housing management. The building was sold to a developer. Activists continued to maintain pressure on the landlord, due to the condition of his other buildings in the area, some of which were also troubled. A local community organization and the beat group in the area drew up plans to expand their hit list, which had the names of bad property owners in the area. This case built a great deal of trust between a network of residents and district officers, and taught them a great deal about how to handle housing issues.

Battling a Halfway House

In August 1994, a resident of the Austin District noticed a newly posted sign on the abandoned Windsor Hotel. The sign indicated that it was going to be converted into a rehabilitation home for drug addicts and newly released prison parolees, under the auspices of an organization dubbed the "Reach Out and Touch Prison Ministry." An investigation revealed that the project had been initiated by two men who, under contracts with the state, were in the business of running recovery homes for newly released inmates and addicts. Inmates under their supervision were known to roam freely in the community, and apparently did not really receive treatment.

Alarmed by the potential consequences that the conversion indicated for the surrounding community, local activists sought police involvement in resisting the reopening of the hotel as a halfway house. Residents were particularly concerned that it would attract more crime to the area. They were suspicious of the founders' motives and the quality of supervision and care that would actually be given at the facility, viewing it as a money-making venture rather than a rehabilitation program.

The proposed venture was repeatedly discussed at area beat meetings, and local groups decided that they and the police should block the reopening of the Windsor Hotel. The police did a title search to learn more about the building—this uncovered the fact that the building was encumbered by $50,000 in unpaid taxes and a string of building-code violations. The title search also revealed that the building was not owned by any of the principals of the prison-ministry group. Police and the community took their findings to housing court. Their persistent efforts resulted in an order to halt reconstruction of the building, since the building permits had been issued under false pretenses. However, the alderman for the ward was not willing to sponsor a rezoning of the area that encompassed the hotel, which would have put a final stop to any plans to convert it into a rehabilitation facility.

According to residents and the police, the Windsor Hotel episode was a catalyst for the creation of a community-police network that had the capacity to tackle future problems as they arose. Through participation in beat meetings and other CAPS activities related to the hotel incident, residents and police in Austin developed a stronger relationship—one that enabled them to leverage additional support from city agencies in their attack on the Windsor Hotel.

Picketing a Landlord's Home

For two years, an irate group of homeowners in Rogers Park picketed the suburban home of a local landlord, and staged demonstrations in front of the bank that held the mortgages for his buildings. Some of the landlord's worst buildings were interspersed among turn-of-the-century homes owned by professional couples with young children. They were fed up with the noise, crime, violence, and general unrest that stemmed from the problem buildings, which reinforced the already slow erosion of property values in the general area. Their efforts were precipitated by a May 1993 shooting incident outside the home of one resident, who quickly organized a meeting attended by 60 people and a beat officer. At this meeting, the group decided to stage a "creative demonstration" in front of the landlord's home. They hoped they could make the building owner as uncomfortable in his home as he was making them in theirs. Things cooled off after the demonstration, until a second shooting—this time a fatal one—occurred in the fall. A new round of picketing ensued, including the first demonstration at the bank. At this point, several state and local politicians got involved. The group also attempted to locate a list of members of the landlord's synagogue in order to place pressure on him from another front.

The picketing did not have a definitive effect, largely because the group was not able to influence investors in the landlord's real estate corporation. The group believed that influencing investors was the key to the problem, but their identities were kept confidential under Illinois law. The group hoped to tell the landlord's backers about the nature of their investment; if they could be convinced to withdraw their support, he might sell his 13 buildings in the area to more responsible parties. However, the group lacked the expertise to identify and contact investors in secret land trusts, for, under Illinois law, this process is a long and complicated one.

Graffiti Cleanup

In the spring of 1994, a young man was shot and injured by a group of gang members in a residential section of the Marquette District. The area where the shooting occurred was a predominantly Hispanic community, known as Little Village. While 31 percent of the families in the community lived in poverty, many of the small homes there were well kept. The community also had a viable commercial district. Gangs had been a problem for the neighborhood for some time, but they had never affected residents of the block involved as greatly as on the day of the shooting. Approximately 60 children live on the block where it occurred, and the incident led to a call for action on the part of frightened parents. One parent circulated a flyer that announced a group meeting, which was attended by 30 people. Prior to this first meeting, residents had never before come together as a result of crime problems.

Upset and frustrated, the residents who attended the first meeting decided to tackle the graffiti and gang markings that had been appearing for some time on garages in the alley behind their homes. They saw this as a place to start—a first step in a fight against gang violence. Residents also hoped that their actions would teach their children respect for the community. With donations from area businesses, and help from the city's graffiti-removal program, the group was able to gather sufficient painting supplies to begin the project. Many children were involved in the Saturday afternoon cleanup. A district police officer attended the cleanup effort, and graffiti on residents' garages was painted over.

However after this show of community involvement, residents of the block did not meet again as a group. No effort was made to monitor the effectiveness of the cleanup. In fact, residents with children who were gang members soon found new graffiti on their garages. The individual who arranged the first block meeting did not want to take an ongoing leadership role, and no one else was willing to step forward and do so. District police did not attempt to contact residents who were initially involved, nor were they visible at later block or beat meetings. Everyone seemed, instead, to be waiting for another incident that would again pull them together.

A Program for Youthful Offenders

Located on the city's southwest side, the Morgan Park district is a homeowning and largely middle-class area that includes the largest urban historic district in the country. It enjoyed a strong and active network of community groups, and during CAPS's first year, their attention turned to delinquency prevention. As a result of constituents' complaints about juvenile crime, a safety committee was formed, which included youth officers, the commander of the district, the ward's alderman, a representative of the prosecutor's office, and staff members of local service-providing agencies. The committee launched a pilot program dubbed the "Alternative Consequence Program for Youth Offenders. July 1993."

Juvenile crime in Morgan Park, especially in the better-off parts of the district, involved graffiti and gang tagging as well as underage drinking in neighborhood parks. The view of the safety committee was that the county's juvenile-justice system was unable to prosecute many offenders in this category because it was overloaded; as a result, youths were receiving the message that their behavior would go unpunished. The philosophy behind the alternative-consequence program was that juvenile offenders should repay the community through community service. The organizers anticipated that if youthful offenders were held accountable in this way, it would deter them from future criminal activity, and would help cement their sense of membership in the community.

Eligibility in the program was limited to youths who committed misdemeanor offenses such as drinking, graffiti and other acts of vandalism, petty retail theft, property damage, and bicycle theft. Offenders had to be between the ages of 12 and 16, and parental consent was required for them to be diverted to this program; otherwise, they would be referred to the juvenile court. Participants signed a contract that stipulated they had to perform a certain number of hours (between 8 and 100) of community service under the supervision of a specific neighborhood agency. Much of their work involved beautification projects in the area. If an offender did not adhere to the contract, his or her case was referred to the juvenile court. People who were knowledgeable about the program felt it was a positive one that ensured that there would be observable consequences for delinquent youths in the area, and that it provided a vehicle for community empowerment within the framework of CAPS.

Gang Unrest at a Bus Stop

The Marquette District is located on the near southwest side of Chicago. A predominantly Hispanic area, it was the fifth most populous district in the city. Two Hispanic gangs plagued the southern edge of the district, and they were engaged in much more serious activities than were youths who were enrolled in Morgan Park's youth-offender program. These gangs gravitated to a Chicago Transit Authority (CTA) bus stop near a local high school, and their members harassed and sometimes beat up high-school students who were waiting for the bus.

The situation eventually led to the fatal shooting of a student by a gang member. This incident became the focus of numerous beat meetings in the district. Citizens who attended the meetings called for action. Various interventions were organized, most of which involved cooperation between the high-school staff and the district police. The first attempt to remedy the problem involved stationing a police car at the bus stop in order to provide a deterrent to intergroup conflict. A second approach to the problem consisted of releasing students from the high school at staggered times in order to increase the monitoring capacities, after school hours, of the police and school officials.

These initial problem-solving attempts did not remedy the situation. Local leaders and the police then decided to meet with CTA officials to establish a more permanent solution to the problem. The CTA decided to close the problem bus stop entirely and to reroute buses to create four new stops that would enable students to avoid contact with the gangs. But this was not a straightforward task: Aspects of CTA bus routing were regulated by federal law, and the process of changing routes that have been officially designated was complicated. In addition to the rerouting, which may or may not be permanent, police cars remain stationed at the original bus stop, and additional patrol officers are often dispatched to do their paperwork in the vicinity of the bus stop, providing further visible police presence in the area.

Despite the substantial effort involved in this apparently modest plan to reduce intergroup tension, interagency communication for the project proved fitful. Police officers who served the area claimed they were unaware of any CTA route changes, and they thought there was still tension and gang harassment at the site of the original stop. There was lingering confusion over whose efforts were responsible for what took place—CTA officials believed they had to do everything without the help of high-school officials. The community's involvement was evident only at the stage of identifying the problem at a monthly beat meeting. However, other Marquette police officers, as well as local political leaders, took a more positive view of the situation, seeing it as an example of community policing in action. Overall, the community believed it had made some progress toward securing a greater level of safety for its children.

Beeping a Beat Officer

Beatlink was a cooperative effort that linked business establishments along a major commercial arterial in the Morgan Park District with officers who were working on foot, using alphanumeric pagers. This effort to increase cooperation between businesses and police in the district reflected two concerns: business owners' dissatisfaction with the prioritization of their calls by the 911 system; and a general interest in finding ways to support faltering small businesses along the area's increasingly troubled commercial strips.

The plan surfaced in the early months of 1993, at a meeting between district police and local business operators. A business owner proposed that area foot-patrol officers carry pagers so that they could be contacted directly by merchants. This suggestion was the stimulus for the pager program, but implementing it was not without obstacles. These included getting department approval, acquiring the pagers, and marketing the program among potential users. District police and the businesses split the responsibility for solving these problems. The businesses looked into ways to pay for it, and in the end, the pagers were donated by the telephone company. Nettlesome issues were resolved, such as how officers could respond if they were sent a telephone number; in this case, part of the program's publicity encouraged merchants to welcome police to step in and use their private telephones. The district commander sought approval from the department for a three-month pilot program designed to test the concept. The top brass were concerned that the pager program would supplant their 911 system; that calls would therefore not be taped, so that officers could not be held accountable; and that area businesses would be unable to determine when to page foot-patrol officers, and when to call 911. The commander countered all of their objections and developed flyers that informed businesses operators about when and how to use the pagers. He eventually received approval for the pilot program, but it was a hard sell.

The Beatlink program went into effect in December 1993. In March 1994, the effectiveness of the effort was examined by informally surveying area businesses. Their responses were positive. Business operators reported feeling safer, and they perceived that their concerns were being better communicated to the police. They believed that the program indeed improved their relationship with district police. Their only negative response involved situations in which foot officers had been temporarily reassigned and were unexpectedly unable to answer their pages. These occurrences, however, appeared to be rare. Police, too, responded positively to the program. The department approved the continuation of the effort beyond its pilot stage. Police also believed that Beatlink improved their effectiveness in handling nonemergency calls, and that it had taken some of the pressure off what they, too, considered to be an overburdened 911 system.

The Police Station with a Bank Inside

Not only was it crime ridden, but Englewood was also one of the poorest communities in Chicago. Many residents of Englewood did not have bank accounts, so they patronized currency exchanges, which charged hefty fees for cashing their checks and issuing the money orders they needed to pay their bills. Residents who left currency exchanges became targets for robbers—street corners that were hot spots in Englewood almost invariably featured currency exchanges. Robberies outside currency exchanges also tended to coincide with the time public assistance checks were received. When the frequency of robberies increased during 1992 and 1993, it became apparent that more than traditional police action would be required. The Englewood district commander joined forces with an area bank and a local foundation to come up with a solution.

The bank had long realized that the Englewood area was underserved, and it had therefore been looking for a location for an automatic teller machine (ATM). The three parties met to discuss the issue, and they concluded that the area would be best served by placing the ATM in the district police station—something new in Chicago. They lobbied the city to get its approval for the installation; after some negotiations, the city granted its approval for a six-month trial. The cost of installing the ATM was assumed by the bank. The bank also mounted an advertising program that drew attention to its banking and direct-deposit services, which were in competition with the currency exchanges. The foundation sponsored information days on banking for residents.

The police were pleased with the results of the program, for it provided a safe haven for bank customers and supported the service-oriented image they wished to establish with residents of the community. The commander hoped that this and other service-oriented ventures that involved the police and the community would help turn around a history of antagonism between police and residents of the area. The bank was satisfied with results, in spite of the fact that transactions were limited to a small number of residents. The educational component of the project did not yield much; most residents of Englewood were still poor, and still did not have bank accounts. However, the incidence of robberies outside currency exchanges leveled off.

Spanish-Language Marketing of CAPS

In the Marquette District, one of the problems for CAPS activists was a lack of Hispanic involvement in CAPS. Before the program began, our surveys revealed that Marquette residents showed the most disenchantment with the quality of police service in Chicago. The surveys found that Hispanics were, by far, the group most likely to report that police in their area were not polite, fair, concerned, or helpful. Animosity toward, and fear of, the police—traditional among people in the area—led many residents to believe that police could not understand or solve their problems. Many residents were fearful of communicating with the police and were reluctant to call 911 because English was not their native language.

To remedy this, Organization Uno, a loose affiliation of Latino leaders, began working with police to improve Hispanic involvement with them and the CAPS program. Organization Uno invited representatives of a Spanish-language radio station to one of their meetings with the police, and it was agreed that the radio station would air a monthly one-hour talk show about CAPS. The show would inform Hispanic listeners about CAPS, beat meetings, and crime prevention. Hosted by a Marquette district neighborhood-relations officer, the show began airing in May 1993. The radio station broadcasted on both the AM and FM bands, and reached a large number of Marquette residents. Neighborhood-relations officers were confident that the radio program improved residents' knowledge about CAPS.

General Lessons about Problem Solving

A major tenet of the CAPS program was that citizens and police needed to develop partnerships in the effort to control crime and reestablish neighborhood security. In many cases, this required that citizens become involved in identifying problems and bringing them to the attention of the police. They could do so through neighborhood-relations offices in each district, at beat or district advisory-committee meetings, or by directly contacting beat officers. In other cases, citizen involvement was expected to go beyond reporting problems to the police; it was anticipated that residents could take personal responsibility for developing and even implementing their own solutions to neighborhood problems. Our case studies illustrated all of these elements, and they pointed to some strengths and weaknesses in the program as it actually operated.

Identifying Problems

In some cases, problem identification was provoked by a single incident. For example, in the case in which residents picketed a landlord's house, a shooting led residents to meet and discuss what they could do about it; gang-related shootings also motivated the graffiti-cleanup and gang-unrest cases. In other situations, a perception of general disorder in the vicinity led citizens to eventually identify a specific problem. Their frustration with panhandling, loitering, and gang activity motivated the launching of Operation Beat Feet, and marchers then began to identify and record the identities of particular troublemakers and to note visible instances of physical decay in their neighborhood. Perceptions that a building was serving as the locus for criminal activities spurred citizen involvement in the bad-building case. Residents' concerns about the neighborhood consequences of the proposed reopening of the Windsor Hotel led them to organize in opposition to its conversion to a halfway house. Finally, a generalized sense that gangs were at the root of the Englewood District's decline motivated residents to undertake anti-drug marches there. The perceived failure of the criminal-justice system ignited other projects. Frustration with the cumbersome and seemingly ineffective operation of the juvenile-justice system sparked the Alternative Consequences Program for Youth Offenders. Business owners' perceptions that the 911 system was not adequately handling emergency calls led to the creation of Beat-link.

Developing and Implementing Solutions

The next step in the problem-solving process—citizen involvement in developing and implementing solutions to a problem—was evident in fewer cases. When citizens were involved in implementing solutions, they adopted different strategies, appropriate to the nature of the problem at hand.

Some citizens' groups sought to build strength by their numbers. Through coordinated public efforts, they attempted to send the message that the community at large would no longer tolerate their plight, and that they knew who was responsible for it. One mechanism for achieving this involved the court-advocacy subcommittees of the district advisory committees, which encouraged volunteers to identify problems in their district and track cases through the criminal-justice system. The Windsor Hotel and bad-building cases demonstrated how important sustained citizen involvement could be in the process of solving problems via the courts. When the solution to a problem potentially involved the courts, the sustained presence of concerned residents and beat officers at hearings helped convince prosecutors and judges of the magnitude of the problem.

Other groups attempted to use their numbers by organizing positive-loitering campaigns and marches. Sometimes, their goal was to establish their presence and support legitimate street activity without directly confronting anyone, as was the case in Operation Beat Feet. At other times, citizens sought to voice their anger and show their strength through direct confrontations, as was illustrated in the March for Peace and the picketing case.

Alternately, a group's goals might be more modest. For example, beautifying the neighborhood is a way of restoring dignity and increasing respect for the community there, and the Marquette District's graffiti cleanup was one example of this type of citizen involvement. Finally, citizens sometimes solved problems by coordinating their efforts more closely with police, as was the case in Beatlink and Operation Beat Feet.

The Role of Community Organizations

While we saw examples of direct citizen involvement in all phases of problem solving, some case studies also demonstrated that their involvement in developing and implementing solutions could be limited to identifying the problems and then relying on neighborhood associations, city service agencies, businesses, or the police to solve them. In these examples, once citizens placed the problem on the public agenda by contacting agencies or organizations, their role in developing and implementing solutions for these problems became secondary. As we noted in chapter 5, Chicago was richly endowed with established community-based organizations of varying kinds. Larger umbrella groups provided assistance in coordinating the actions of smaller block clubs, and could make referrals to, and provide technical support for, beat groups.

In Morgan Park, a large and powerful community organization was instrumental in bringing together members of the police youth division and the neighborhood-relations office, the alderman's office, the county prosecutor's office, along with local businesses, in order to form the Alternative Consequences Program for Youth Offenders. In Beatlink, a local merchants' association took responsibility for securing funding for the pagers that foot-patrol officers carried in Morgan Park. In the Rogers Park District, another established and powerful community organization coordinated what had been a loose network of block clubs into a powerful resident coalition, to fight a slum landlord and push for the sale of a bad building. Another group coordinated building inspections; provided a representative to the district's court-advocacy group; and helped residents with title searches in their continuing battle to rid the area of an irresponsible landlord.

Beat associations were also instrumental in creating and implementing solutions to problems because they provided residents an opportunity, usually through beat meetings, to weigh alternatives and make suggestions to district police and the ward alderman. Beat meetings played a central role in bringing people together to organize both Operation Beat Feet in Rogers Park and the program to stop the reopening of the Windsor Hotel in Austin. Even when an area nonprofit organization took partial responsibility for implementing a solution, as was the case in Beatlink, beat meetings provided an opportunity for concerned residents to make suggestions about possible remedies for problems.

The March for Peace in the Englewood District illustrated the role that area churches can take in coordinating the actions of residents, particularly when there is a weak network of beat associations and block clubs in the area. The church, in cooperation with district police, established the timing and locations of the march. It also transported residents to and from the march sites and provided a safe haven in which citizens could voice their fears and frustration. An area philanthropic organization played a central role in Englewood's ATM project. The foundation, a nonprofit community-development agency, worked with district police commander in placing the automatic teller machine in the police station.

The Role of City Services

Problem solving also involved the cooperation of city service agencies, and from the beginning, the intensification and better coordination of their efforts were an integral part of CAPS. Two important sources of city service support were the Department of Streets and Sanitation and the Department of Buildings. These departments provided assistance for citizens and community groups that attempted to rid their neighborhood of decrepit buildings and to improve the safety of their streets. In the bad-building case, the Department of Streets and Sanitation became involved with garbage and Dumpster problems, while the Department of Buildings arranged for site inspections to determine code violations. Streets and Sanitation was also contacted by activists from Operation Beat Feet, and the department responded to calls about abandoned cars, broken streetlights, and overflowing garbage that the group noted during its patrols.

The graffiti-cleanup program provided an important service in support of neighborhood improvement projects. Many residents and community groups view graffiti as the first sign of neighborhood decline. Contacting the city for graffiti removal—whether by use of a graffiti blaster or paint—was an important step in neighborhood improvement for many beat organizations. Citizens' efforts to remove graffiti in the Marquette District were facilitated by the donation of paint by the city's graffiti-removal program.

The city attorney's office played a role in developing the Alternative Consequences Program for Youth Offenders, by verifying the legality of various aspects of the program. The city attorney also advised neighborhood groups—which were willing to provide work for juvenile offenders—that they could be liable for on-the-job accidents. The parks in the district were also involved in this program, providing opportunities for juvenile offenders to perform their community service in the public parks of the district.

Finally, the transit authority played a central role in implementing a solution to a problem with gang unrest at a high school bus stop. When parents complained to the high school, the police and the alderman's office attempted to solve the problem. When their attempts proved insufficient, the agency was contacted. Its decision to reroute the bus that serviced the high school reduced the potential for gang clashes and racial unrest in the area.

The Role of Businesses

Businesses also played a role in problem solving. The telephone company was integral to the success of the Beatlink pager program. Its donation of pagers, as well as its commitment to fund the operating costs for an indefinite period, were determining factors in the original approval of the pilot program by police headquarters. In the ATM case, a bank shouldered responsibility for the operating costs of the station-house ATM. It also instituted a program that gave residents of Englewood numerous incentives to open low-fee checking accounts. The Hispanic radio station, broadcasting on both the AM and FM bands, donated one hour per month to beat officers in the Marquette District. The program provided an outreach mechanism to Chicagoans who were not fluent in English; it was a call-in show, and the station also provided phone lines, enabling residents to talk to a representative of the police department about concerns or questions they had about CAPS. Finally, in the Marquette District's graffiti cleanup, various local businesses contributed brushes, paint, and refreshments to residents who cleaned up the area.

Police Involvement

The complement to citizen involvement in community policing involved efforts by police to adapt their organizational structure and operational routines to support their new role in the community. Three elements within the police department played major roles in devising and implementing solutions to problems in the prototype districts. They included district commanders, who took leadership roles in some cases; neighborhood-relations officers, who, operated as liaisons between the police department and the public; and beat officers, who, in some situations, established close and cooperative relationships with residents, businesses, and community groups in their beats. Under the CAPS model, the goal of the police is, first and foremost, to control crime. But in addition, the case studies illustrate some unique methods by which the police attempted to improve not only their crime-fighting capabilities, but also their relationships with the community. These included providing improved services to the community, and improving the quality of information and cooperation given by beat officers and community groups.

Four cases illustrated the police department's efforts to provide improved community services. In the ATM project, Englewood's district commander was responsible for coming up with the idea, and working with a foundation to identify a bank that would get involved in the project. He thought it was important to communicate to residents that the police station was more than a jail—that it was not simply a place where people are taken after being arrested. The commander believed that residents of Englewood could come to see the station as the home for new and different kinds of community service, beginning with the ATM. Police in this district also held seminars to assist people in getting off welfare, and to convey the importance of education.

Beatlink served as an example of the police department's efforts to improve its service to the business community. While a local business association took responsibility for the pagers, it was the district commander's job to secure approval for the pilot program. This process took several months, and it involved convincing the department's top brass that the program would not undermine the 911 system. In order to accomplish this, the commander had to establish clear guidelines concerning what constituted an emergency, as opposed to a nonemergency, and to ensure that procedures for using the pagers would be readily available to businesses. The commander believed that Beatlink indeed improved the quality of communication between area businesses and foot-patrol officers. By emphasizing the role of foot-patrol officers, the commander also viewed this as an example of the department's commitment to establishing beat integrity. It was an example of police responding to a demand for improved services for the community, and adopting and implementing the community's proposed solution to a problem.

To staff the Marquette District's effort in the CTA/gang-unrest case, the department created a program called "Voluntary Special Employment." Through this program, police officers, on their days off, worked in a patrol car stationed at the troubled bus stop, from 2:30 P.M. until 5:00 P.M. The patrol car provided a visual deterrent to gang activity there. At other times, area police officers were dispatched to complete their paperwork near the stop—again, in order to provide a visible police presence in the area. This was one way for the police to show their willingness to work with concerned residents to help provide a safer environment for children. Furthermore, in the Marquette District, beat officers hosted a radio show, hoping the effort would increase the involvement of Hispanics in CAPS. The program also allowed the Marquette District to demonstrate its interest in providing services to a segment of the population that had a long-standing fear of the police.

Other cases illustrated the ways in which police attempted to increase their cooperation with the community. The two problem-building cases, while different, documented ways in which neighborhood-relations officers, beat officers, and district commanders approached problem solving. In the Windsor Hotel case, Austin District police first learned about the issue from residents at a beat meeting. When the case was turned over to the courts, the police helped by transporting activists to and from court, and by distributing information about court dates to residents. At court-advocacy meetings, the police and residents active in Austin discussed what their next collaborative steps would be. Police volunteered to conduct title searches in regard to the property, and because of these title searches, the police and community were able to get this case into housing court. In the bad-building case, there was visible police presence from all levels of the organization. When the community informed police about problems in and around the building, it became a priority location in officers' beat planners. Later, the district commander took a personal interest in the case and toured the building with a police photographer. Photos sent by the commander to the prosecutor provided evidence of criminal housing management. The commander also sent a police escort when residents picketed the offices of the building's owner.

The district commander was also visible in the case in which activists picketed a landlord's home. He made personal visits to the buildings involved and attended meetings in residents' homes to investigate new avenues for pressuring the landlord to sell his buildings. Beat officers and tactical units in the district flagged the landlord's buildings in their beat planners, and attempted to make as many arrests as possible in these buildings in order to persuade the prosecutor's office to send the landlord a nuisance-abatement notice. (Landlords who do not comply with the order can be prosecuted on both civil and criminal charges, including a Class 4 felony, and can lose their building.) Police officers and residents also cooperated in the surveillance of suspected drug activity in the buildings.

Foot-patrol and beat officers in the Rogers Park District developed a cooperative relationship with participants in Operation Beat Feet. While their coordination was informal, the marchers had nightly contact with foot-patrol officers, whom they came to know on a first-name basis. Residents supported the police through court advocacy, by appearing at hearings when their beat officers made arrests. Problems in the neighborhood were discussed at monthly beat meetings, and officers' beat planners were updated to reflect citizens' concerns.

In Morgan Park, neighborhood-relations officers and the district commander were involved in setting up the committee that created the Alternative Consequences Program for Youth Offenders. Neighborhood-relations and youth-division officers presented the option of program participation to juveniles and their parents at the time of an arrest. Officers also selected young offenders likely to benefit from the program, and determined the number of community-service hours they would work. After these decisions were made, police contacted participating community organizations and passed the cases on to them for supervision.

The March for Peace illustrated the role of police in offering protection to residents when they take direct action against neighborhood problems. District police in the crime-ridden Englewood community protected marchers by transporting them from their church to the march area, and by providing escorts during the march. Because the path took participants directly past known drug dealers and gang members, it is unlikely that they would have been willing to march without police protection and the support they received from the district.

Sustaining Citizen Involvement

While some of these cases illustrate the ability of police and citizens to mobilize around neighborhood problems and win some victories, other efforts we examined turned out to have little staying power. The case studies suggest that long-term involvement was facilitated by work on problems that were discrete and had easy-to-define targets, and by those that attracted the attention of established organizations that could lend continuity to problem-solving efforts.

The bad-building case study illustrated a very concrete problem: a building in disrepair that had attracted criminal elements, and that was owned by a landlord whose office was nearby. Everyone involved understood the problem, had theories about its origins, and had some understanding of concrete actions that could be taken against it. Ordinary citizens had clear roles: to report crimes and building-code violations, and to join court-watching sessions when the cases came up. Police could generate crime reports on the building, inundate it with requests for inspections, and lean heavily on squatters living there. Likewise, Operation Beat Feet could sustain involvement because it was tied to a network of organizations active in the area, and it called for specific commitments of time to perform a clearly defined task. The volunteers walked spiritedly together in groups, recorded names of problem people and locations, interacted occasionally with foot officers, and worked on keeping up their morale. They reported regularly at the beat's meetings about their activities and progress. On the other hand, the March for Peace focused on gang and drug problems—both diffuse problems, and ones that are deeply rooted in disintegrative social and economic forces that go far beyond the capacity of neighborhoods to solve. The marches that Englewood could sustain could not hope to make more than an hour-long dent in the problem. The neighbors who came together to fight an outburst of garage graffiti had no organization at all; so despite the fact that they lived in close proximity to the graffiti, they could not sustain even the simplest efforts when the problem reappeared.

As noted previously, the Hispanic communities that we observed had particular difficulty sustaining citizen involvement in problem solving. This doubtless reflected the same social forces that hindered Hispanic participation in beat meetings, and limited the involvement of groups that served them in support of CAPS. Their personal experiences with police (both in the United States and other countries); their assessments of how police treat people in their community; language barriers; and the different agendas of the groups that served them—all of these conspired to undermine Hispanic involvement in CAPS. In light of this, it will not be surprising when we note in chapter 7 that few of the benefits of CAPS accrued to the Hispanic community in Chicago. Largely, they did not know about the program; they had little contact with it; and they perceived little change in the condition of their lives, as a consequence of it.

7

The Impact of CAPS on Neighborhood Life

This chapter examines the impact of CAPS in the prototype districts. It details changes, over time, in program recognition, popular assessments of the quality of police service, and trends in neighborhood problems. We find that the program did not appear to market itself effectively, for there was little increase in the recognition of CAPS as a special police-community program. On the other hand, residents of most prototype districts detected positive changes in policing during its first year of operation. The visibility of community-oriented projects and activities went up, and residents of most of the prototype districts found the police more responsive to community concerns. Perceptions of police misconduct declined in several areas, and especially among African-Americans. There was also evidence that the program led to a significant decline in crime-related problems in three prototypes; drug- and gang-problem declines in two districts; and significant decreases in levels of physical decay in two areas.

Discerning the impact of CAPS on visible police activity was important because sustaining visible patrol drives the resource-allocation decisions of all police administrators. In the 1970s, Charles Bahn (1974: 340) stressed the importance of what he dubbed "the reassurance factor" in police patrolling. He defined this as "the feeling of security and safety that a citizen experiences when he sees a police officer or police patrol car nearby." After reviewing the evidence of the day—which was mixed—about the impact of police patrol and response time on deterring crime, he noted that "the need for reassurance, in fact, is behind both the public call for more police and the public acceptance of political cries for money for police. When the man in the street asks for more police, he is really asking for the police to be on hand more frequently and more conspicuously when he is going about his daily business" (1974: 340–341).

The belief that seeing police on patrol in their community makes a difference in how citizens feel about both their personal safety and the quality of police service influences numerous executive police decisions. Indeed, routine motorized patrol is the backbone of policing, for departments spend billions of dollars each year maintaining their presence on the streets. Of course, providing reassurance is only one of the functions of patrol. Police agencies field motorized patrols because (if properly done) this tactic can position officers close to the scenes to which they are likely to be dispatched. They also do so because it is believed to deter crime. But equally important, they invest in patrols because police administrators fear the political consequences of cutting back on visible patrols.

As we noted in earlier chapters, the competing resource demands made by routine patrol and new community-policing efforts led to program-implementation crises in several cities. In view of this, Chicago was determined to avoid any perception that community policing had led to a deterioration of popular police services. Members of the city's police management consulting team played an important role in this regard—they calculated the staffing levels that CAPS would require to sustain routine police operations, while at the same time maintaining beat integrity and freeing beat officers from driving around in response to 911 calls, so that they could do alternative things. Key city and department officials also played an important role—they not only found sufficient existing resources to staff the prototype districts at the required levels, but also, they generated the new resources required to expand the program to encompass all 25 of the city's police districts.

Ironically, some researchers would have been skeptical about the perception problem the police thought they faced. The assumption that people would notice changes in the levels of routine patrolling can run counter to one version of common wisdom in research on policing—that visible policing does *not* make a difference in citizens' fears, or in attitudes toward police. This notion stems

from early experiments conducted in Kansas City, where police
were selectively withdrawn from some experimental precincts, and
police numbers were beefed up in other precincts in order to gauge
the effect of the extension of (largely motorized) routine patrol on
crime and fear. Researchers there found no differences in the subsequent views or the victimization experiences of residents of the experimental areas and of those of other areas. They also did not notice that the number of police assigned to the other areas had
changed. There certainly was previous research that ran counter to
the Kansas City conclusions about the effects of police visibility.
For example, people who report that they have seen police breaking
traffic laws, drinking on duty, or showing brutality are generally
unhappy about their efforts (Smith and Hawkins, 1973). However,
the Kansas City findings became famous (for details, see Kelling et
al. [1974]; Sherman [1986]).

Documenting the impact of CAPS on the frequency and quality
of citizens' encounters with police was important because research
suggests that these factors can play an important role in undermining public support for the police. Not surprisingly, people who are
pulled off the road, or stopped by police while on foot, are generally unhappy about the experience, and it affects their general attitudes toward the police. For example, Southgate and Ekblom (1984)
found that field interrogations and vehicular stops generated three
times as much "annoyance" (as they labeled it) as did other encounters with police (see also Maxfield [1988]). Those people who
recall having been the targets of rude or abusive behavior are also
dissatisfied (Smith and Hawkins, 1973).

People who contact the police, as opposed to being stopped by
them, also may have cause to complain. Victims who contact police
are typically less satisfied as a result of doing so (Skogan, 1990;
Smith, 1983; Walker et al., 1972; Bordua and Tifft, 1971). Roger
Parks (1976) found that victims who received the most thorough
service were the only ones whose attitudes resembled those of non-
victims; otherwise, victims were decidedly negative about police
performance. Generally, it is hands on police assistance that people
want—police are evaluated primarily in terms of their performance
as helpers and comforters, and, secondarily, in terms of their crime-
fighting process. The hands-on assistance by police includes paying
careful attention to what the people who contacted them have to
say, attending to their immediate needs, conducting any necessary
in-depth investigations, and sharing with citizens any follow-up information about a case (Skogan, 1989). Unfortunately, the more

deeply involved ordinary citizens become with the criminal-justice system, the more unhappy they are (Shapland, et al, 1985). There is also limited but important evidence that the impact of police contacts may not be symmetrical—that is, favorable contacts may have few positive consequences in terms of people's generalized view of the police, while unfavorable contacts deflate their overall rating (Jacob, 1971). This is significant because contacts of all types produce both favorable and unfavorable outcomes, as rated by the citizens who are involved (Southgate and Ekblom, 1984; Bayley and Mendelsohn, 1968).

Finally, it was important to document the impact of CAPS on the quality of life in the city's neighborhoods. While there is a great deal that is attractive about the concept of community policing, its proponents must develop better answers to the inevitable question: Does it work? The evidence is mixed. The most consistent finding of evaluations to date is that community policing improves popular assessments of police performance. This is certainly an accomplishment, especially if it occurs in African-American and Hispanic neighborhoods, where relations with the police are most evidently in need of repair. However, the limited scope of documented impacts to date makes community policing vulnerable to the charge that it is mostly a public-relations triumph.

Methods for Assessing Change

Most of the evidence examined here is drawn from survey interviews that involved random samples of residents of Chicago's neighborhoods. The first survey took place during April and May of 1993, and it was completed before the program began. To prepare for the surveys, we used 1990 census data as a source for selecting sections of the city that closely matched the demography of the five newly announced prototype areas. Surveys and other data-collection efforts were conducted in these selected areas as well as in the five prototype districts. Conditions in these comparison areas are used here to (roughly) represent what would have happened in the prototype districts if there had been no CAPS program, for (as noted previously) it was not put in motion in other parts of the city until the end of the prototyping period. In a true experiment, these areas would have served as control groups, against which changes in the program areas could be strictly benchmarked. However, none of these areas were randomly selected (a feature of a true experiment), and they all have a distinctive character, population, and history. As a result, they are employed more modestly in this analysis, as a background against which to judge the extent of changes we observed in the prototype districts. Each of the comparison areas spanned as many police districts as possible, so that we could account for any efforts by local commanders to get a head start by experimenting on their own with CAPS-related strategies (none did so in the comparison districts). Comparison areas were much larger than police districts, and, together with the five prototype districts, spanned about 60 percent of the populated area of the city. Two of the prototype districts—Englewood and Austin—shared an area used for the comparison, to reduce survey costs; this was possible because of their very similar demographic profiles and crime rates.

The first evaluation survey (which we called wave 1) was conducted in the prototype districts, and in the matched comparison areas, before the program began (as already noted). Residents of four areas—Morgan Park, Rogers Park, and their comparison areas—were then reinterviewed (wave 2) in June 1994. Residents of the remaining areas were questioned again in September 1994. The period between the two waves of interviews thus varied, from about 14 months for the first set, to 17 months for Englewood, Austin, Marquette, and their comparison areas. Because of police vacations, the large number of neighborhood festivals that take place during Chicago's brief summer, and a soaring number of calls for service during the warmer months, we concluded that there were relatively few differences between the two sets of districts, in terms of community-policing efforts that took place during this period.

All of the interviews were conducted by telephone, in English or Spanish. The respondents for the first set were selected using a combination of sampling techniques designed to reach respondents who were living in the relatively small areas involved. Half of the respondents were selected, at random, from telephone-directory listings of households in each of the targeted areas, while the other half were contacted by calling randomly generated telephone numbers. The second approach ensured that households that did not have listed phone numbers would be included in the data. The reinterview rate, when we attempted to recontact the original respondents, was 59 percent. Men, Hispanics, younger respondents, those with less education, and renters were less likely than others to be successfully recontacted. A total of 1,506 people were interviewed on each of the two occasions; there was an average of 180 reinterviews in each of the prototype districts and 150 in their comparison areas (for more information on the surveys, see Skogan [1995]).

The analyses that follow compare the results of the two waves of interviews. We used the data in three ways. First, before-and-after data for prototype-district and comparison-area respondents monitored changes in each pair of places. When there was a change in a prototype district but no comparable shift in its comparison area—or vice versa—it can be evidence that CAPS made a difference, especially if we can reasonably link it to specific elements of the program. Second, we were concerned throughout with issues of race and class—we examine the impact of the program and other issues among subgroups in the population, principally those defined by race and class. To do this, responses in all of the analysis areas were combined, and the data were examined statistically for evidence of race or class differences in the changes found in the prototype and comparison areas. Finally, the fact that we questioned individuals twice gave us the capacity to look at the impact of events or experiences in their lives in the period between the two waves of interviews. For example, we look at the impact of being stopped by police during the period between the interviews on changes in people's views of the police. All of the statistical analyses control for race and other demographic characteristics of our respondents, including sex, age, length of residence in the area, and marital status. Statistical tests of the impact of the program were conducted using multiple regression and repeated-measures analysis of variance.

Recognition of the Program

Limited marketing efforts were launched along with the program. A horde of public-officials and top department brass attended "roll out" ceremonies in each of the prototype districts, and the first few of these captured the media spotlight. A CAPS newsletter was devised, and the first issue (August 1993) included a description of the program and success stories from the prototype districts. A copy went to every member of the department, and hundreds were distributed in each of the prototype districts. A CAPS logo graced the front of every publication. These included brochures in English and Spanish, and fact sheets for activists and city workers. During the early months, the CAPS managers relied on neighborhood-relations officers to distribute these materials.

Our evaluation surveys addressed the issue of whether Chicagoans knew about the program. To monitor this we asked:

Now we have a few questions about a new program that has been announced by the Chicago Police Department. It is a *community policing program* that calls for more cooperation between police and the residents of Chicago. Have you heard about this new policing program? [emphasis in the original]

Although CAPS did not officially begin until after the conclusion of our first neighborhood survey, there had already been public meetings about the program as well as coverage of it in the media. In the first survey, 36 percent of those interviewed indicated that they had heard of the program. In a follow-up question, most indicated that they had heard about it on television or radio (57 percent); read about it in a citywide or neighborhood newspaper (42 percent); or heard about it "from someone else" (27 percent—note that multiple sources could be mentioned). There was already a substantial difference in program recognition between residents of the prototype districts (40 percent) and those of other areas (31 percent).

While this is a seemingly high recognition rate for a new program, questions like this typically overestimate people's knowledge of policies or programs because respondents want to appear helpful and knowledgeable. The question also was positioned well into the questionnaire, following many items about crime and the police, so respondents should have been as focused as possible on the topic and might have guessed what kind of response we wanted to hear from them.

Like a great deal of the data we discuss in this chapter, therefore, an important question is that of *change* over time. In this case, the second survey found there was not very much change at all. A little more than a year later, the overall recognition figure was virtually unchanged, standing at 38 percent. Program recognition was still higher in the prototype districts than in the comparison areas (41 percent versus 34 percent), but there had already been about the same difference a year earlier. After more than a year of operation, the level of knowledge about the program was still relatively low in Englewood (30 percent), Marquette (32 percent), and Austin (30 percent). In the less-troubled districts (Morgan Park and Rogers Park), more than half of residents had heard about CAPS. Almost as many residents of these districts had heard about the program before it began, however, so this did not represent any increase in program visibility over time. In parallel citywide surveys in 1993 and 1994, we found that recognition of CAPS actually dropped by nine percentage points.

In the 1994 citywide survey, we found that program recognition declined more among African-Americans than among whites. Within most prototype districts, homeowners were more likely than renters to know about the program, and whites were more familiar with CAPS than were blacks. Program recognition was also linked to higher levels of education and income, and it was more frequent among older respondents. There were persistent differences, for the visibility of the program did not increase significantly among any of these subgroups during the first year. Together, these results suggest that CAPS was not effectively marketed as a visible and unifying symbol of change during the first year, even in the prototype districts.

The Impact of CAPS on Everyday Policing

This does not mean that residents of the prototype districts did not sense that "something was up" in their neighborhoods. Across a number of measures, there is evidence that they observed changes in police activity that reflected the increased staffing and beat work that was taking place in their districts. In most of the prototypes, they saw police more often, and certain police activities became more visible. This was important because enhanced visibility had positive consequences in regard to their views of the quality of police service in their neighborhoods. On the other hand, many elements of routine policing did not change in the prototypes—the rate at which people contacted the police and were stopped by them did not change; and there was no evidence of a change in the quality of routine police services.

Impact on Visibility

This section examines the visibility of various kinds of police activity in Chicago, and the impact of CAPS on who saw police, and what the consequences of this visibility were in terms of people's views of the quality of police service and their concern about crime. As in many surveys, we find modest effects of the visibility of police—in this case, while they are engaging in community-oriented activities—on fear of crime, and stronger effects of visibility on assessments of the quality of police service.

To assess the *quantity* of policing activity that people observed around them, we asked respondents if they had seen a police officer in their neighborhood in the preceding 24 hours or—failing this—

in the past week. Compared to the year before, visibility of police in the past 24 hours went up in every prototype district. The increase was smallest in Rogers Park (just six percentage points), but recent sightings of police went down in its comparison area by a similar figure. In the other prototypes, visibility was up by 10 percentage points or more, all differences that were statistically significant. The only comparison area where residents reported seeing police more often was the one for Marquette.

To assess the *quality* of visible policing people saw around them, we asked seven questions about "specific situations in which you might have seen the police in the past month"; the questions all referred to a respondent's neighborhood. It was useful to examine these questions in three groups. Two questions asked about *enforcement* situations: "[Did you see police] pulling someone over for a traffic ticket," and "police officers searching or frisking anyone here in your neighborhood, breaking up any groups, or arresting anyone?" Responses to these questions varied a great deal, by district. In high-crime Englewood, 48 percent of those interviewed for the first time had observed searches or arrests in just the past month; in Morgan Park, the figure was only 18 percent, and in Rogers Park, 20 percent. Under CAPS, they noted few changes in the level of enforcement activity. The biggest change was a decrease in awareness of enforcement activity in the comparison area for Englewood and Austin; elsewhere, modest (5 percent) increases and declines in awareness of enforcement in the prototypes and comparison areas largely canceled each other out. The survey also asked about the visibility of *motorized patrol:* Residents were asked if they had seen a police car driving through their neighborhood. The vast majority had seen one, and a year later, visibility had changed only slightly (2 to 3 percent) in the prototypes; in every case, this was matched by small parallel changes in the comparison areas. The program does not appear to have increased the visibility of the core elements of traditional policing—patrol and enforcement.

On the other hand, there were large and significant increases in the visibility of other forms of police activity in several of the prototypes. These were all more *community-oriented* forms of patrol. Residents of all areas were quizzed about the visibility of foot patrols in two different situations: "a police officer walking or standing on patrol," and an officer "walking on patrol in the nearest shopping area." In total, about 17 percent recalled seeing a foot officer in their neighborhood, and 35 percent recalled seeing one in a shopping area, during the month prior to the first evaluation survey. These figures were in accord with usual practices, for Chicago traditionally made extensive use of foot officers around rapid-transit stops and along busy commercial corridors, but rarely along residential streets. About one-third of those we interviewed recalled seeing police doing close neighborhood patrol ("officers patrolling in the alley or checking garages or in the back of buildings"), and about one-quarter had spotted them having informal contact with citizens ("a police officer chatting or having a friendly conversation with people in the neighborhood"). Changes in these figures can be illustrated by responses to the last question—about the visibility of informal contacts.

Figure 7-1 indicates that in four of the five prototype districts, there were significant increases in the visibility of informal police-citizen contacts, which accumulated in most areas to a fairly high level. The presentation format employed in figure 7-1 will be repeated in several later figures: It depicts wave 1 and wave 2 survey results (labeled W1 and W2) for the prototype districts and their comparison areas, so as to facilitate comparisons between over-time changes in the results. The values given in parentheses near the bottom of figure 7-1 present the statistical significance of wave-1 to wave-2 changes within an area. This is the likelihood that the change recorded in figure 7-1 actually reflects a chance fluctuation in the survey, and we only want to pay attention to changes that

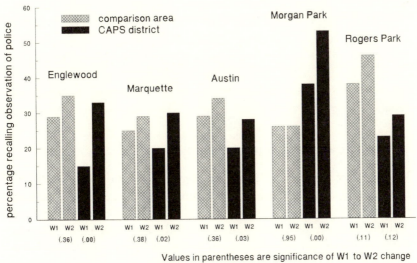

Figure 7-1 Changes in visibility of informal contacts with police.

were probably *not* due to chance. The usual cutoff is a probabil-ity—of the finding being due to chance—of .05 or less (that is, only 5 times in 100), although in this book, we also pay attention to patterns of results that lie within the .05-to-.10 range as well.

Figure 7-1 depicts significant increases in informal contacts in all districts but Rogers Park; there they were also up, but less so. In Morgan Park, the visibility of informal contacts climbed from 38 percent to 53 percent; it doubled in Englewood (where contacts were very infrequent prior to CAPS), and it was up by about one-third in Marquette and Austin. Changes in visible informal contacts in the districts' comparison areas were statistically insignificant; and except for Rogers Park's comparison area, they were consider-ably smaller in magnitude than were the districts' changes.

The results presented in figure 7-1 illustrate a general pattern: A score based on all four questions about the visibility of the po-lice's community-oriented activity went up significantly in all five prototypes. It also increased significantly in the comparison area shared by Englewood and Austin, but it went up by more in these two prototypes. Further analyses of various demographic groups re-vealed the same pattern: The visibility of community-oriented po-licing practices went up, according to respondents, among all major categories, including those defined by race, home ownership, length of time in a residence, gender, age, education, and income.

In sum, residents of the prototype districts saw police more of-ten. From their vantage point, the new officers assigned to beat work in the prototypes increased the visibility of foot-patrol offi-cers, neighborhood patrolling, and informal contacts with citizens. They did not notice any significant changes in traditional motorized-patrol or enforcement efforts. The increased visibility of community-oriented policing was nearly a universal experience—one shared by every major demographic subgroup in the proto-types.

Significance of Increased Visibility

Why is this significant? First, it offers some evidence that CAPS made a real difference in police activity at the street level. It is an indicator that police activities in the prototypes were to some ex-tent focused—as intended—on efforts to bring police closer to ordi-nary people in the community. It is possible that many of the ef-fects of CAPS might have been achieved just by adding more cops to the districts, and having them perform their routine duties. From this perspective, the rest of the program could be considered just window dressing. However, we have seen evidence that police were actually doing something visibly different and, from the point of view of the general public, CAPS was not just "more of the same thing."

The increased visibility of policing that we found in the prototypes is also important because it had consequences of its own. These effects were independent of, and in addition to, those of CAPS. Across all of the areas surveyed, people who observed more police activity were more satisfied with the quality of police service and felt safer in regard to crime.

Unlike research in Kansas City, which suggested (as noted previously) that changing levels of police patrol does not make much of a difference, our evidence here is correlational rather than experimental. But it also involved a program that increased—this time visibly—the level of police activity in selected areas. The apparent consequences of police visibility in Chicago run counter to the Kansas City results. To illustrate the magnitude of the effects that are involved, figure 7-2 charts wave-2 responses to one question asked of all respondents: "How good a job are the police doing in dealing with the problems that really concern people in your neighborhood?" The percentage of respondents in each race category that replied that police were doing a "very good" job is presented in the figure. The visibility of community-oriented policing during the period between the two sets of interviews is represented by a count, ranging from zero to four, of the number of sightings of community-oriented activities. We can see in figure 7-2 that whites were more satisfied than African-Americans or Hispanics—most notably, when the police-visibility level was very low. However, levels of satisfaction were higher for all groups when the police were more visible. The gap in satisfaction levels between white and minority respondents averaged about 10 percentage points, while the gap in satisfaction between respondents recalling lower levels of police visibility and those recalling higher levels was about 15 percentage points. Although harder to discern, the upward slopes of the lines for African-Americans and Hispanics also were somewhat steeper than the slope for whites. They tend to converge a bit at higher levels of police visibility. This suggests the effect of police visibility was greater for minorities than for white respondents. (Note that all of the effects of visibility illustrated in figure 7-2 were reflected with great consistency in more elaborate statistical analyses of multiple-item attitudinal measures.)

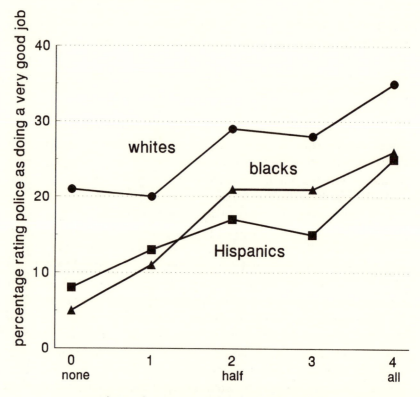

Figure 7-2 Visibility of and satisfaction with police.

To examine the impact of police visibility, we took advantage of the two-wave nature of our data. We examined people's views on crime and the police a year after CAPS began, controlling statistically for their views as reflected in the wave-1 survey. This directly measured changes in their attitudes. We then added to the model the measure of the visibility of community-oriented policing that is used in figure 7-2; this was the variable we were primarily interested in. We also controlled for a list of other factors known to affect people's view of police, including race, sex, age, length of time in a residence, marital status, and home ownership. As a further control, we included the visibility of community-oriented police activity before the program began, along with an indicator of whether each respondent lived in a prototype district or a comparison area.

We assessed residents' views of police and crime in several

ways, using measures that are employed throughout this chapter. Assessments of police *responsiveness to community concerns* were measured by four questions:

- "How responsive are the police in your neighborhood to community concerns?"

- "How good a job are the police doing in dealing with the problems that really concern people in your neighborhood?"

- "How good a job are the police doing in working together with residents in your neighborhood to solve local problems?"

- "When dealing with people's problems in your neighborhood, are the police generally very concerned, somewhat concerned, not very concerned, or not concerned at all about their problems?"

Responses to these four questions were single factored, and a scale that was constructed by summing them had an alpha reliability of 0.86. Before the program began, African-American and Hispanic respondents were less convinced than were whites that police were responsive to local concerns; young people and renters were also less satisfied than their counterparts. Long-term neighborhood residents were more positive about the police on this measure.

Assessments of police *effectiveness at dealing with crime* were measured by two questions:

- "How good a job do you think they [police] are doing to prevent crime in your neighborhood?"

- "How good a job are the police in your neighborhood doing in keeping order on the streets and sidewalks?"

Respondents replied by choosing from four response categories, ranging from a "poor job" to a "very good job." The correlation between the two sets of responses was +.70. African-Americans and renters were more likely to think that police did not do a very good job at dealing with crime before the program began.

Fear of crime was measured by responses to three questions, using quite diverse response categories:

- "How safe would you feel being alone outside in your neighborhood at night?" (Four categories were used, ranging from "very safe" to "very unsafe.")

- "Is there any particular place in your neighborhood where you would be afraid to go alone either during the day or after dark?" (The responses were yes or no.)

- "How often does worry about crime prevent you from doing things you would like to do in your neighborhood?" (Four categories were used, ranging from "very often" to "never at all.")

The reliability of the composite scale that combined these items was 0.66. Before CAPS began, levels of fear were higher among women, low-income and less-educated people, African-Americans, and renters.

The statistical analysis found that the impact of visible community-oriented police efforts was great and highly significant in each instance. Controlling for other factors (including what they thought about crime and the police in 1993), residents who subsequently observed them in action were more satisfied with police responsiveness to community concerns, thought they were more effective at dealing with crime, and felt safer. The effect of police visibility on attitudes about the police was larger than that of age or sex, and was about the same as the effect of those factors in relation to fear.

Table 7-1 summarizes all of these findings. It presents coefficients that describe the impact of police visibility and their statistical significance. The coefficients can be compared to one another

Table 7-1 Impact of Police Visibility on Three Outcome Measures

Respondents	Regression Coefficients and their Significance			
	Responding to Concerns	Dealing with Crime	Fear of Crime	Number of Cases
Total	+.15 **	+.18 **	−.04 **	1,498
Whites	+.10 **	+.11 **	+.02	480
Blacks	+.17 **	+.22 **	−.08 **	736
Hispanics	+.18 **	+.17 **	+.01	235
Renters	+.17 **	+.22 **	−.07 **	620
Owners	+.14 **	+.16 **	−.03	886

Note: Racial breakdown excludes other and unknown races. ** indicates $p \leq .05$; the others were not significant (all $p \geq .15$). Controls are for demographic factors, prototype residence, and wave-1 measures of the dependent variables and police visibility.

in each column in terms of the size of their apparent impact. Most of the relationships indicated in this table were very significant. The first row of data in table 7-1 summarizes the overall impact of police visibility on fear and assessments of the quality of police service; the signs there indicate that assessments of police were more positive, and fear was lower, among those who had seen the police in action. Further, the data document that the effect of visible community-oriented activity was almost generic: In the case of assessments of police service, it persisted among respondents of all races, and among both homeowners and renters. Lower levels of crime were linked to police visibility because of its positive effects among renters and African-Americans. Members of both of these groups felt safer when they spotted police doing community-oriented things. But there was no apparent effect of visibility on homeowners, whites, or Hispanics—this is a forerunner of many findings in this chapter, for CAPS did not appear to make much of a difference in their lives.

CAPS's Impact on Public Satisfaction

Did residents of the prototypes grow satisfied with the quality of police service as they gained experience with community policing? To examine this, our surveys included questions that assessed a number of aspects of the quality of police service. One of the central tenets of CAPS was that police must become more responsive to neighborhood priorities, so that their efforts will reflect the diversity of problems in different communities. As already noted, the survey included four questions that assessed perceived police responsiveness. We have also already discussed the questions that comprised an index of perceived police effectiveness at dealing with crime. As a final measure, the surveys included three questions that probed perceptions of *police demeanor:*

- "In general, how polite are the police when dealing with people in your neighborhood?" (Four response categories were used, ranging from "very impolite" to "very polite.")
- "In general, how helpful are the police when dealing with people in your neighborhood?" (Four categories were used, ranging from "not helpful at all" to "very helpful.")
- "In general, how fair are the police when dealing with people in your neighborhood?" (Four categories were used, ranging from "very unfair" to "very fair.")

The reliability of the composite scale that combined these items was 0.78. Respondents with a high score thought police were fair, helpful, and polite. Before the program began, African-Americans and Hispanics were less satisfied with how police treated people in their neighborhood, as were younger respondents. Homeowners, long-term neighborhood residents, and the elderly were much more satisfied.

Figure 7-3 depicts average responses to the police-responsiveness measure in each of the evaluation areas. It indicates that a year or so after the implementation of CAPS, perceived police responsiveness was up in four of five districts. There were no significant changes in three of their comparison areas. Opinion also grew significantly more favorable in Rogers Park, but parallel changes took place in its comparison area, making it more difficult to attribute them to the program. Only in Marquette were public assessments of police responsiveness unchanged. Figure 7-3 presents average scale scores, which often do not appear to vary much, but in the multivariate analyses, the effects of living in the prototypes were strong and significant in three of the districts.

To be sure, the successes wrought by the program were not overly dramatic. A horizontal line in figure 7-3 indicates where respondents who gave, on average, a neutral response would fall. A neutral response would fall, for example, between "fair job" and

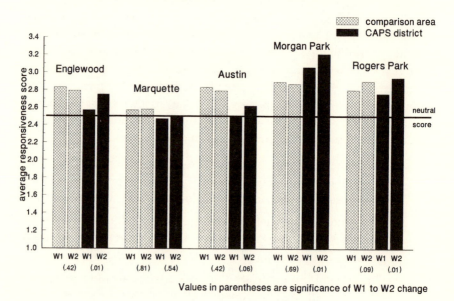

Values in parentheses are significance of W1 to W2 change

Figure 7-3 Changes in police responsiveness by district.

"good job," or between "somewhat responsive" and "somewhat un-responsive," for the various questions. In Austin and Englewood, changes during the first year of CAPS succeeded in driving public opinion barely over the neutral mark, but, at least, out of the negative range and into the positive. Residents of Rogers Park and (especially) Morgan Park were more positive even before the program began, but there was still room for improvement in their ratings of police service. Those who were living in Marquette were neutral about police responsiveness before the program began, and afterward as well.

Figure 7-4 examines the same data, but divides respondents into demographic categories. Hispanics were concentrated in the Marquette District but, otherwise, people of different backgrounds could be found in several districts, so figure 7-4 paints a fairly general picture of the impact of CAPS on groups in the city. As it indicates, perceived police responsiveness went up significantly among whites and blacks who lived in the prototypes, but stayed virtually stable or declined in areas of the city still served by traditional policing. The attitudes of both renters and owners were significantly affected as well. Only Hispanics concentrated in Marquette—and black residents of the same district—did not change their views significantly during the course of the program.

Other changes in popular views of the police did not show

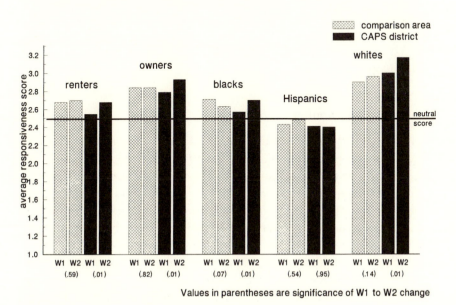

Figure 7-4 Changes in police responsiveness by group.

such a sharp contrast between the prototype districts and the comparison areas. Our measures of how effective people thought police were at fighting crime showed very slight gains in every area, including the comparison neighborhoods. In two districts (Englewood and Austin), there were significant improvements in how effective people thought police were at keeping order on the streets and sidewalks, and these were coupled with a corresponding significant decrease in their shared control area. There was no clear pattern in small changes in popular perceptions of police demeanor, including the measures of helpfulness, fairness, and politeness. Beliefs about the fairness with which police treat people went up significantly in Englewood and Austin, and did not change in their comparison area. However, the remainder of the questions did not point to any systematic change in police demeanor.

In sum, CAPS appears to have enhanced the visibility of foot-patrol officers, close neighborhood patrol, and informal contacts with citizens. Residents of the prototypes saw police more often, but they did not notice any significant changes in traditional forms of patrol or enforcement efforts. They were reassured when they saw police doing community-oriented patrol. Controlling for many factors, police visibility was linked to positive changes in people's views of the quality of police service, and—at least for blacks and renters—reduced fear of crime. Perceptions of the responsiveness of police to neighborhood concerns improved in four of the five prototype districts; in three of the four, there were no parallel shifts in the views of residents of the comparison communities, and only in one district does it seem likely that assessments of the police did not change very much because of CAPS.

Impact on Routine Operations

There was little evidence that CAPS had any impact on the visibility of routine police operations. These included the frequency with which people contacted police about various matters, and how the calls were handled. How well their calls were handled influenced people's views, but CAPS did not appear to change the frequency with which they contacted police, or the reasons that they did so. Police also do "proactive" work: They make stops and conduct searches and interrogations. Not surprisingly, when people were stopped, they were unhappy about it. However, the professionalism with which incidents were handled deflected some of this dissatisfaction, and there was no evidence that CAPS increased the rate of proactive policing in the prototypes.

The program had no apparent impact on routine proactive policing. Our surveys monitored the frequency with which residents were stopped by police while driving or on foot, and whether they were stopped in their neighborhood. Overall, about 10 percent were stopped in their neighborhood during the year preceding the first survey, and about the same number—8 percent—during the first year of CAPS. These numbers did not vary between the prototypes and other districts. Virtually all the stops involved motorists, and young African-American and Hispanic males were overrepresented in these data by a wide margin. Before the program began, about 15 percent of Hispanics recalled being stopped, as did 11 percent of African-Americans and 8 percent of whites. Men were more than twice as likely to be stopped as women. But the biggest variation in the rate of people who recalled being stopped was reserved for age groups: Fully 34 percent of all respondents under age 25 recalled being stopped, as opposed to 9 percent of everyone else. When controlling for the relationship between these three factors, racial differences disappeared, and age and sex were the predominant factors. There was also no change over time in the proportion of respondents that reported receiving a parking ticket (slightly more than 25 percent) or a summons for speeding or some other moving violation (a little under 10 percent, mostly young males).

The program had no apparent impact on the frequency with which people contacted the police, or why they did so. Our surveys questioned everyone about nine different reasons for which they might have contacted police during the past year: to report a crime, an accident, or a medical emergency; to report one of three kinds of suspicious circumstances; to contact police about neighborhood problems; or to give them information or get information from them. Both in 1993 and 1994, about half of those we interviewed had contacted the police about some matter. In each year, about 30 percent said they had contacted them more than once. And people had called the police about a broad range of concerns. In both years, about 25 percent had called to report a crime; another 15 percent to report an accident or a medical emergency; and 25 percent had contacted them about suspicious persons or noises, or about some other event they thought "might lead to a crime." An overlapping 25 percent had contacted police to ask for information or advice, or to give the police information.

It is interesting to note that the program had no apparent impact on the willingness of victims to report their experiences to the police. Victimization research has found that half or more of most common crimes are not reported to the police. Reporting is typically affected by several factors: the seriousness of the reported incident, any relationship between the parties involved (as in domestic-violence cases), whether victims are insured against loss, and whether anyone is injured. The discretionary and highly variable rate at which victims do report crimes is an issue of some concern for evaluators, for it distorts official crime statistics. Research conducted in Portland by Anne Schneider (1976) found that involvement in an effective crime-prevention program *increased* the official burglary rate because victims were substantially more willing to step forward and contact police when they were victimized. This would have made the program look bad had she not been able to monitor this change using resident surveys.

Our Chicago survey included an extensive victimization component. When people recalled any incident from a long list of recent experiences with crime, they were asked if the experiences had been reported to the police. Following the national pattern, about 68 percent of successful burglaries were reported, as were 41 percent of attempted burglaries, 30 percent of incidents of household vandalism, and 39 percent of physical assaults. However, there were no differences over time in victims' reporting practices, or between prototype-district residents and those living in the comparison areas. For example, when it occurred, the reporting of completed and attempted burglaries went down a few percentage points in both the prototype districts and the comparison areas. Assault reporting was up a bit in the prototypes, but not significantly.

Finally, there was no evidence that CAPS had any impact on the quality of service delivered when people did call the police. When residents recalled contacting the police, we asked them a series of follow-up questions about the encounter. (If they had called them many times, we asked about the most recent contact.) We asked them if police paid careful attention to what they had to say, if they explained what action they would take in response to the incident, if the police were helpful and polite, and how satisfied they were with the way police handled the matter. Other research has found that these factors are powerful predictors of general attitudes toward police—an important dimension on which police managers can evaluate the quality of the service they are delivering

(Skogan, 1990, 1994). Using a statistical model that controlled for experiences with the police before 1993, their prior attitudes about the police, and a list of demographic factors, we found very limited differences between prototype-district and nonprototype-district residents' assessments of how well their problems were handled when they contacted police during the first year of CAPS. Under the CAPS plan, the bulk of these contacts should have been handled by rapid-response teams rather than beat officers, and we found no evidence that these teams were going about their business any differently than they had before CAPS began.

Impact on Perceptions of Police Misconduct

We were also concerned about the potential impact of CAPS on police misconduct. One concern was corruption. Community policing involves establishing long-term relationships between beat officers and the diverse groups in the communities they serve. And among these groups are potential corrupters, including those who violate liquor or health ordinances; who need to evade environmental and land-use regulations; or who wish to protect gambling and prostitution. Some of the organizational problems that community policing is supposed to address are the results of policies created expressly to counter corruption, including the frequent rotation of officers from place to place (Skogan, 1995). Corruption was a topic that officers' immediate supervisors seemed best positioned to assess. In chapter 4, we noted that actual experience serving in the prototypes helped alleviate their concern about the potential for corruption in a community-policing program.

Another potential issue was police abuse of authority in dealing with citizens. For example, chants of "Rodney King" were still greeting beat officers in Chicago when CAPS was first unveiled, and during the course of its first year, at least two major incidents of police abuse of power surfaced in the citywide media. Community policing extends at least two worrisome powers of street officers: It increases their use of discretion, and it increases the scope of their authority. Community policing increases their use of discretion because it involves decentralizing authority in the organization in order to encourage more flexible, creative, and wide-ranging police work. Because it expands the scope of the police mandate, police will more often find they are working on problems that lie outside the confines of criminal law and its careful delineation of their powers and responsibilities. In these instances, they may find it easier to act on their prejudices or stereotyped notions, or to be tempted to act when they lawfully cannot.

To monitor abuse of authority, we asked residents "how big a problem" three potential police practices were in their neighborhood:

- Police stopping too many people on the streets without good reason?
- Police being too tough on people they stop?
- Police using excessive force; that is, being verbally or physically abusive to people in your neighborhood?

The reliability of the composite scale that combined responses to these items was 0.85.

Despite widespread discussion of these issues, most people thought they constituted "no problems" in their own area: In fact, 82 percent thought that police stopping too many people was not a problem, and 81 percent agreed that being too tough on people they stop and using excessive force were not problems, either. Not surprisingly, the differences that existed in views of these problems were most noticeably related to race and age. Among the youngest respondents (18 to 26 years of age), 17 percent of those interviewed in 1993 thought police use of excessive force was a big problem in their community; among those over age 40, the comparable figure was 5 percent; 13 percent of African-Americans, 8 percent of Hispanics, and only 3 percent of whites agreed.

Another factor that was linked to perceptions of police aggressiveness was being stopped by them during the past year. The negative effect of being stopped was apparent even in statistical analyses that controlled for three factors: being stopped in the past (before the first survey), people's demographic profiles, and their earlier views of police misconduct. The effect of being stopped more than once between the two waves of interviews was even larger, almost twice the effect of being stopped only once. Being stopped had this negative effect among whites, African-Americans, and Hispanics.

It helped to be treated well. Those who recalled having been stopped were asked five follow-up questions about their most recent encounter with police. We asked if police clearly explained why they wanted to talk to them; if police paid attention to what they had to say; if they clearly explained their actions; and how fair and how polite they were. People who reported being well treated along these lines were substantially more positive about police misconduct than those who were stopped but not treated as well. Likewise, those who had themselves contacted police and felt their case was well handled (along the lines discussed in the previous section) were more sanguine about possible police abuse of authority. The same strongly positive effects of being professionally treated could be observed across a broad range of attitudes toward police in Chicago.

During CAPS's first year, living in a prototype district had fairly limited effects on public views of police abuse of authority. The effects were largely confined to African-Americans, who were somewhat more positive about police in every prototype district after the first year of the program. This parallels, to a certain extent, the impact of police visibility on fear of crime, which was largest among African-Americans. Given the depth of concern about these issues in all communities, and the often deep divisions among the races over police conduct, this improvement in the views of African-Americans is of some significance.

At the outset, the views of whites were more positive about police misconduct, but their assessments did not change much, regardless of where they lived. Overall, the percentage of African-Americans living in the prototypes that thought police use of excessive force was either some problem or a big problem dropped from 28 percent to 20 percent. The percentage that thought they stopped too many people dropped from 29 percent to 22 percent, and the proportion that felt they were too tough on those they stopped dropped from 30 percent to 21 percent. Parallel declines in the comparison areas were about half of those figures. Furthermore, the views of Hispanics living in the prototypes did not change much at all. In Marquette—which, in our survey, was half Hispanic and half African-American—the views of blacks grew more positive, and those of people of Hispanic origin did not change. In Morgan Park—which was split fairly evenly among white and black residents—the views of African-Americans grew more positive while those of whites remained the same. Concern about police abuse of authority went down the most in Englewood and Austin, two districts that were overwhelmingly African-American in composition. For example, the percentage that thought that police use of excessive force was a big problem declined from 17 percent to 8 percent in Englewood, and from 12 percent to 8 percent in Austin. It also went down by 4 percentage points in the comparison area that they shared.

The Impact of CAPS on Neighborhood Life

In describing CAPS, the department's vision statement noted:

> It is this focus on prevention through a stronger government-community partnership that holds real hope for addressing some of the City's most difficult neighborhood problems—and for doing so in a way that is far less expensive than constantly reacting to those problems after the fact. (Chicago Police Department, 1993: 12)

We will examine here the effectiveness of the program in addressing local problems. We will examine the impact of the program in two ways: first, by describing wave 1–wave 2 changes in specific problems in each area; and then by identifying clusters of problems and examining general patterns of change in those problems across all of the districts. Most of the discussion focuses on survey respondents' ratings of the extent of various problems in each community. This is appropriate because many of the problems that concerned neighborhood residents cannot easily be counted as discrete incidents, and most are either not captured by any official record-keeping system or are very poorly recorded when they *are* captured. For example, street-level drug dealing surfaces in official statistics only when arrests are made, and these numbers simply did not reflect the wide-open drug dealing that plagued several of our study neighborhoods. Graffiti was only rarely reported to police (most people do not connect it with making a 911 call), and was not dealt with very intensively when it *was* reported. No one kept official statistics on problems like junk-strewn vacant lots.

Using surveys enabled us to employ uniform and comparable measures of the impact of a broad mix of problems, and to go directly to the public rather than having to rely on second-hand sources of information about the quality of their lives. There is some evidence that individuals are fairly reliable informants about the extent of these problems (Skogan, 1990). However, for some issues, it is also possible to examine alternative measures. As noted above, our surveys included systematic measures of the victimization experiences of the individuals and households we surveyed, and this produced a second look at problems that fell into conventional crime categories. We also examined officially reported crime figures at the district level when they could be compared to the problems identified by neighborhood residents as priority issues.

Impact on the Most Serious Neighborhood Problems

In chapter 2, we discussed the varied nature of the problems in the CAPS neighborhoods. Some problems, including drugs and gang violence, were common across many or most of the prototypes. The others differed from place to place, and issues that loomed large in some districts were scarcely problems at all in others. One goal of community policing is to open departments up to local input so that they can effectively discern these differences and tailor their operations to respond to them. In turn, our evaluation also needed to be responsive to these local variations. We wanted to focus on the concerns expressed by neighborhood residents and track what happened to them during the first year of CAPS.

To do this, we concentrated on the issues cited by neighborhood residents as the most serious problems in their communities. In the wave-1 survey, respondents were quizzed about 18 specific issues that we anticipated—before the program began—might be problems in various parts of the city. Residents were asked to rate each of them as either a "big problem," "some problem," or "no problem" in their neighborhood. The analyses here identify the *four* biggest problems that residents of each district cited in the first survey, and track the ratings they gave these issues a year later when we interviewed them again. This approach lets residents set the agenda for the evaluation, through their expressions of concern about events and conditions in their communities.

Figures 7-5 to 7-9 identify the problems that were cited by residents of each of the CAPS prototype districts. Two problems on the list were of virtually universal concern: Street-level drug dealing was one of the top-ranked problems in every district we studied, and "shooting and violence by gangs" was one of the leading problems in four of the five prototypes (the lone exception was Rogers Park). More than 60 percent of the residents of Englewood, Marquette, and Austin rated street-level drug dealing a big problem. Gang violence was the number-two or number-three problem in Englewood, Austin, and Marquette, and the most highly rated problem in Morgan Park. Ratings of drug dealing and gang violence also clustered together tightly when people assessed conditions in their neighborhoods; the correlation between the two measures was +.72. Gangs and drugs are challenging issues that lay near the core of the city's crime problems in the 1990s. They present a difficult target for community policing and, indeed, policing strategies of any style.

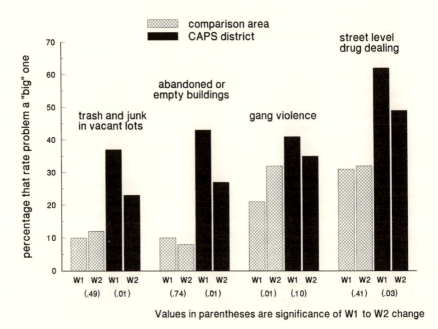

Figure 7-5   Neighborhood problems in Englewood.

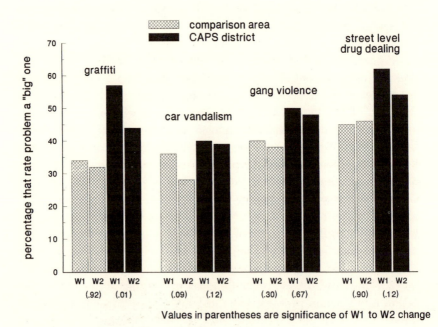

Figure 7-6   Neighborhood problems in Marquette.

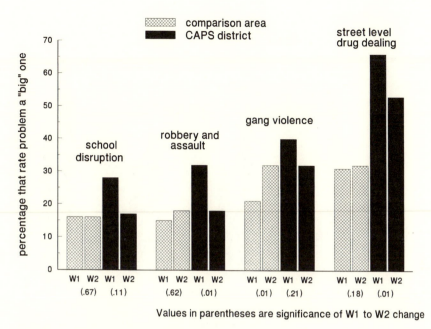

Figure 7-7 Neighborhood problems in Austin.

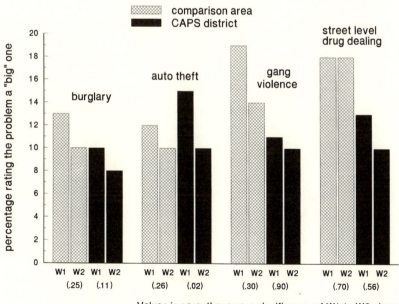

Figure 7-8 Neighborhood problems in Morgan Park.

221

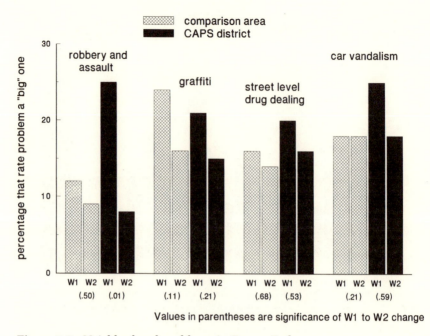

Figure 7-9 Neighborhood problems in Rogers Park.

Otherwise, a wide range of problems were identified as vexing. Car vandalism was near the top of the list in Marquette and Rogers Park, as was graffiti. Street crime (people being attacked or robbed) was also highly rated in two districts—Austin and Rogers Park. Auto theft, burglary, disruptions around schools, abandoned buildings, and vacant lots that were filled with trash and junk—each of these stood near the top of the list in one district. It is interesting to note that only in one district—Morgan Park—did conventional crimes constitute all four of the most highly ranked problems. In the other four prototypes, two of the top four problems were quality-of-life concerns rather than conventionally serious criminal offenses.

Because each district's top problems are presented separately, it is easy to overlook the fact that the initial level of these biggest problems varied considerably from district to district. For example, street-level drug dealing was rated a big problem by 60 percent or more of residents of Englewood. On the other hand, only about 13 percent of the residents of Morgan Park and 20 percent of those we interviewed in Rogers Park thought this was a big problem, even though it was one of the districts' top-ranked issues before CAPS was initiated. In Morgan Park, burglary was a top-ranked problem, but only 10 percent of those we interviewed gave it a high rating. In Morgan Park, in particular, there was not much room for improvement in many problem areas, and expectations about the potential impact of CAPS on problems there must be tempered by this fact.

Figures 7-5 to 7-9 present problem ratings for the prototype districts and their comparison areas, for both the wave-1 and wave-2 surveys. As in figure 7-1, the statistical significance of each over-time change is presented as well. Further statistical analyses of the data controlled for the wave-1 measure of each problem, and assessed the additional effect of living in a prototype district rather than in its comparison area. The analyses were done using repeated-measures analysis of variance, which focuses on the significance of differential changes in the means of the outcome measures over time.

The findings can be summarized as follows.

Englewood. All four of this community's biggest problems declined from 1993 to 1994, while none went down significantly in Englewood's comparison area. The biggest problems in Englewood included drugs, gang violence, abandoned buildings, and trash-strewn lots. Street-level drug selling was ranked as a big problem by 62 percent of Englewood residents in 1993, but by only 49 percent in 1994. Abandoned-building problems dropped—they were reported by 43 percent in 1993 and by 27 percent in 1994. Gang violence was down only modestly (the percentage who thought it was a big problem declined from 41 percent to 35 percent), but it increased significantly in Englewood's comparison area.

These findings may reflect the relative vigor with which Englewood used the CAPS service-request process. Englewood's residents and police were extremely successful at mobilizing city services to respond to both of its decay problems. During the 16-month period ending in August 1994, they generated 1,314 CAPS service requests for attention in regard to abandoned buildings, and 2,379 requests for special service from the Department of Streets and Sanitation. In both cases, Englewood's service-request count ranked number one among the five prototype districts, both absolutely and relative to the size of their population. For every 85 Englewood residents, there was a request to deal with an abandoned building. As figure 7-5 illustrates, perceptions of the extent of both decay problems went down significantly in Englewood during the 1993–1994 period. Gangs and drug problems were the focus of the

March for Peace, and efforts such as the first-offenders program of the district's advisory committee.

Marquette. Graffiti, this district's second-ranked problem before CAPS began, went down in Marquette, but not in its comparison area. A reported decline in street-drug dealing, from 62 percent of respondents to 54 percent, was not significant, but it did not change in Marquette's comparison area. Gang violence and car vandalism both remained stable between 1993 and 1994. Only the drop reported in graffiti problems (from 57 percent of respondents to 44 percent) was statistically significant. As we noted in chapter 6, residents and police in Marquette generated the largest number of service requests for graffiti removal, both absolutely and per capita.

Austin. Street-level drug dealing and assault and robbery went down significantly in Austin. The percentage that rated street-level drug dealing a big problem declined from 66 percent to 53 percent; for street crime, the comparable figures were 32 percent and 18 percent. A reported decline in gang violence, from 40 percent to 32 percent, was also significant when a substantial increase in gang problems in the comparison area was taken into account. A reported decline in school disruption, from 28 percent to 17 percent, was not significant, although this problem remained constant in Austin's comparison area.

School disruption was one of the foci of BADGE (Buddies against Drug and Gang Environment), a project developed by Austin's advisory committee's school subcommittee—parents established an escort program for children entering and leaving the schools; and the escorts remained on school grounds during these periods. Eleven of the district's 19 schools participated in the program. PAG (Parents against Gangs) was also active in the area, integrating police, parents, and schools.

Rogers Park. Reports that street crime was a big problem declined precipitously in Rogers Park, from 25 percent of respondents to 8 percent. This drop far outweighed a parallel decline in this prototype's comparison area. Reports of all three of the district's other biggest problems (drugs, graffiti, and car vandalism) also declined somewhat, but those shifts could not be attributed to the program because of parallel declines in the comparison area.

As we noted in chapter 6, Rogers Park did not succeed in mobilizing support for dealing with graffiti. In fact, overall, this district made the least effective use of the CAPS service-request process. Graffiti was the third-ranked problem there, but residents and police in Rogers Park came in last in terms of generating CAPS service requests—they filed one graffiti service request for every 2,250 residents. As figure 7-9 documents, graffiti problems did not decline significantly in Rogers Park. On the other hand, Rogers Park featured many efforts aimed at street crime. In Operation Beat Feet, people patrolled the decaying core of the district, and a series of successful campaigns was mounted against buildings concentrating troublemaking tenants. The Good Guys Loitering Program mobilized neighbors to retake street corners after dark. In a dramatic move, the roll-call assemblies that took place during shift changes in Rogers Park were moved from the district station to a series of hot spots around the area. Dubbed "Rolling Roll Calls," this activity flooded these spots with uniformed officers and police vehicles and presented a highly visible show of force on the street.

Morgan Park. Every reported problem in Morgan Park declined at least slightly. The largest drop reported by respondents was that for auto-theft problems—reports went from 15 percent to 10 percent. However, none of these declines could be clearly attributed to CAPS. Burglary, auto theft, and gang violence also went down in Morgan Park's comparison area. The scale in figure 7-8 reminds us that problems in Morgan Park were already lower than in any other district we studied before the program began.

Alternative Measures of Crime

When common crimes were involved, two alternative measures of the extent of neighborhood problems could be directed toward the analysis of change in the prototypes. Common crimes were among the top-ranked issues in Morgan Park (auto theft and burglary), Rogers Park (robbery and assault), and Austin (robbery and assault). In each case, both official crime figures and reports of victimization could be compared to the problem ratings. In the case of official crime statistics, we examined the average monthly crime rate for the 17 months that preceded CAPS (that is, from December 1991 through April 1993), and compared it to the rate for the 17 months that followed the inauguration of CAPS in the prototype districts. To measure crime victimization, we calculated the percentage of survey respondents that were victimized during the year preceding each wave of surveys.

Official crime statistics include both attempted as well as successful crimes, so in the surveys, burglary was measured by responses to two questions:

- "During the past year, has anyone broken into your home or garage to steal something?"
- "(Other than that), have you found any sign that someone tried to break into your home?"

Attempted and completed robberies were also measured by responses to two questions:

- "During the past year, has anyone stolen something directly from you by force, or after threatening you with harm?"
- "(Other than that), has anyone tried to steal something from you forcefully, even though they did not get it?"

Auto theft was measured by first asking if the household had a car or truck (22 percent of the entire sample did not), and then asking, "Did anyone steal that car (or truck), or try to, during the past year?" Assault victimization was probed by the following question: "Has anyone physically attacked you or actually been violent with you in an argument or fight?" The best official analogue to this measure is that for "aggravated" assault, which typically involves injury to the victim. Because assaults, robberies, and car thefts could take place virtually anywhere, we asked victims if the incident took place in their neighborhood—only neighborhood crimes (which presumably took place in the prototype district) are examined here.

Table 7-2 compares the results of three different measures of trends for the two common crimes that were identified as among the biggest problems in Morgan Park. In the case of auto theft, popular perceptions of the extent of the problem went down by one-third; the victimization rate dropped to more than half its original rate; and officially recorded crime dropped by 26 percent. It was thus very likely that auto theft went down in Morgan Park. On the other hand, burglary probably did not decline noticeably: The victimization measure dropped to a rate that was 60 percent of its former figure, but neither popular impressions of the extent of the problem, nor the official crime count, dropped much at all.

In Austin and Rogers Park, a question about "people being attacked or robbed" identified one of the most highly ranked problems. This question involves two distinct official crime categories—robbery and assault. These two offenses are also probably quite dif-

Table 7-2 Three Measures of Crime Trends in Morgan Park

Area and Crime Type	Percentage That Rate Crime as a Big Problem	Official Crimes per Month	Survey's Percentage of Victims
Morgan Park:			
Auto Theft			
Before	15	146	8.0
After	10	108	3.2
	p = .02	−26%	p = .02
Morgan Park:			
Burglary			
Before	10	107	10.1
After	8	102	6.0
	p = .11	−5%	p = .11

Note: Official-crimes-per-month average is for a 17-month period before CAPS and for 17 months following CAPS's implementation; tests of significance are for before/after changes in problem ratings and victimization rate; percentage change is given for monthly recorded crimes.

ferently amenable to community-policing programs. Robbery is typically an economically predatory, stranger-to-stranger crime perpetrated in public places. Assault, on the other hand, often involves people who know one another, and official assault figures reflect a subset of disputes that has escalated to the point where they reach official notice. Alcohol is often involved in these offenses, and they frequently take place in private, rather than public, places. We would expect that the kinds of programs mounted in Chicago would have the most potential for deterring robbery and would have less impact on assault.

Table 7-3 examines detailed crime trends for robbery and assault in Austin and Rogers Park. In both instances, the survey problem measures went down a great deal. The robbery-victimization rate dropped by half in Austin (from 8 percent to 4 percent), and officially recorded robbery there went down 8 percent. In Rogers Park, officially recorded robbery went down 20 percent, and the robbery-victimization rate was probably down as well (the statistical significance of the change was marginal, but the initial robbery rate was so low that it did not have much further to go). Thus, robbery went down noticeably in both Austin and Rogers Park. On the other hand, measures of assault did not change very much in either district. The victimization rate was cut in half in Austin, but the numbers involved were low before the program began, and the official rate was essentially unchanged. Neither assault measure pointed in a hopeful direction in Rogers Park.

Table 7-3   Three Measures of Crime Trends in Austin and Rogers Park

Area and Crime Type	Percent That Rate Crime as a Big Problem	Officially Recorded Robberies per Month	Survey's Percent of Robbery Victims	Officially Recorded Assaults per Month	Survey's Percent of Assault Victims
Austin: robberies and assaults					
Before	31	197	9.0	169	4.0
After	18	181	4.0	168	2.0
	p>.01	−8%	p=.03	−0.6%	p=.48
Rogers Park: robberies and assaults					
Before	25	97	2.8	83	1.7
After	8	78	0.5	84	1.1
	p>.01	−20%	p=.10	1%	p=.66

Note: Official-crimes-per-month average is for a 17-month period prior to CAPS, and for 17 months following CAPS's implementation; tests of significance are for before-after changes in problem ratings and victimization rate; percentage change is given for monthly recorded crimes.

Impact on Problem Clusters

It should be noted that the approach we used above in evaluating CAPS's impact—following the fate of each prototype's most highly ranked problems—poses the risk of a methodological flaw. Because we examined only problems that were ranked high in the wave-1 survey, there was a potential bias toward concluding that they would decline in the next survey. Because every social measurement includes a significant random-error component, some of these problems may have been high-ranking ones due to chance fluctuations; when this was true, there was a high likelihood that chance factors would bring them down when they were measured again. This is called regression (e.g., movement) toward the mean (which is a lower figure), and a discussion of it can be found in Cook and Campbell (1979). Because problem measures for the comparison areas were not selected for their extreme values, they were less likely to fall (other things being equal) by chance. This tendency toward misleading differential changes threatens evaluations like this one, which focus on changes in program and comparison areas over time.

One defense against regression artifacts is to examine the fate of all of the problems examined in the survey, not just the most extreme. This approach to gauging the impact of CAPS on neighborhood problems is conservative and actually biases us *against* finding any effects of the program (for reasons discussed below), but avoids the potential bias created by examining only an area's worst problems. Here, we do this by creating summary scores that combine assessments of multiple, closely-related issues into measures of general clusters of problems. Through statistical analysis, three clusters of neighborhood problems were identified: We dubbed these *major crimes, gang and drug problems,* and signs of *physical decay.* The clusters encompass almost all of the neighborhood problems that were assessed in the surveys. Because we kept all of them and did not select individual problems because they were particularly high at Wave 1, they should not be biased downward for the wave-2 survey. The actual measures should also be more statistically robust because they combine responses to multiple questions; this helps cancel out random measurement errors.

This approach brings with it other problems, however. An analysis of the impact of CAPS on generic issue clusters is useful for drawing general lessons about the impact of community policing, but the summary scores take into account topics that were not always a focus of public concern. For the wave-1 survey, some of them turned out to be rated scarcely above "no problem" in many of the prototypes. They thus presented a difficult test for CAPS, for problems that were not very big ones in the first place (and Morgan Park and Rogers Park had several of them) did not have very much room to show improvement. This is called a "floor effect," because, for the wave-2 survey, the ratings could not drop below the bottom of the survey scale (a rating of "no problem"). For some problems, in some areas, the bottom was not very far away. This biased the analysis a bit *against* identifying any program effects.

The problem clusters and their specific components were as follows:

- Major crimes: problems with car vandalism; auto theft; burglary; street crime; and rape or other sexual assaults. The reliability of this measure was 0.85.

- Gangs and drugs: problems with street-level drug dealing; and shootings and violence by gangs. The correlation between these two measures was $+.72$.

- Physical decay: problems with vacant lots filled with trash and junk, abandoned cars in the streets and alleys, abandoned houses or other empty buildings, and graffiti. The reliability of this measure was 0.75.

To examine the impact of CAPS on these problems, we employed the analysis strategy described previously. Instead of using responses to questions about individual problems, however, we averaged responses to all of the questions in each cluster and used the summary score. Statistical controls were used for wave-1 measures of the cluster scores, and the independent effect of living in a prototype district rather than in its comparison area was assessed by using repeated-measures analysis of variance. In addition, figures 7-10, 7-11, and 7-12 present average problem-cluster scores for the prototypes and their comparison areas, for both the wave-1 and wave-2 surveys.

Major Crimes. Figure 7-10 depicts the average major-crime score in each district before CAPS began and, again, 14 to 17 months later. By this score, crime problems during this period declined significantly in each of the five prototypes. The decline was smallest in Morgan Park, where issues noted above already ranked relatively low in intensity (averaging about halfway between "no problem" and "some problem"). Statistically, the apparent decline in major-crime problems in Marquette and Morgan Park did not outpace parallel shifts in their comparison areas, so it is chancy to attribute these declines to CAPS. In the three remaining areas, statistical analyses confirm that declines in major-crime problems in the prototypes outweighed any changes in their comparison areas, and they could well have been caused by the program.

Drugs and Gangs. Figure 7-11 depicts district-level changes in drug and gang problems. This measure declined significantly in Englewood, Marquette, and Austin. Each type of problem was, in fact, down significantly in Englewood and Austin; and in these problems, there were significant *increases* in their comparison neighborhoods, lending credence to the inference that the program made a difference in these prototype districts.

Physical Decay. Figure 7-12 illustrates trends in physical decay in all the survey areas. Decay was down significantly in three districts—Englewood, Marquette, and Austin—but a parallel decline in decay in Marquette's comparison area makes it difficult to attribute the Marquette trend to the program. Three of the four physical-decay measures were down significantly in Englewood, but none were down in its comparison area.

Were Problems just Displaced?

While there clearly is evidence of significant declines in a wide range of problems in Chicago's prototype police districts, there is

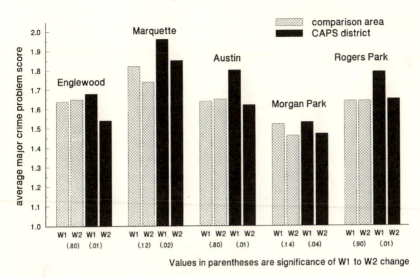

Figure 7-10 Changes in crime problems, by district.

still the possibility that some or all of the problems were simply displaced or moved elsewhere rather than truly being solved. In fact, the possibility of displacement questions the results of virtually *every* crime-prevention program, but rarely are researchers in a good position to assess displacement. The possibilities of it are wide ranging. For example, depending on the problem, displacement might be geographical—the program may push it into another neighborhood, or somewhere down the highway. Geographical dis-

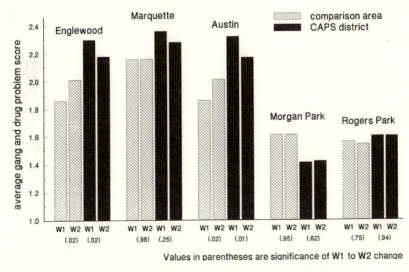

Figure 7-11 Changes in gang and drug problems, by district.

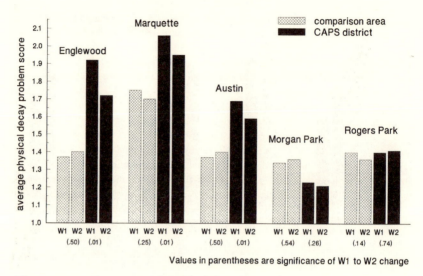

Figure 7-12 Changes in physical decay, by district.

placement is indeed the most widely discussed alternative, but the program might instead displace the problem in terms of time to a period when residents or police are not patrolling; or offenders might switch to another activity, with no guarantee that the neighborhood will be better off due to their new line of work.

Of these possibilities, we were able to consider only the possibility of geographical displacement, and even then only tentatively. To monitor displacement, we identified the instances in which problems that we judged to be the most displaceable—gang violence, street-level drug sales, and street crimes—declined significantly. This occurred in Englewood, Austin, and Rogers Park. We then identified potential displacement zones around these prototype districts that were areas where we had also conducted evaluation surveys (these were parts of the comparison areas for this study). These potential displacement areas were defined as constituting the first two tiers of census tracts along the borders of Englewood, Austin, and Rogers Park. In our surveys, 78 respondents lived in areas that were potential displacement zones for drug problems and gang problems, and 77 lived in areas that were the potential targets of displaced street crime. Respondents living in areas further away from the prototype districts continued to be used for comparison areas.

We then examined wave 1–wave 2 changes in the data for the three "displaceable" crimes, accounting separately for changes in the prototype districts, the displacement areas, and the (now shrunken) comparison areas. We examined simple change scores for the three subareas and used multiple regression combining all the data. In no case was there evidence of a significant increase in drug, gang, or street-crime problems in a potential displacement zone. If anything, there was a hint of a scattering of benefits, rather than a displacement of crime. In the aggregate, gang problems went up in the relevant comparison areas, but remained steady in the displacement areas near the prototype districts. Street crime remained steady in the comparison areas, but went down in the displacement areas adjoining the prototypes. There were no apparent shifts in drug problems, other than their significant decline in Austin and Englewood. None of the gang-problem or street-crime changes in the displacement zones were statistically significant, and the number of survey respondents who were living in the displacement areas was not a large one, so we are not tempted to claim that the benefits of CAPS spilled over from the prototypes into surrounding areas, but in this case this hypothesis is at least as credible as are fears about displacement.

Summary

Our examination of the impact of CAPS in the five prototype districts found evidence of success in regard to several important dimensions. First, there were changes in many residents' views of the quality of police service. In fact, residents of Englewood, Austin, and Morgan Park perceived that police were growing more responsive to their concerns and were working with them to solve neighborhood problems; significantly more felt that way in Rogers Park as well, but so did residents of its nearby comparison area. In Englewood and Austin, they were more optimistic about future trends in policing as well. Visibility of police was up in every prototype, but in only one comparison area.

What became more visible was community-oriented police activity—walking in residential areas and along commercial strips, checking buildings and alleys, and engaging in informal conversations with ordinary citizens. This kind of activity was more visible in every prototype, and the prototype-district increases were much greater than changes in the two comparison areas where visibility also increased. Residents of the prototypes did not see more motorized patrol or more enforcement activity, despite increases in police staffing there. We took this as further evidence that CAPS indeed made a difference in what was happening in the streets of the prototype districts.

Residents who saw community-oriented activity were more positive about the police. They were more likely to believe that police were being responsive to community concerns, and that they were effective in dealing with crime. Overall, they also felt safer in regard to crime. The effect of greater visibility on perceived responsiveness of police was a general one. It was an additional positive force in the prototypes, where, in the main, even controlling for police visibility, people still felt better about the quality of police service.

It is very important to note that, in the aggregate, the views of both African-Americans and whites grew more positive in the prototype districts. Hispanics were concentrated in Marquette, where the fewest changes occurred in anyone's views. Also, the perceptions of both homeowners and renters changed for the better. This is significant because in almost every study that covers the matter, race and class are deeply enmeshed in people's views of police and of their experiences with routine policing. For example, in Smith and Hawkins' study (1973), personal characteristics such as age, and experiences like being arrested, were related to attitudes toward police only among whites; blacks were almost monolithic in their views, which were much more negative. While social class also made a difference, Jacob (1972) found that blacks were more likely than whites of all backgrounds to report being unhappy about how they were treated when they were stopped by police. And Apple and O'Brien (1983) note that context matters: In heavily black areas, perceptions of the police among blacks were much more negative than the views of African-Americans living in more racially diverse areas, perhaps because of the growing accumulation of neighborhood grievances.

Community policing also threatens to become a racially polarized program. An evaluation of community policing in Houston found that the way in which programs in various areas were run favored the interests of homeowners and established interests in the community. Police worked well with members of these groups, but less affluent residents did not hear about the programs and did not participate in them. The positive effects of community policing were therefore confined to whites and homeowners (Skogan, 1990). This suggests that policing by general consent can be difficult in places where the community is fragmented by race, class, and lifestyle. If, instead of trying to find common interests in this community diversity, the police deal mainly with elements of their own choosing, they will appear to be taking sides. It is, in fact, very easy for them to focus community policing on supporting those with whom they get along best and who share their outlook. If they do so, the "local priorities" that they represent will be those of some in the community, but not all.

We found that Chicago's program enjoyed fairly inclusive recognition, and fairly widespread benefits. The visibility of community-oriented police activity rose among all racial groups, and irrespective of income, education, or home ownership. Increased visibility was linked to higher levels of satisfaction among whites, blacks, Hispanics, homeowners, and renters. Visibility was related to reduced fear of crime only among African-Americans and renters, who were much more fearful than their counterparts when the program began. Perceptions of police responsiveness to neighborhood concerns went up among blacks and whites living in the prototype districts, and among renters and homeowners. Only Hispanics, who were concentrated in a district that evidenced generally lower levels of program impact, seemed unaffected. Finally, perceptions of police misconduct went down the most among African-Americans, and showed significant district-level declines in the two largely African-American districts—Englewood and Austin. And again, Hispanics seemed left behind.

Our second major purpose was to assess the impact of CAPS on the everyday lives of Chicago's residents. We focused on the fate of the problems that residents of the prototype districts identified as their greatest concerns. There was some evidence of improvement in the lives of residents of every program area. A survey-based measure of the extent of major crime problems went down in all five prototype districts, although they declined in the comparison areas for Marquette and Morgan Park. The victimization survey pointed to decreases in the two biggest crime problems in Morgan Park—burglary and auto theft. Street violence dropped in Rogers Park and Austin, according to several measures. Reports of drug and gang problems declined in Englewood and Austin, where the widest range of decreases was recorded in the area's top problems. Reported perceptions of the extent of physical decay declined in these two districts, and in Marquette and its comparison area. Graffiti, a big issue in Marquette, was down significantly there. The fewest program impacts were recorded in Morgan Park, but it is important to note that most problems measured in the surveys were already at low levels there, so there was less room for improvement than in the other districts.

8

Reinventing Policing, Chicago Style

$\mathbf{T}$his book documents Chicago's effort to develop a community policing strategy that works. Over time, the city's CAPS program developed into one of the most substantial and closely watched experiments in 1990s policing. As we noted earlier, we followed the program from its inception through its implementation in five test districts and took advantage of the fact that the department's prototyping process let us compare what happened in these districts with trends in areas where change had not yet occurred.

It was clearly a big program. While Chicago's prototyping approach to formulating a workable program relied on the experience gained in just five districts, together they constituted a very large "city." If the five prototype districts had indeed been a city, it would have been one of the largest in the country, for more people (568,000) lived in the prototypes than in Seattle, and they were only slightly outnumbered by the population of Boston. If the 1,800 police officers in the five districts were to form their own department, it would have been a bit bigger than Cleveland's, and far larger than those serving Atlanta, Miami, Kansas City, or New Orleans. The sheer scale of Chicago's reform effort was one of its most significant features.

This chapter summarizes some of the accomplishments that we observed. It also comments about things that did *not* go so well, and about some of the resulting challenges that the department would have to face when the program later expanded to encompass the entire city.

Chicago's Accomplishments

Chicago's first accomplishment was that something happened: Major alterations were made in the way police went about their business. In a world where programs often do not progress further than the press releases that announce them, this was significant. Entire districts were drafted for the effort, and we have noted that they were big and diverse places. Furthermore, CAPS was built on the districts' original complement of officers, not on volunteers or special-duty officers showered with overtime pay. The personnel in their management structures also were used (except for captains, who had to go), and we judged that two of the five original district commanders did not care for the idea of community policing at all. Officers' jobs were restructured, so that when they went to work every day, they did different things than they had done in the past. Teams of officers were assigned to beats for at least a year, and the dispatching system was changed so that the volume and character of their workload was different. They had more time to engage in community-oriented work; they responded mostly to calls from their beat; and they were sent to many calls that were relevant to their turf orientation. Other calls were picked up by free-ranging rapid-response officers, and they could handle the load because more police were assigned to the districts, on the basis of the consulting firm's calculations.

Not everything got done during the first 16 months of prototyping. For one thing, CAPS was based in the uniformed-patrol division and did not really involve the rest of the department. Chicago was committed for the long term to involving all elements of the organization in community policing—including detectives and other special units—However, little progress was made toward integrating them into the program in the prototype districts. The city's plan also included computerized crime analysis, which was to provide the department's knowledge base for problem identification. R&D staff members devised an extremely useful computer program that could have done the job. However, bureaucratic snafus kept the department from acquiring the right equipment on a timely basis; nobody could set the computers up or train users; and the hardware's electrical-power demands threatened to black out some of the older district stations. Beat profiles were another problem-solving tool that did not see the light of day. Notebooks (beat planners) maintained by beat officers were supposed to record the results of a systematic canvas of each beat's problems, resources, institutions, and contact people. These were to be the basis for drawing up profiles of beat problems and identifying potential solutions to them. However, the beat planners got tangled up in legal problems; decades earlier, the city had signed a consent decree agreeing not to maintain illegal intelligence files (this had been the task of the department's Red Squad), and the city's attorney feared that beat planners fell into this category. Districts that did experiment with the planners found it difficult to get officers interested in filling out new forms, and little progress was made on beat profiling during our evaluation period.

Citizen Involvement

Structural changes were also made to facilitate the involvement of neighborhood residents in CAPS. Some are surprised that this has proven to be a stumbling block in many cities. Participation in, and even sympathy for, community policing has been at low levels in neighborhoods that need it most. Perhaps the most unique feature of Chicago's program was the beat meeting. During the prototyping period 15,000 people assembled to meet with police who were serving their area. The meetings were held on a regular basis and in prominent neighborhood locations. We found that, to a certain extent, Chicago avoided the middle-class bias that has plagued volunteer-based crime-prevention efforts (Skogan, 1988, 1989). Attendance indeed proved to be higher in higher-crime and poorer beats, and rates of attendance were highest in areas heavily populated by African-Americans (albeit due in part to low participation rates among Hispanics). The bad news was that attendance in black and poor areas was principally driven by crime problems.

What happened at the meetings had mixed results. Too many were dominated by neighborhood-relations specialists or did not involve a productive dialog between police and residents. Residents identified many local problems, but police dominated the solution side of the equation, and they clung to traditional enforcement-oriented approaches to resolving issues. The districts' success rate ranged from 10 to 60 percent in terms of how effectively the meetings were conducted, and from 7 to 38 percent, on the basis of how much problem solving went on. Everyone knew that they had to become more productive, and, to tackle this issue, a training program for residents was begun in 1995.

When the CAPS program was first announced, organizations all over the city were enthusiastic about bringing the program to their communities. We found that many groups in the selected prototype districts invested heavily in support of CAPS. Depending on the area, up to 90 percent of groups sent representatives to beat meetings; over 80 percent encouraged people to attend the meetings, worked with beat officers, and identified service needs; as many as two-thirds distributed newsletters or flyers about CAPS; and up to half held their own anticrime meetings. This was important, because CAPS depended on community activists to get people to turn out for beat meetings; to get involved in activities sponsored by the district advisory committees; and to play a role in problem solving.

However, our study of these organizations, and our case studies of problem-solving efforts, highlighted some very real difficulties in sustaining citizen involvement in community policing. Organizations serving white and home-owning constituencies got involved quickly, because it fit their volunteer-based, block-oriented, neighborhood orientation. Organizations serving the poor and African-Americans were heavily skewed toward providing them with individualized services, and they were staffed by paid employees rather than volunteers. Community policing did not help them much. Organizations serving Hispanics fit this profile; in addition, they pursued cultural, legal, and family-oriented goals that also did not fit well with CAPS's beat orientation. This was important, because our case studies suggested that unorganized individuals found it difficult to sustain even simple problem-solving efforts. Ad hoc groups emerged in reaction to specific threats, but even with some police support, the people who got involved did not stick with the effort.

Officer Buy-In

We identified a number of strategies for encouraging officer commitment to community policing, and during the first 16 months, the department tried most of them. As noted previously, all manner of policing reforms—community policing among them—have foundered on the rocks of police culture and resistance to change, so this was of great concern. Officers (and many of their bosses) were concerned about the potential loss of police autonomy, the diversion of resources from the traditional core functions of policing, the imposition of unrealistic programs by civilians and the out-of-touch brass downtown, and any demeaning of their status as tough-minded enforcers of the law. To counter this threat, CAPS's managers restructured officers' jobs, tackled the department's very traditional management style, avoided conflict with the union and the social-work label, and made a very significant commitment to training.

There was evidence of modest success on this front. Figure 8-1 summarizes many of the changes that we detected in officers' attitudes. Unlike our analysis of the impact of CAPS on the public, there was no comparison group of officers without any involvement in the program. By the time we interviewed them again in 1995, all of the officers questioned in 1993 had been through roll-call training and had at least a little actual experience with community policing. And, of course, the department had been buzzing about the program for years. We anticipated that there would be more changes among officers serving in the prototypes, since they had more training and actual experience with the program. This turned out to be the case.

Figure 8-1 presents changes in the summary officer-attitude scores described in chapter 4— separately for prototype-district officers and for those serving in other districts. Each pair of scores describes their views in 1993 and 1995. The dividing line for the

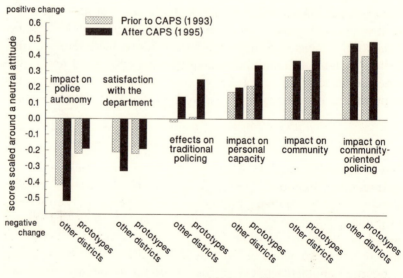

A higher positive score is more optimistic.

Figure 8-1 Changes in officer optimism in prototype and other districts.

scores is the neutral-attitude position. Those below the zero line describe opinions that were negative; for example, the opinion that, on average, they disagreed that the department was a good place to work. Those above the zero line describe opinions that were, on the whole, positive. Officer-satisfaction views regarding the department as a place to work, and their views about the impact of CAPS on police autonomy, were fairly negative even after almost two years of CAPS; prototype-district officers became very slightly less negative over time, while those serving in other areas grew more negative. At the other end, both prototype-district and other officers were more positive about CAPS in the spring of 1995 than they were in early 1993. They were more optimistic about the impact of CAPS on traditional policing and on the community; about their personal capacity to engage in problem solving; and about the viability of community-oriented policing activities.

However, the department did not succeed in finding a way to link an officer's aptitude for community policing to any of the organization's performance measures, nor to their pay or chances for promotion. This is a generic problem, not just Chicago's, and it is one that will continue to plague policing. There is a need for rewards for doing a good job, especially in organizations in which civil service regulations and union contracts constrain the ability of managers to decide who will work for them, or to match people to positions. During the evaluation period, there was also an obvious disjunction between the official new mission of the department and the views of key members of the senior command staff. Officers who were looking for a rationale for withholding a commitment to the program could point to these views as evidence that the organization was not completely committed to its new course of action.

Integrating Service Delivery

Another distinguishing feature of Chicago's program was its effective integration of city services into the structure of community policing. CAPS inevitably involved an expansion of the traditional police mandate, so finding a way to deliver on the promise of neighborhood problem solving was high on the mayor's agenda as well as on the agenda at police headquarters. The mayor used his clout with city-agency executives, while at the street level, his office monitored the responsiveness of the bureaucracies to special service needs that were identified and prioritized by district officers. The districts varied in terms of how effectively they used this process, and our surveys found evidence of declines in specific problems in the districts that focused their attention on them. Overall, physical decay (including combined reports of abandoned cars and buildings, trash and junk, and graffiti) went down significantly in two districts but not in their comparison areas, and in another district decay declined in tandem with the comparison area. Morgan Park was aggressive about pursuing selected services, but its decay problems were so small that they could not go down much further, while Rogers Park simply did not make effective use of the CAPS service-delivery system.

The real challenge will be to make this process work when the program expands to encompass the entire city. The prototypes were special places that got special treatment, but after CAPS becomes a citywide program, every district cannot be singled out. In principle, CAPS could make the existing service capacity of the city more effective because it helps target the most significant problems, and it could make them more responsive because street officers, beat-meeting participants, and community activists have a say in how services are prioritized. Behind the scenes, the mayor and his advisers anticipate that the resource targeting and computerized monitoring that his office conducts, regarding how long it takes agencies to fix problems, will also enhance their general efficiency, a spin-off benefit of community policing for his hard-pressed budget.

Program Impact

To judge the impact of CAPS, we compared changes in the five prototypes to trends in their matched comparison areas. We used this approach to examine residents' assessments of the quality of police service, and to gauge the impact of community policing on the quality of life in the city's neighborhoods.

While our surveys did not find any evidence of growing awareness of the CAPS program, residents of the prototype districts did spot changes in the frequency and character of policing in their communities. They saw officers more frequently, and in four of the five prototypes, they saw them doing informal and community-oriented work more often. There was no evidence that they noticed a decline in the frequency of motorized patrol or enforcement activity—a potential trade-off that in other cities has ignited a political backlash against community policing. In four districts, residents reported significant improvements in police responsiveness to neighborhood concerns. These changes were general ones: Whites,

African-Americans, renters, and homeowners living in the prototypes grew more positive about the police; only Hispanics appeared to be unaffected by the program. An analysis of the impact of CAPS on perceptions of police misconduct found that the views of African-Americans grew more positive. Whites (who were already very positive) and Hispanics (who were even more negative than blacks) did not change their opinions.

We also found evidence that CAPS improved neighborhood conditions. There was at least one positive change in every district. Victimization went down in Morgan Park and Rogers Park. Street crime dropped in Rogers Park and in Austin, according to several measures. Drug and gang problems declined in Englewood and in Austin, and graffiti went down in Marquette. Problems with abandoned buildings and trash-filled vacant lots declined in Englewood, which made the most extensive use of the city agencies responsible for these problems. To summarize all of this, figure 8-2 describes the impact of the program on the three clusters of neighborhood problems and presents the summary of perceived police performance that we examined in detail in chapter 7. It presents "net" scores that deduct changes in the comparison areas from the "gross," or over-time changes in the program areas. Where the values drop below zero, problems went down more in the prototypes than in the comparison areas; the bars go up when police responsiveness improved more in the prototypes. Figure 8-2 also indicates which of the changes were statistically significant. The fewest

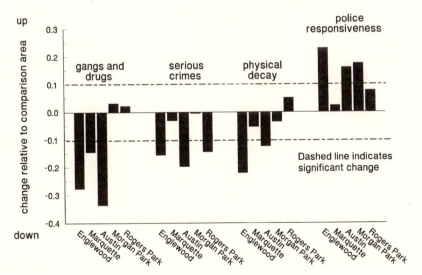

Figure 8-2 Changes in problems and police responsiveness.

changes took place in Morgan Park, where problems were of considerably smaller magnitude than in the other districts.

By these measures, Chicago's success rate was close to that of other cities that have conducted carefully evaluated community-policing programs. A review of 11 community-policing projects found that they had a success rate of just over 50 percent (Skogan, 1994). These projects targeted victimization, fear of crime, casual social disorder (like loitering, panhandling, public drinking, and street harassment), drug availability, and the perceived quality of police service. They were carried out in experimental neighborhoods in Houston, Newark, Oakland, Birmingham, Madison, and Baltimore. Each was evaluated using roughly the same approach that we employed in Chicago: matched comparison areas; two waves of resident surveys; and the collection of census, crime, and other official data. To give an example of the findings, fear of crime was a target of all 11 projects, and it went down—probably as a result of the program—in 6 of them. Overall, compared to what happened in the comparison areas, changes like the one related to fear occurred in 27 of the 51 outcomes that were monitored—a success rate of 53 percent.

Because we evaluated the impact of the program in two different ways, we calculated two success rates, but they turned out to be almost identical. Our first approach was to monitor the fate of the four biggest problems in each of the five districts, as identified by the people who lived there. There was evidence of program impact on 9 of these 20 problems, for a success rate of about 45 percent. Our second approach to assessing the impact of CAPS on the neighborhoods was to examine over-time changes in four clusters of problems: drugs and gangs, serious crimes, physical decay, and police responsiveness. The results of this analysis are summarized in figure 8-2. Of the 20 outcome changes summarized, there was evidence of significant program effects in 10 instances, for a success rate of 50 percent.

In other words, Chicago seems to be about at the national mark. It fielded somewhat different community-policing efforts, of varying quality, in five experimental districts; the programs we cited previously also varied considerably from city to city. In every city, some projects were well conceived and well executed, while others did not get very far. In the aggregate, they all succeeded about half the time.

But one important difference to keep in mind is that in every other city considered here, the evaluators were looking at small pilot projects. They all focused on very small areas; they typically involved no more than a dozen volunteer officers; and they often were run directly out of the chief's office. In contrast, Chicago's prototype districts were large and diverse, and the project was staffed by regular units and not-always-sympathetic managers. The scale of the city's prototyping experiment exceeded the change effort that would be involved in totally remaking policing in many of the nation's largest cities.

One of the biggest challenges to community policing in Chicago will be to find ways to involve the Hispanic community in it. Recall that our analysis of the roots of the program stressed the importance of Hispanics in the balance of political power in the city— the political winner needs to keep them in the fold. However, they were more unhappy even than African-Americans about the quality of police service in their neighborhoods, and they faced serious crime problems. While rates of crime in Hispanic neighborhoods were somewhat lower than those in black areas, crime counts there were still two-to-four times the rate for white Chicago.

But at almost every point, we found that Hispanics were left out of CAPS. Heavily Hispanic beats had the lowest rate of attendance at beat meetings; in a multivariate statistical analysis, we found this was the strongest factor working against participation. Our observations of who came to meetings indicated that they did not turn out in large proportions unless the beat was at least 75 percent Hispanic. And organizations serving Hispanics were the least likely to be involved in supporting beat meetings. The prototype district where most of the Hispanics were concentrated did not have very effective top-level leadership during the early months of the project. The district advisory committee there was deeply divided by race and spent a great deal of its energy on resolving internal matters. We even found that rank-and-file Hispanic police officers tended to share the skepticism of white officers, rather than the enthusiasm about community policing that was expressed more often by black officers.

Perhaps as a result, our surveys found that Hispanics knew the least about the program, and that their lives were not much touched by it. The most heavily Hispanic district was the only one in which there was no discernible improvement in ratings of police responsiveness, and the views of police expressed by Hispanics living in all the prototypes did not change over time. Except for a reduction in graffiti problems, they did not observe any benefits of the program for their neighborhoods.

Implications for Community Policing

What are the implications of Chicago's experience for the country? We think there are two: It is hard to get community policing off the ground, but it can be made to work.

The first challenge to police and municipal executives is to get something concrete to happen on the street. The obstacles to reinventing policing, involving municipal agencies, and engaging the public in a meaningful way, have filled many chapters of this book. For mayors or the attentive public to demand that the police "go do it" is inadequate. Community policing has to be the community's program, representing a commitment by the city's political leaders and taxpayers. It still can easily fail, for a dozen reasons, so it will require adroit leadership as well as broad support. Learning from the successes and failures of other cities should be part of the process.

A related problem is *sustaining* commitment to the enterprise. The six cities already mentioned in this chapter are instructive in this regard. Of the 11 experimental projects that were carried out in these cities, only one survived: Madison kept its experimental district station open and expanded its beat-officer program. All of the other projects closed down—victims of lapsed federal funding, pressure to respond to surging 911 calls, opposition from officers and midlevel managers, and city politics (Skogan, 1994). Chicago's capacity to stay the course has not yet been demonstrated, although the signs of it are favorable.

If community policing gets off the ground, it can be made to work. While there is an ample supply of failed experiments and of cities where the concept has gone awry, there is evidence in Chicago and elsewhere that it can succeed at tackling tough issues. Evaluations find that a public hungry for attention has a great deal to tell police, and it is grateful for the opportunity to do so. When people see more police on foot or working out of a local substation, they feel less fearful. Officers have become committed to making community policing work, and where they have developed sustained cooperation with community groups and fostered self-help programs, they have witnessed declining levels of crime, social disorder, and physical decay. However, the making-it-work stage primarily requires something that many cities have too little of—patience. One of Chicago's biggest lessons for other cities is that they may have to stick with the effort for many years. If their success rate is also only 50 percent, it means that they too will have to engage in an iterative, make-it-work development process in order to get it right in future attempts.

References

Chapter 1

Boydstun, John, and Michael Sherry. 1975. *San Diego Community Profile: Final Report.* Washington, D.C.: Police Foundation.

Crank, John P. 1994. "Watchman and Community: Myth and Institutionalization in Policing." *Law and Society Review* **28,** 325–351.

Kerner, Otto. 1967. *Report of the National Advisory Committee on Civil Disorders.* Washington, D.C.: U.S. Government Printing Office.

Mastrofski, Stephen D. 1988. "Community Policing as Reform: A Cautionary Tale." In Jack R. Greene and Stephen D. Mastrofski (eds.), *Community Policing: Rhetoric or Reality?* New York: Praeger.

Sherman, Lawrence W. 1992. "Attacking Crime: Policing and Crime Control." In Michael Tonry and Norval Morris, (eds.), *Modern Policing,* 159–230. Chicago: University of Chicago Press.

Skogan, Wesley G. 1990. *Disorder and Decline: Crime and the Spiral of Decay in American Cities.* New York: Free Press.

Skogan, Wesley G. 1995. "Community Policing in the United States." In Jean-Paul Brodeur (ed.), *Comparisons in Policing: An International Perspective,* 86–112. Aldershot, Eng.: Avebury.

Chapter 2

Block, Carolyn Rebecca, and Richard Block. 1993. *Street Gang Crime in Chicago.* Washington, D.C.: National Institute of Justice, U.S. Department of Justice.

Fuchs, Ester R. 1992. *Mayors and Money: Fiscal Policy in New York and Chicago.* Chicago: University of Chicago Press.

Glastris, Paul. 1993. "Chicago's Hands-On Mayor." *City Journal* **3** (no. 4, Autumn), 78–84.

Holli, Melvin G., and Paul M. Green. 1984. *The Making of the Mayor: Chicago 1983.* Grand Rapids, Mich.: Eerdmans Publishing.

Illinois Advisory Committee. 1993. *Police Protection of the African-American Community in Chicago.* Chicago: Illinois Advisory Committee of the United States Commission on Civil Rights.

Illinois Criminal Justice Information Authority. 1995. *Major Trends in Chicago Homicide: 1965–1996.* Chicago.

Judd, Dennis R., and Todd Swanstrom. 1994. *City Politics: Private Power and Public Policy.* New York: HarperCollins.

Ladd, Helen F., and John Yinger. 1989. *America's Ailing Cities: Fiscal Health and the Design of Urban Policy.* Baltimore: Johns Hopkins University Press.

Reardon, Patrick. 1993. "More Chicagoans Find it isn't Their Kind of Town." *Chicago Tribune,* November 28.

Rodriguez, Alex. 1996. "The Future of Chicago." *Chicago Sun Times,* February 28.

Skogan, Wesley G. 1979. "Citizen Satisfaction with Police Services." In Ralph Baker and Fred A. Meyer, Jr. (eds.), *Evaluating Alternative Law-Enforcement Policies,* 29–42. Lexington, Mass.: Lexington Books.

Skogan, Wesley G., and Andrew C. Gordon. 1982. "A Review of Detective Division Reporting Practices." In *Crime in Illinois 1982,* 167–182. Springfield, Ill.: Illinois Department of Law Enforcement.

Washington, Laura. 1983. "Black Disticts Lose Out in Police Deployment Policy." *Chicago Reporter* 12 (No. 9, September), 1–3, 6.

Chapter 3

Booz, Allen & Hamilton, Inc. 1992. "Improving Police Service: Summary of Findings To-Date." Consulting report for the city of Chicago.

Chicago Police Department. 1993. *Together We Can: A Strategic Plan for Reinventing The Chicago Police Department.* Chicago: Chicago Police Department.

Dantzker, Gail, Arthur Lurigio, Susan Hartnett, Sirgulina Davidsdottir, Kristin Donovan, and Sheila Houmes. 1994. *Preparing Police Officers for Community Policing: An Evaluation of Training for Chicago's Alternative Policing Strategy.* Community Policing Program Paper no. 6. Evanston, Ill.: Institute for Policy Research, Northwestern University.

Kass, John and Sharman Stein. April 12, 1992. "Daley Weighs Racial Politics in Picking Police Chief." *Chicago Tribune.*

Kass, John. February 21, 1993. "Daley Saved on Taxes, But it Still Costs Him." *Chicago Tribune.*

Recktenwald, William and George Papajohn. August 18, 1992. "Seven Police Districts Facing Last Roll Call." *Chicago Tribune.*

Recktenwald, William. January 22, 1993. "Police Drop Plan to Close Seven Stations." *Chicago Tribune.*

Sadd, Susan, and Randolph Grinc. 1993. *Issues in Community Policing: An Evaluation of Eight Innovative Neighborhood-Oriented Policing Projects.* New York: Vera Institute of Justice.

Sadd, Susan, and Randolph Grinc. 1994. "Innovative Neighborhood Oriented Policing: An Evaluation of Community Policing Programs in Eight Cities." In Dennis P. Rosenbaum (ed.), *The Challenge of Community Policing,* 27–52. Thousand Oaks, Calif.: Sage Publications.

Spielman, Fran. February 2, 1993. "The Beat Cop is Back." *Chicago Sun-Times.*

Stein, Sharman. June 21, 1992. "Sink or Swim Named Top Cop on the Day the Loop Flood, Matt Rodriguez Still Faces some Tidal Waves." *Chicago Tribune.*

Weisel, Deborah. 1995. "The Implementation of Community Policing in Six Cities." Paper presented at the 1995 National Institute of Justice Evaluation Conference, Washington, D.C.

Chapter 4

Bouza, Anthony V. 1985. "Police Unions: Paper Tigers or Roaring Lions?" In William Geller (ed.), *Police Leadership in America,* 241–280. New York: Praeger.

Chicago Police Department. 1993. *Together We Can: A Strategic Plan for Reinventing the Chicago Police Department.* Chicago: Chicago Police Department.

Goldstein, Herman. 1990. *Problem-Oriented Policing.* New York: McGraw-Hill.

Holdaway, Simon. 1995. "Modernity, Rationality and the Baguette." In Jean-Paul Brodeur (ed.), *Comparisons in Policing: An International Perspective,* 145–160. Aldershot, Eng.: Avebury.

Law Enforcement News, September 30, 1991.

Law Enforcement News, June 30, 1994.

Lurigio, Arthur J., and Dennis P. Rosenbaum. 1994. "The Impact of Community Policing on Police Personnel: A Review of the Literature." In Dennis P. Rosenbaum (ed.), *The Challenge of Community Policing,* 147–166. Thousand Oaks, Calif.: Sage Publications.

Lurigio, Arthur J., and Wesley G. Skogan. 1994. "Winning the Hearts and Minds of Police Officers: An Assessment of Staff Perceptions of Community Policing in Chicago." *Crime and Delinquency* **40** (July), 315–330.

McElroy, Jerome E., Colleen Cosgrove, and Susan Sadd. 1993. *Community Policing: The CPOP in New York*. Newbury Park, Calif.: Sage Publications.

Muir, William K. 1977. *Police: Streetcorner Politicians*. Chicago: University of Chicago Press.

Pate, Antony M., Marlys McPherson, and Glenn Silloway. 1987. *The Minneapolis Community Organizing Experiment*. Washington, D.C.: Police Foundation.

Rubenstein, Jonathan. 1973. *City Police*. New York: Farrar, Straus and Giroux.

Sadd, Susan, and Randolph Grinc. 1993. *Issues in Community Policing: An Evaluation of Eight Innovative Neighborhood-Oriented Policing Projects*. New York: Vera Institute of Justice.

Sadd, Susan, and Randolph Grinc. 1994. "Innovative Neighborhood Oriented Policing: An Evaluation of Community Policing Programs in Eight Cities." In Dennis P. Rosenbaum (ed.), *The Challenge of Community Policing*, 27–52. Thousand Oaks, Calif.: Sage Publications.

Silverman, Eli, and Carmen Solis. 1994. "Community Policing Training," *Law Enforcement News*, November 15.

Uchida, Craig, Brian Forst, and Sampson Annan. 1990. *Modern Policing and the Control of Illegal Drugs: Testing New Strategies in Two American Cities* (Final Technical Report). Washington, D.C.: Police Foundation.

Van Maanen, John. 1983. "The Boss: First-Line Supervision in an American Policy Agency." In Maurice Punch (ed.), *Control in the Police Organization*. Cambridge: MIT Press.

Weisburd, David, Jerome McElroy, and Patricia Hardyman. 1988. "Challenges to Supervision in Community Policing." *American Journal of Police* **7**, 29–50.

Wycoff, Mary Ann. 1988. "The Benefits of Community Policing: Evidence and Conjecture." In Jack R. Greene and Stephen D. Mastrofski, (eds), *Community Policing: Rhetoric or Reality?* 103–120. New York: Praeger.

Wycoff, Mary Ann, and Timothy Oettmeir. 1994. *Evaluating Police Officer Performance Under Community Policing*. Washington, D.C.: National Institute of Justice.

Wycoff, Mary Ann, and Wesley G. Skogan. 1993. *Community Policing in Madison: Quality from the Inside Out*. Washington, D.C.: National Institute of Justice.

Wycoff, Mary Ann, and Wesley G. Skogan. 1994a. "Community Policing in Madison: An Analysis of Implementation and Impact." In Dennis P. Rosenbaum (ed), *The Challenge of Community Policing*, 75–91. Thousand Oaks, Calif.: Sage Publications.

Wycoff, Mary Ann, and Wesley G. Skogan. 1994b. "The Effect of a Community Policing Management Style on Officers' Attitudes." *Crime and Delinquency* **40,** 371–383.

Chapter 5

Austin, D. Mark. 1991. "Community Context and Complexity of Organizational Structure in Neighborhood Associations." *Administration and Society* **22** (February), 516–531.

Chicago Police Department. 1993. *Together We Can: A Strategic Plan for Reinventing the Chicago Police Department.* Chicago: Chicago Police Department.

Chicago Police Department. 1994. *CAPS Roll-Call Training Bulletin No. 5.* Chicago: Chicago Police Department.

Grinc, Randolph M. 1994. " 'Angels in Marble': Problems in Stimulating Community Involvement in Community Policing." *Crime and Delinquency* **40** (no. 3, July), 437–468.

Hope, Tim. 1995. "Community Crime Prevention." In Michael Tonry and David Farrington (eds.), *Building a Safer Society: Strategic Approaches to Crime Prevention,* 21–90. Chicago: University of Chicago Press.

Lovig, Justine, and Robert Van Stedum. 1995. *Community Organization Survey Methods Report.* Chicago Community Policing Evaluation Consortium, Project Paper no. 11.

Skogan, Wesley G. 1986. "Fear of Crime and Neighborhood Change." In Albert J. Reiss Jr. and Michael Tonry (eds.), *Crime and Justice: A Review of Research, vol. 8,* 203–230. Chicago: University of Chicago Press.

Skogan, Wesley G. 1988. "Community Organizations and Crime." In Michael Tonry and Norval Morris (eds.), *Crime and Justice: A Review of Research, vol. 8,* 39–78. Chicago: University of Chicago Press.

Skogan, Wesley G. 1990. *Disorder and Decline: Crime and the Spiral of Decay in American Cities.* New York: Free Press.

Chapter 6

Crawford, Adam, and Matthew Jones. 1995. "Inter-Agency Co-Operation and Community-Based Crime Prevention." *British Journal of Criminology* **35,** 17–33.

Gilling, Daniel J. 1994. "Multi-Agency Crime Prevention: Some Barriers to Collaboration." *The Howard Journal* **33,** 246–257.

Sadd, Susan, and Randolph Grinc. 1993. *Issues in Community Policing: An Evaluation of Eight Innovative Neighborhood-Oriented Policing Projects.* New York: Vera Institute of Justice.

Skogan, Wesley G. 1990. *Disorder and Decline: Crime and the Spiral of Decay in American Cities.* New York: Free Press.

Spelman, William. 1993. "Abandoned Buildings: Magnets for Crime?" *Journal of Criminal Justice* **21,** 481–495.

Whelan, Dominique. 1995. *Partnerships in Action.* Evanston, Ill.: Center for Urban Affairs and Policing Research.

Chapter 7

Apple, Nancy, and David J. O'Brien. 1983. "Neighborhood Racial Composition and Residents' Evaluation of Police Performance." *Journal of Police Science and Administration* **11,** 76–84.

Bahn, Charles. 1974. "The Reassurance Factor in Police Patrol." *Criminology* **12,** 338–345.

Bayley, David H., and Harold Mendelsohn. 1968. *Minorities and the Police.* New York: Free Press.

Bordua, David, and Larry L. Tifft. 1971. "Citizen Interviews, Organizational Feedback, and Police-Community Relations Decisions." *Law and Society Review* **6,** 155–182.

Chicago Police Department. 1993. *Together We Can: A Strategic Plan for Reinventing the Chicago Police Department.* Chicago: Chicago Police Department.

Cook, Thomas D., and Donald T. Campbell. 1979. *Quasi-experimental Designs for Research.* Chicago: Rand McNally.

Jacob, Herbert. 1971. "Black and White Perceptions of Justice in the City." *Law and Society Review* **6,** 69–90.

Jacob, Herbert. 1972. "Contact With Government Agencies: A Preliminary Analysis of the Distribution of Government Services." *Midwest Journal of Political Science* **16,** 123–146.

Kelling, George L., et al. 1974. *The Kansas City Preventive Patrol Experiment: Technical Report.* Washington, D.C.: Police Foundation.

Maxfield, Michael. 1988. "The London Metropolitan Police and Their Clients: Victim and Suspect Attitudes," *Journal of Research in Crime and Delinquency* **25,** 188–206.

Parks, Roger. 1976. "Police Response: Effects on Citizen Attitudes and Perceptions." In Wesley G. Skogan (ed.), *Sample Surveys of the Victims of Crime,* 89–104. Cambridge, Mass.: Ballinger.

Schneider, Anne L. 1976. "Victimization Surveys and the Criminal Justice System." In Wesley G. Skogan (ed.), *Sample Surveys of the Victims of Crime,* 135–150. Cambridge, Mass.: Ballinger.

Shapland, Joanna, John Wilmore, and Paul Duff. 1985. *Victims in the Criminal Justice System.* Aldershot, Eng.: Gower.

Sherman, Lawrence. 1986. "Policing Communities: What Works?" In Michael Tonrey and Albert J. Reiss, Jr. (eds.), *Communities and Crime,* 343–386. Chicago: University of Chicago Press.

Skogan, Wesley G. 1989. "The Impact of Police on Victims." In Emilio Viano (ed.), *Crime and Its Victims,* 71–78. Washington, D.C.: Hemisphere Publishing.

Skogan, Wesley G. 1990. *Disorder and Decline: Crime and the Spiral of Decay in American Cities.* New York: Free Press.

Skogan, Wesley G. 1990. *The Police and the Public in England and Wales.* Home Office Research Study no. 117. London: Her Majesty's Stationery Office.

Skogan, Wesley G. 1994. *Contacts Between Police and the Public: A British Crime Survey Report.* Home Office Research Study no. 134. London: Her Majesty's Stationery Office.

Skogan, Wesley G. 1994. "The Impact of Community Policing on Neighborhood Residents: A Cross-Site Analysis," In Dennis P. Rosenbaum (ed.), *The Challenge of Community Policing: Testing the Hypotheses,* 167–181. Newbury Park, Calif.: Sage Publications.

Skogan, Wesley G. 1995. "Community Policing in the United States." In Jean-Paul Brodeur (ed.), *Comparisons in Policing: An International Perspective,* 86–112. Aldershot, Eng.: Avebury.

Skogan, Wesley G. 1995. *Evaluation Design and Survey Methods Report.* Community Policing Project Paper no. 7. Evanston, Ill.: Institute for Policy Research.

Smith, David J. 1983. *Police and People in London I: A Survey of Londoners.* London: Policy Studies Institute.

Smith, Paul E., and Richard O. Hawkins. 1973. "Victimization, Types of Citizen-Police Contacts, and Attitudes Toward the Police." *Law and Society Review* **8,** 135–152.

Southgate, Peter, and Paul Ekblom. 1984. *Contacts Between Police and Public.* Home Office Research Study no. 77. London: Her Majesty's Stationery Office.

Walker, Darlene, et al. 1972. "Contact and Support: An Empirical Assessment of Public Attitudes Toward the Police and the Courts." *North Carolina Law Review* **51,** 43–79.

Chapter 8

Skogan, Wesley G. 1988. "Community Organizations and Crime." In Michael Tonry and Norval Morris (eds.), *Crime and Justice: A Review of Research,* vol. 8, 39–78. Chicago: University of Chicago Press.

Skogan, Wesley G. 1989 "Communities, Crime and Neighborhood Organization." *Crime and Delinquency* **35,** 437–457.

Index